ADVANCE PR…

Learning That Matters: A Field Guide to Course Design for Transformative Education

"Bold and empowering! A compelling guide on learning-centered teaching that demands a shift from status-quo…from deep-seated, colonized practices that have long infected the professoriate and crippled success by generations of students. If you seek powerful forms of inquiry through capacious issues that matter, this book is for you. If you desire evidence-based strategies to bring coherence to each student's learning, this guide is crucial to that goal. If you seek insight into a liberated academy…rooted in democracy and equity to activate meaning-making by all students, this guide is a fresh glimpse into provocative possibilities for higher education."

Rosalie A. Richards, Ph.D.
Associate Provost for Faculty Development
Stetson University

"Designing and facilitating learning experiences is an essential part of the work of faculty throughout higher education. In *Learning That Matters: A Field Guide to Course Design for Transformative Education*, readers are gifted with abundant opportunities to reflect on our teaching and ample guidance for taking action on what we discover through the process. Designed to be used either as a group or by an individual, this resource charts a path for taking sound educational theory and turning it into practice in our pedagogy. The authors have embedded equity and social justice throughout each page of this important book. They have given us ways to be more intentional in aligning our instructional design with our values."

Bonni Stachowiak
Dean of Teaching and Learning at Vanguard University
Host of the Teaching in Higher Ed *podcast*

"Recent events have thrown into sharp relief the inequities that exist in education. We, who care about our students' learning, may not be able to wait for those in leadership positions to make critically-needed changes to higher education. But educators can start where the learning happens and let necessary changes rise from there. This book can help you walk that path and be that change. This book gathers key topics and takes an accessible, practical approach to implementing impactful, meaningful change in your teaching. You can apply the concepts and exercises to a whole course design or re-design or focus on a module. You can approach this book by reading it from the beginning to the end, or you can jump to specific sections when those principles apply to the acute challenges you are facing. This book is applicable to educators of all levels and all disciplines and at all stages of their careers—as long as they share the goal of improving teaching and learning. You will feel inspired, invigorated, and motivated, and you will feel empowered to make an impact."

Melinda Maris, Ph.D., Assistant Dean
Foundation for Advanced Education in the Sciences
National Institutes of Health

"The succinct and compelling chapters of *Learning That Matters: A Field Guide to Course Design for Transformative Education* provide a taxonomy of the well-designed learning experience for students. Readers may benefit from a sequential reading of chapters or simply dip into the guide at any place for conversation starters, tips, and evidence-based strategies. These authors presented at the annual institute that my teaching center organized at Emory's Oxford College, and I have followed them most recently in a new position at the University System of Georgia, the Board of Regents. Strong thanks to them for furthering the noble and aspirational work, aligned with the social justice work at Emory, which ultimately translates to one fundamental idea: all means all. Our goal is to successfully deepen the learning of all the students in our courses. This book makes that goal achievable."

Jeffery Galle, Ph.D.
Associate Vice Chancellor for Academic Affairs
University System of Georgia, Board of Regents

"*Learning That Matters: A Field Guide to Course Design for Transformative Education* is an important toolbox for all of us in higher education who strive to help students engage in deep and meaningful learning. This practical guide is chocked full of useful content, supplemented by author experiences. It also includes suggestions for activities as well as reflections on teaching and learning. It's a great resource for aspiring, new, and seasoned college and university faculty."

Claire Major
Professor of Higher Education
The University of Alabama

Learning That Matters

Learning That Matters

A Field Guide to Course Design for Transformative Education

By Caralyn Zehnder, Cynthia Alby, Karynne Kleine, and Julia Metzker

GORHAM, MAINE

Published by Myers Education Press, LLC
P.O. Box 424 Gorham, ME 04038

> **Myers Education Press** is an academic publisher specializing in books, e-books, and digital content in the field of education. All of our books are subjected to a rigorous peer review process and produced in compliance with the standards of the Council on Library and Information Resources.

Library of Congress Cataloging-in-Publication Data available from Library of Congress.

13-digit ISBN 978-1-9755-0451-9 (paperback)
13-digit ISBN 978-1-9755-0450-2 (hard cover)
13-digit ISBN 978-1-9755-0452-6 (library networkable e-edition)
13-digit ISBN 978-1-9755-0453-3 (consumer e-edition)

Printed in the United States of America.

All first editions printed on acid-free paper that meets the American National Standards Institute Z39-48 standard.

Books published by Myers Education Press may be purchased at special quantity discount rates for groups, workshops, training organizations, and classroom usage. Please call our customer service department at 1-800-232-0223 for details.

Cover design by Teresa Lagrange.

Visit us on the web at **www.myersedpress.com** to browse our complete list of titles.

CONTENTS

ACKNOWLEDGMENTS

THIS BOOK ENJOYS THE creative and intellectual labor of too many wonderful educators to name here. We are indebted to the many members of the Innovative Course-building Group over the last 15 years for their inspiration, willingness to share ideas, and ability to make teaching a more collaborative and joyful experience. We must acknowledge our friend and colleague Rosalie Richards, who provided important ideas, especially in the initial stages of writing, and asked lovingly critical questions that helped us be better and aim higher.

Thank you to all of our past, present, and future students—we believe in designing transformative courses because we believe you deserve this type of learning experience, because we want you to become your best selves, and because your success brings us joy.

Caralyn would like to thank all the amazing faculty she has worked with including the Environmental Science program faculty at Georgia College and the Intro Bio group at the University of Massachusetts Amherst. I admire your willingness to reflect, take risks, and be humble about your teaching, and for doing such amazing work for students. And for my parents, who have always been supportive and excited about my work. And special thanks to Wren and Will Duncan. Wren—your creativity and joy motivate me; may you always love learning. Will—thank you for your unwavering support, for always bringing me a hot cup of coffee, and for taking Wren outside so I could write.

Cynthia would like to thank all the Governor's Teaching Fellows and the faculty and staff of Georgia College; your commitment to education that truly transforms has been the foundation and inspiration for my work for nearly 20 years. Ideas I learned from you all permeate these pages. It has been a glorious ride, and I am looking forward to 20 more. And to my husband, Charlie Vaughn, who makes everything possible and the finest friends anyone could ask for.

Karynne has the good fortune to enjoy a diverse host of colleagues who are also great friends. Throughout the years of traversing miles of proverbial backroads together, they have provided recursive intellectual stimulation, continual emotional support, and transformational equanimity for which I will always be grateful. Special thanks to Mike Gleason, my "salad guy," who has abided by our pledge to sustain one another in all circumstances with especially good lunches. I am the lucky one.

Julia would like to acknowledge the incredible mentors who have been generous with their time, talents, and love—namely, Rosalie Richards and Jen Drake—and of course my talented coauthors. I owe much to the colleagues and friends that have sustained me in my journey as an educator and an educational developer who are too many to name. To Kathleen Eamon, Karen Gaul, Rachel Homchick, and Elizabeth Williamson—your support over the past year allowed me to contribute to this book, so a little piece of it is yours. And to my partner in life, Joe Metzker, for keeping me fed, having late-night conversations about our work, making me smile, and never waning in your support.

Thank you to the colleagues who provided feedback on our manuscript as we developed it: Christina Lunsmann, Mindy Maris, Monica Miller, Jeanne Sewell, Andrew Spracklen, and Bridget Trogden.

Finally, we thank Chris Myers and everyone at Myers Education Press for believing in this book and guiding it to completion.

FOREWORD

Each fall, a new crop of hopeful students arrives at our institutions eager to learn, but in a matter of weeks, hopes wane for some when they learn they have to get through core requirements before they get to the good stuff. Some may begin to doubt whether they have the tools necessary to persevere in meeting outcomes for which the purpose is unclear. What if the "good stuff" was infused throughout from day one? What if the purpose and meaning for every course were the first things on the syllabus? What if learners knew how each lesson fit into their big-picture plan? What if every course addressed a real-life issue, dilemma, or problem in some way? What if students were making a difference in their communities throughout their college careers? How might this focus change the student experience? Who could make this vision a reality? You could. Whether you are a veteran professor or a novice instructor, a faculty developer or a committed administrator, it could be you.

This book is built on the idea that meaningful learning experiences don't just happen—they have to be intentionally designed. We, like many of you, have each experienced poorly designed courses that we struggled through—not really understanding the point until much later in life, if at all. More important, this book's authors have experienced their own transformative learning experiences that ultimately led them to pursue a lifelong passion as educators. We have all created and taught courses intentionally designed to challenge and engage diverse groups of students. We understand the work that goes into good teaching, as well as the impact that innovative, well-designed courses, can have on student learning and on our own professional satisfaction. Our goal is to use our own experience, combined with research and a multitude of evidence-based teaching strategies, to provide you with a road map towards developing meaningful courses that integrate these strategies and promote learning for *all* students.

CHAPTER ONE

Teaching Matters

This We Know

WHY DO YOU NEED this book right now? The past decades have seen the publication of multiple articles and books detailing challenges faced by higher education with calls for reform to close equity gaps. Simultaneously, advancements in the science of learning from researchers in neuroscience, psychology, and education have resulted in new, evidence-based teaching practices that have not seen widespread adoption. The research base grows. Students change. We change. The world changes. We felt it was time for a practical guide to course design that also addresses where we are as a nation.

We won't have long strings of citations through most of this book, but in this chapter, we want to make clear the extent of the agreement on some crucial points.

Students entering college now, and the ones likely to enter in the future, are going to be different from the students you taught last year. Higher education in the United States is already experiencing large-scale demographic and socioeconomic shifts in student populations (Cahalan & Perna, 2015; Espinosa et al., 2019; Prescott, 2019). These changes are compounded by the unsustainability of an increasingly expensive educational model that widens the inequities between "successful" and "unsuccessful" learners (Addo et al., 2016; Choy, 2001; Ladson-Billings, 2006; McNair et al., 2016; The National Task Force on Civic Learning & Engagement, 2012; Witham et al., 2015).

There is tension over the value institutions place on teaching versus research. You may feel pulled, or stretched to the breaking point, by these tensions yourself. Many institutions, even smaller "teaching-focused" ones, are directing more resources toward research outputs (Blakey et al., 2017; Fairweather, 2005). Yet the success of universities is increasingly dependent on hiring faculty with the ability to support student success by having robust pedagogical knowledge in addition to specialized content knowledge (Berman, 2014; J. Brown & Kurzweil, 2018; Jankowski, 2017). However, most faculty still complete their graduate and postdoctoral work with very little pedagogical training (Beach et al., 2016; De Vlieger et al., 2017; Rossing & Lavitt, 2016).

Survey after survey of employers highlights demands for graduates who can communicate, problem-solve, and have the capacity to address complex problems independently and in teams (Bridgstock, 2009; Flores et al., 2012; Gallup-Purdue Index, 2014, 2015; Hart Research Associates, 2015a, 2015b, 2018; Pascarella & Terenzini, 2005; Trilling & Fadel, 2009). What many instructors want for students and what employers want have become strikingly similar. In fact, there are good arguments to be made that honoring the "economic imperative" helps address inequities in educational outcomes (Ludvik, 2020).

A persistent opportunity gap exists between Black, Indigenous, and people of color (BIPOC) and their White counterparts. This gap has remained despite decades of work, efforts to foster student success, and billions of dollars in funding (Becker et al., 2017; Carnevale & Strohl, 2013; Espinosa et al., 2019; Trapani & Hale, 2019). We now see the lack of legitimate progress coming to a head in the Black Lives Matters protests occurring literally as we write. We need to reflect on our positions of power in the classroom and evaluate our courses for, among other limitations, racism, biases, and barriers while focusing on incorporating more diverse content and culturally sustaining teaching. We must replace the deficit-based narrative that the low success rates of Black and Brown students are based on an inability to learn and succeed when the truth is that these low success rates are due to racism and bias. We need to identify and dismantle the institutional and systemic racism that holds back BIPOC students.

Research in education, cognitive science, psychology, and neuroscience has taught us so much about how people learn, moving us beyond the limited understanding of education as a transactional process. We now understand more fully the power of active learning, the types of studying strategies that actually work for retaining concepts and principles that are transferable across contexts, the importance of student self-motivation and their development of academic identities, and how factors such as a sense of belonging all contribute to enduring learning outcomes for individuals and learning communities. Yet sadly, we also know that these practices are not being deployed widely or equitably (Aronson & Laughter, 2016; Blaich & Wise, 2011; P. Brown et al., 2014; Carnevale & Strohl, 2013; Finley & McNair, 2013; Harackiewicz & Priniski, 2018; Hattie, 2012; Kilgo et al., 2015; Kuh, 2008; Lang, 2016; McConnell & Rhodes, 2017; National Research Council, 2000, 2001; Roksa & Arum, 2011; Winkelmes et al., 2016)

Moreover, institutions of higher education are ill prepared structurally to accommodate rapid change, even as the demands and expectations placed on higher education are changing at an ever-faster rate (Delbanco, 2012; McNair et al., 2016; Mehaffy, 2012). The effect of the COVID-19 pandemic on higher education is a clear example of this. From online learning to ethical teaching practices regarding student surveillance to the many ways in which teaching online has heightened inequities among students *and* faculty, the virus is impacting higher education in ways that we haven't yet fully realized or measured. The effect is surely going to be long-lasting and deep (C. Brown, 2020; Flaherty, 2020; Inside Higher Ed and Hanover Research, 2020; Kandri, 2020; Patel, 2020; Zhai & Du, 2020).

Based on these facts and observations, we believe that higher education needs to change, and we assume that you share this belief. If we continue to educate through a curricular and pedagogical model developed more than 100 years ago—the model that brought us to this moment of unacceptably low success for so many students—we will fail to realize the change these trends and reports call for. We believe there is no more critical place for these changes to be enacted than through the courses we create and teach.

Why We Teach

Most of us come to teaching with aspirational goals. We truly want the learners we work with to develop the skills necessary for critical evaluation of complex issues; to think creatively; to be able to collect, analyze, and interpret data; to work collaboratively as members of diverse teams; and to communicate clearly and effectively. Not surprisingly, these aspirational teaching goals are well aligned with nationwide initiatives, employer feedback about student career readiness (Gallup-Purdue Index, 2014, 2015; Hart Research Associates, 2015a, 2018), and the mission statements of so many of our own colleges and universities. Higher educators echo the common sentiment—we really want students to become lifelong learners—even as we recognize that we may not be able to see if this actually happens. Collectively, we long for the students we teach to become the civic leaders, inventors, creators, and caretakers that our world needs, even if this may be an all-too-infrequent outcome of the work done at colleges and universities.

But, when it comes down to the occasionally mundane and exhausting work of teaching our classes, we sometimes lose sight of these goals. Maybe we sell ourselves short and think that we couldn't possibly have an impact on students' futures when we only see them a few times a week for a semester. Perhaps we sell students short and think they couldn't handle big projects or the uncertainty associated with unpeeling the layers necessary for understanding complicated issues. Or possibly we just don't know how to be a transformative teacher, even if we entered the profession precisely to play such a role. After all, few of us have benefited from an education in how to teach. Whatever the reason, the student learning that occurs in our courses is too often not well aligned with our own aspirational goals.

In this field guide, we propose a cohesive process to bridge this gap: building courses around transferable learning outcomes that require students to engage with big questions facing our society. You will learn to connect your disciplinary content knowledge and skills to students' application of content and principles. With practice, you'll be able to intentionally incorporate meaningful learning outcomes in your courses through the design of learning experiences that support students in achieving these outcomes. You'll teach students how to collaborate, listen, and learn from each other by creating opportunities that intentionally challenge and engage students in tackling complex, real-world problems. It is these engaging challenges that lead to transformative learning. We define transformative learning similarly to Mezirow (1991); it is a quality of learning in which a student encounters an idea, a theory, or evidence that changes their perspective. Transformative learning makes a significant, long-term impact on the life of the student that can't be "shaken off" because it is part of the learner.

We propose that all students deserve transformative learning experiences and that they all should have the opportunity to succeed in their courses. By this we don't mean that students should skate through their education, coming out the same as they went in. In fact, the testament of transformation is that it changes the self and identity. We recognize that this has often not been the case for many because of the effect of systemic racism, sexism, and elitism in institutions of higher education and in college courses. Therefore, we intentionally create courses that are antiracist; utilize elements of affirming, decentering pedagogies; and are culturally inclusive.

This We Believe

Here we place our stake in the ground, a "stake" forged through our nearly 100 years of combined experiences in teaching and learning. These belief statements encapsulate our philosophy about course design, faculty professional development, and the future we envision for higher education.

We believe that

- courses that are intentionally designed result in more robust, transferable learning.
- all students are able to make important contributions in our classrooms.
- societal needs must inform decisions regarding the educational activities students engage with to develop students' internal motivation and provide purpose.
- faculty are ideally positioned to inspire students to change their communities and the world.
- faculty bring a wellspring of expertise and humanity to their teaching, which can provide a vitalizing source needed in this crucial work.
- empowering faculty with the knowledge, skills, and agency to mentor others leads to innovative courses that change students' lives.

Who We Are

It's no surprise that we have found in each other critical coauthors, esteemed colleagues, and valued friends. Working closely in many settings begets fond feelings, but in our case, we believe our type of teaching, which encourages vulnerability, emphasizes relationship building, and is premised on collaboration, has created the sturdy bonds that we enjoy. We see ourselves as partners, each with unique offerings yet stronger together than any one of us is alone. We don't guarantee that as you work through this book in pursuit of transformative education you will end up building unwavering friendships and brilliant collaborations. Yet we are convinced that transformative educators are marvelous folks that you'll be eager to know. Pause with us here as we introduce each other, and share a bit about ourselves, including our individual "whys" that brought us together to write this book.

Cynthia (she/her/hers) is a voracious reader across a multitude of subject areas with a talent for "cross-discipline idea synthesizing." Fortunately for the field of education, Cynthia applies her creative prowess to improving the art and science of teaching, which she does through a consistent inquiry as to how to reenchant learning for both students and faculty. As you might suspect, Cynthia's academic degrees span a wide spectrum from classical languages, philosophy, archaeology, and language education. She is also the lead lecturer for Georgia's "Governor's Teaching Fellows," a program she has worked with since 2001. As such, Cynthia has positively influenced college teaching nationally. Like others on the team, Cynthia is well connected to and rejuvenated by nature—she and her husband raise a critically endangered breed of sheep on their farm, Shangri-Baa.

Karynne (she/her/hers) is the veteran of the group, having over 35 years' experience in education. She has taught at every grade level from primary school to doctoral studies, where she has noted remarkable similarities in the integrative thinking processes exhibited by learners despite age differences. The field of education has provided her endless intellectual stimulation, which she cherishes. Karynne is the chatty one, and she enjoys nothing more than the opportunity to have conversations with others as a way of discovering and generating knowledge. She finds her best ideas come when she is in contact with others. Her educational philosophy continues to be hammered out, yet she focuses on finding out "what is" and then imagines and works to realize "what could be." As a strong advocate for democratic education, Karynne concentrates on addressing her own and others' biases that have fostered inequitable educational outcomes that serve to reinforce the status quo and limit life choices.

The member of this team who traverses the most miles is Julia (she/her/hers), whose journey from teaching chemistry at a public liberal arts college to a career as an educational developer started in Georgia. After a few years in Florida, she landed in Washington State, where she serves as the director of the Washington Center for

Improving Undergraduate Education at The Evergreen State College. Julia herself had a transformative undergraduate liberal arts education at Evergreen from which she launched to obtain a doctorate in inorganic chemistry—solidifying a professional identity that blends the value of scientific inquiry with the critical importance of valuing humanity. As is true for each of us, Julia sees learning that taps one's social network as powerful, and she consistently helps others connect to community resources that build interdependent webs. She has a special interest in seeing that attaining a college degree is something every individual can achieve—a goal she believes requires our colleges and universities to critically interrogate their structures and curricula. Julia and her partner (a speech pathologist) share a passion for helping every learner achieve their goals while caring for a household of four-legged friends, who also help them raise chickens and bees.

As captain for this adventure and consummate juggler, Caralyn (she/her/hers) is the one who kept us going among the myriad projects we're all knee-deep in and that threaten to obstruct us from our goal. Caralyn was the last of the team to come to Georgia College as a newly minted professor with a PhD in ecology, where the group first coalesced. After a stint as a professional development coordinator, she is now a flourishing faculty member in the Department of Biology at the University of Massachusetts Amherst. Caralyn's arrival at Georgia College was auspicious for her as well as for us as it was through collaboration that she uncovered her passion for transformative teaching and developed her identity as a professional educator. A delightful ally from the start, Caralyn added an analytic yet quieting perspective to the group's work. Caralyn takes her love of nature beyond her work as an ecologist, and on a good weekend, you'll find her out hiking and birding with her husband and daughter.

You may notice from this section that we are an optimistic group committed to improving our corner of the world by applying our various talents as teachers and learners. Although we each have particular disciplinary expertise, as a team we tend to be solution-oriented, holistic thinkers who focus on leverage points that offer the potential for change. Another characteristic we share is a strong work ethic. It is also important for us to claim our privilege as White women with roughly similar middle-class upbringings who had access to higher education because that experience is a lens through which our perspective toward education has been formed. We hope that from knowing about our commitments you will see why you would want to do the same and then make such commitments yourself. As we have supported each other in this journey, we would be gratified to support you on yours.

How to Use This Book

Now that you know a bit more about us, we want to provide some detail about how to use this book. This book is called a "field guide" because it is meant to be used in a much more interactive way than most books, even the most practical among them. We have led workshops on course design for many years, and over and over we see the same thing—people are excited about making a change and get started with course design, and then after the workshop is over, they lose steam. For our workshops, we developed a solution in which we asked faculty to work in pairs or teams to hold one another accountable and check in, long after the workshop has concluded. These teammates help brainstorm ideas, provide support, offer feedback, and check in with one another. They are often the secret to success. We designed this book to be used in pairs or teams, perhaps in a faculty learning community or part of a faculty development course. Obviously, it can be used alone, but if you can find a friend, we suspect you will have a more meaningful experience. After all, collaboration is one of the great joys of teaching. We invite you to connect with a greater community by sharing your progress on social media using the hashtag #learningthatmatters or commenting on our website https://learningthatmatters.weebly.com/. Enlisting others is a tried-and-true method for keeping motivation strong.

We also designed this book to be worked through slowly, ideally over a summer or a semester. Read a chapter. Think deeply. Follow up on some of the wonderful resources. Complete the activities, which will help you build your course step by step. Repeat. Enjoy.

You may also find this book a little unusual because we have endeavored to make it conversational and personal. While everything we recommend is informed by research, it has all been carefully field-tested and refined over time in our own classrooms. You will hear our voices throughout the text as we share our own experiences.

The chapters are structured in a way that models our view of excellent teaching practices. We open each chapter with a "preflection" to activate your thinking or prime you to identify current beliefs that you hold that will connect to the topic. We follow that initial connection by sharing our intentions for your learning—what we intend for you to know or be able to do after reading the chapter and completing the activities. The intended outcomes let you know where you are heading.

Throughout the chapters, you will find "Reflect to Learn" prompts. These are designed to be answered individually at first and then serve as discussion points when you come together with your partner or team. Or, for those of you working through the book alone, we invite you to use these reflective moments to initiate a conversation with us and others on social media (#learningthatmatters). Most chapters also include one or more activities, which are designed to help you practice or think through a concept. You'll encounter "Make It Happen" activities, which we created to lead you as you move step by step toward designing your course and put your learning into concrete action. We've carefully written each chapter so that you'll be able to take the ideas presented and apply them to the work you are currently doing.

We end each chapter with "Wonderful Resources to Extend Learning," and they are crucial. We wish this book could be everything you need to be an exceptional educator. We believe it will help you develop a transformative mindset and provide much-needed tools to get yourself rolling. The discipline of education is as complex as any other discipline. If only professors could have higher degrees in both their content field and education! There is no getting around it—you will have to continue to build your expertise in this area. Between the four of us, we have read an absurd number of resources on teaching in higher education. There were many that were forgettable, but a handful rise to the top. Throughout this book, we list our favorites, which we hope you will check out. You can also visit our website to learn more about other resources. There you can learn about what we are all currently up to, and maybe you'll invite us to visit with your faculty learning community now that COVID-19 has turned us all into Zoom experts.

Welcome. We are excited that you are now on this journey with us, helping us make a difference in the life outcomes of yourself and others!

Wonderful Resources to Extend Learning

The Courage to Teach **by Parker Palmer** (2017) provides an inspirational and thought-provoking foray into exploring the role of the educator in the classroom. Parker offers a gentle challenge to reduce the authority gap between teacher and learner by creating classrooms as communities of truth.

In the 16 essays penned in ***Teaching to Transgress: Education as the Practice of Freedom,*** **bell hooks** (1994) uses a feminist approach to education and offers a radical shift from dominant paradigms in education. This book will challenge you to interrogate how you teach and invite you into a liberatory practice.

References

Addo, F. R., Houle, J. N., & Simon, D. (2016). Young, Black, and (still) in the red: Parental wealth, race, and student loan debt. *Race and Social Problems, 8*(1), 64–76. https://doi.org/10.1007/s12552-016-9162-0

Aronson, B., & Laughter, J. (2016). The theory and practice of culturally relevant education. *Review of Educational Research, 86*(1), 163–206. https://doi.org/10.3102/ 0034654315582066

Beach, A. L., Sorcinelli, M. D., Austin, A. E., & Rivard, J. K. (2016). *Faculty development in the age of evidence: Current practices, future imperatives.* Stylus Publishing.

Becker, A. S., Cummins, M., Davis, A., Freeman, A., Hall Giesinger, C., & Ananthanarayanan, V. (2017). *NMC Horizon report: 2017 higher education edition.* The New Media Consortium.

Berman, R. A. (2014, September). Engaging students requires a renewed focus on teaching. *Chronicle of Higher Education, 61*(3), B28–B30.

Blaich, C. F., & Wise, K. (2011). *From gathering to using assessment results: Lessons from the Wabash National Study* (NILOA Occasional Paper, 8). National Institute for Learning Outcomes Assessment.

Blakey, E., Khachikian, C., & Lemus, D. (2017). Increasing research requirements for tenure at teaching universities: Mission creep or mission critical? *Teacher-Scholar: The Journal of the State Comprehensive University, 8*(1), Article 3. https://scholars.fhsu.edu/ts/vol8/iss1/3

Bridgstock, R. (2009). The graduate attributes we've overlooked: Enhancing graduate employability through career management skills. *Higher Education Research and Development, 28*(1), 31–44. https://doi.org/10.1080/07294360802444347

Brown, C. (2020, April 9). *Readying for the future: COVID-19, higher ed, and fairness.* Lumina Foundation. https://www.luminafoundation.org/news-and-views/readying-for-the-future-covid-19-higher-ed-and-fairness/

Brown, J., & Kurzweil, M. (2018). *Instructional quality, student outcomes, and institutional finances.* American Council on Education.

Brown, P. C., Roediger, H. L., & McDaniel, M. A. (2014). *Make it stick: The science of successful learning.* Harvard University Press.

Cahalan, M., & Perna, L. (2015). *Indicators of higher education equity in the United States: 45 year trend report.* Pell Institute for the Study of Opportunity in Higher Education. www.pellinstitute.org

Carnevale, A. P., & Strohl, J. (2013). *Separate & unequal: How higher education reinforces the intergenerational reproduction of White racial privilege.* Georgetown University Center on Education and the Workforce.

Choy, S. (2001). *Students whose parents did not go to college: Postsecondary access, persistence, and attainment* (NCES 2001–126). U.S. Department of Education, National Center for Education Statistics.

De Vlieger, P., Jacob, B. A., & Stange, K. (2017). Measuring up: Assessing instructor effectiveness in higher education. *Education Next, 17*(3), 68–74.

Delbanco, A. (2012). *College: What it was, is, and should be.* Princeton University Press.

Espinosa, L. L., Turk, J. M., Taylor, M., & Chessman, H. M. (2019). *Race and ethnicity in higher education: A status report.* American Council on Education.

Fairweather, J. S. (2005). Beyond the rhetoric: Trends in the relative value of teaching and research in faculty salaries. *The Journal of Higher Education, 76*(4), 401–422. https://doi.org/10.1080/00221546.2005.11772290

Finley, A., & McNair, T. (2013). *Assessing underserved students' engagement in high-impact practices.* Association of American Colleges and Universities.

Flaherty, C. (2020, May 11). Big Proctor. *Inside Higher Ed.* https://www.insidehighered.com/news/2020/05/11/online-proctoring-surging-during-covid-19

Flores, K. L., Matkin, G. S., Burbach, M. E., Quinn, C. E., & Harding, H. (2012). Deficient critical thinking skills among college graduates: Implications for leadership. *Educational Philosophy and Theory, 44*(2), 212–230.

Gallup-Purdue Index. (2014). *Great jobs, great lives: A study of more than 30,000 college graduates across the U.S.* (Gallup-Purdue Index Report, 22).

Gallup-Purdue Index. (2015). *Great jobs, great Lives: The relationship between student debt, experiences and perceptions of college worth* (Gallup-Purdue Index Report, 24).

Harackiewicz, J. M., & Priniski, S. J. (2018). Improving student outcomes in higher education: The science of targeted interventions. *Annual Review of Psychology, 69*(1), 409–435. https://doi.org/10.1146/annurev-psych-122216-011725

Hart Research Associates. (2015a). *Falling short? College learning and career success.* https://www.aacu.org/leap/public-opinion-research/2015-survey-falling-short

Hart Research Associates. (2015b). *Optimistic about the future, but how well prepared? College students' views on college learning and career success.* https://www.aacu.org/leap/public-opinion-research/2015-students

Hart Research Associates. (2018). *Fulfilling the American dream: Liberal education and the future of work.* https://www.aacu.org/research/2018-future-of-work

Hattie, J. (2012). *Visible learning for teachers: Maximizing impact on learning.* Routledge.

hooks, b. (1994). *Teaching to transgress: Education as the practice of freedom.* Routledge.

Inside Higher Ed and Hanover Research. (2020). *Responding to the COVID-19 crisis, part II: A survey of college and university presidents.*

Jankowski, N. A. (2017). *Unpacking relationships: Instruction and student outcomes*. American Council on Education.

Kandri, S.-E. (2020, May 12). *How COVID-19 is driving a long-overdue revolution in education*. World Economic Forum. https://www.weforum.org/agenda/2020/05/how-covid-19-is-sparking-a-revolution-in-higher-education/

Kilgo, C. A., Sheets, J. K. E., & Pascarella, E. T. (2015). The link between high-impact practices and student learning: Some longitudinal evidence. *Higher Education, 69*(4), 509–525.

Kuh, G. D. (2008). *High-impact educational practices: What they are, who has access to them and why they matter*. Association of American Colleges and Universities.

Ladson-Billings, G. (2006). From the achievement gap to the education debt: Understanding achievement in U.S. schools. *Educational Researcher, 35*(7), 3–12. https://doi.org/ 10.3102/0013189x035007003

Lang, J. M. (2016). *Small teaching: Everyday lessons from the science of learning*. Jossey-Bass.

Ludvik, M. B. (2020). A new era of accountability: Resolving the clash of public good and economic stimulation performance. In J. P. Freeman, C. L. Keller, & R. L. Cambiano (Eds.), *Higher education response to exponential societal shifts* (pp. 251–274). IGI Global.

McConnell, K. D., & Rhodes, T. L. (2017). *On solid ground: VALUE report 2017*. Association of American Colleges and Universities. https://www.aacu.org/OnSolidGroundVALUE

McNair, T. B., Albertine, S. L., Cooper, M. A., McDonald, N. L., & Major, T. (2016). *Becoming a student-ready college: A new culture of leadership for student success*. John Wiley & Sons.

Mehaffy, G. L. (2012). Challenge and change. *Educause Review, 47*(5), 25–42.

Mezirow, J. (1991). *Transformative dimensions of adult learning*. Jossey-Bass.

National Research Council. (2000). *How people learn: Brain, mind, experience, and school* (J. D. Bransford, A. L. Brown, & R. R. Cocking, Eds.). National Academies Press. https://doi.org/ 10.17226/9853

National Research Council. (2001). *Knowing what students know: The science and design of educational assessment* (J. W. Pellegrino, N. Chudowsky, & R. Glaser, Eds.). National Academies Press. https://doi.org/10.17226/10019

The National Task Force on Civic Learning and Democratic Engagement. (2012). *A crucible moment: College learning and democracy's future*. Association of American Colleges and Universities.

Palmer, P. J. (2017). *The courage to teach: Exploring the inner landscape of a teacher's life*. John Wiley & Sons.

Pascarella, E. T., & Terenzini, P. T. (2005). *How college affects students: A third decade of research* (Vol. 2). Jossey-Bass.

Patel, V. (2020, April). Covid-19 is a pivotal moment for struggling students. Can colleges step up? *Chronicle of Higher Education*. https://www.chronicle.com/article/Covid-19-Is-a-Pivotal-Moment/248501

Prescott, B. T. (2019). Recent trends in several key metrics in higher education. *Change: The Magazine of Higher Learning, 51*(1), 22–27. https://doi.org/10.1080/00091383.2019.1547075

Roksa, J., & Arum, R. (2011). The state of undergraduate learning. *Change: The Magazine of Higher Learning, 43*(2), 35–38. https://doi.org/10.1080/00091383.2011.556992

Rossing, J. P., & Lavitt, M. R. (2016). The neglected learner: A call to support integrative learning for faculty. *Liberal Education, 102*(2), 34–41.

Trapani, J., & Hale, K. (2019). *Higher education in science and engineering. Science and engineering indicators 2020* (NSB-2019-7). https://ncses.nsf.gov/pubs/nsb20197/

Trilling, B., & Fadel, C. (2009). *21st century skills: Learning for life in our times*. John Wiley & Sons.

Winkelmes, M.-A., Bernacki, M., Butler, J., Zochowski, M., Golanics, J., & Weavil, K. H. (2016). A Teaching intervention that increases underserved college students' success. *Peer Review, 18*(1/2), 31–36.

Witham, K., Malcom-Piqueux, L. E., Dowd, A. C., & Bensimon, E. (2015). *America's unmet promise: The imperative for equity in higher education*. Association of American Colleges and Universities.

Zhai, Y., & Du, X. (2020). Addressing collegiate mental health amid COVID-19 pandemic. *Psychiatry Research, 288*(1), Article 113003. https://doi.org/10.1016/j.psychres.2020. 113003

CHAPTER TWO

From the Foundation Up

MOVING FORWARD, WE WILL start each chapter with "pre"flection, which is the act of engaging in serious and careful thought about an event before it occurs (Falk, 1995). As an activation technique, preflection helps learners anticipate and prepare for learning by thinking about an idea or experience before they know much about it or go on to deepen their understanding. We encourage you to avoid the temptation to rush ahead, but rather give yourself the gift of a moment of preflection.

Preflection

Would you consider teaching as an art? A science? Neither? Both?

As you read this chapter, reflect on it, and engage with the activities both independently and with fellow readers, note that it has been designed to support you in the following:

- Exploring the concept of teaching perspectives in order to determine the perspective you most strongly identify with
- Familiarizing yourself with the anchor concepts utilized throughout the book
- Examining how your teaching perspective integrates with these anchor concepts

Creativity abounds in teaching—from performance in the classroom to designing the curriculum to meeting the needs of diverse learners. This degree of creativity means that transformative teaching requires much improvisation. You might think that improvisation suggests no structure, but improvisation requires one to have a set of guiding principles that can be extracted and applied to evolving contexts (Sawyer, 2011). Taking on the metaphor of teaching as improvisation calls for a balance of identity exploration, a strong foundation, and an ability to adapt while shepherding each learner toward their goals. In this chapter, we explore some principles or key concepts for learning that provide a strong core for improvisation, including knowing your current stance toward teaching, foundational pedagogies and practices that foster learning, and, ultimately, integrating practice and theory with your identity as a professional educator who continuously seeks to hone your craft. We start our journey through the course design process in what might seem like an unlikely place—*you*—by asking you first to consider who you are as a teacher and then to think about how some key foundational concepts either fit into that identity or require that identity to expand or explode.

Who Are You?

We presume you are a professional educator who cares deeply about students and their learning and that one reason you are reading this book is to further develop in this role. That is why we begin by asking you to turn inward as a starting point to consider who you are now and, looking ahead, who you'd like to be as an educator. We are firm believers that this type of learning about yourself matters.

In his groundbreaking book *The Courage to Teach*, Parker Palmer (2017) asks us to consider an interesting proposition—namely, that educators teach who they are. Because we have gained so much from reflecting on how our own identities and values inform how (and what) we teach, we have become advocates for the introspective process of self-discernment. Here, we offer you a space to examine how the values you bring to the classroom inform your decision-making. Having an awareness of your identity as a professional will help you align your beliefs and values with your teaching practices, bringing a sense of cohesion and integrity to your work.

Have you ever been asked to write your story as a professional educator? Have you interrogated the assumptions you carry about teaching or about student learning? How might your responses to these questions uncover the values you hold or your reasons for choosing teaching as a vocation? Here you will get closer to writing your story and, thus, to fulfilling your aspirations as a teacher by reflecting on five teaching perspective categories that have been operationalized through the Teaching Perspectives Inventory (Pratt et al., 2001).

Through decades of observational qualitative studies of higher educators, Collins and Pratt (2011) have found that despite the many variations in personal style, educators conceive of teaching in ways that fall predominantly into five categories, or perspectives. Each perspective represents a distinctive complement of actions, intentions, and beliefs about learning, teaching, and knowledge. No one perspective is "better" than another, but becoming aware of your conceptions of "good teaching" will allow you to be more successful on your own and in work with colleagues, no matter your dominant perspective.

Activity: Your Teaching Perspective

Read through the following fictional scenarios and consider which seems most like you. Each scenario connects to one of the five teaching perspectives to help you think about your own actions, intentions, and beliefs about teaching.

(As you read these stories, remember to focus on the approach and values, not the subject matter.)

Niko Jackson (they/them/theirs) took up art in high school and tinkered in a range of media before committing themself to training as a muralist. Recently, Dr. Jackson was excited to find a site just beyond the outskirts of the campus for students to complete their capstone project—beautifying an abandoned appliance factory. Before beginning the collaborative design, Niko modeled their thinking for students by juxtaposing the ways appliances from the factory improved quality of life for many nationwide with the poverty experienced by factory workers and the local community after the factory was closed to move production to Thailand. Niko used samples of interviews they had conducted with elders of another blighted community as a lesson for understanding how murals could be art while also honoring the experiences of those who had lived and worked in the area.

Margot Rideau (she/her/hers), an experienced and highly respected historian, was preparing for two upcoming courses: an introductory Survey of American Government and an upper level seminar on the American presidency. Dr. Rideau was considering using some common readings because she wanted students to critically read primary and secondary sources in both classes. However, when she reread the texts, Margot determined that several complex concepts were implied throughout them that she didn't think were explicit enough for the students in the survey course. Ultimately, she selected less complicated texts with similar themes to foster and scaffold the development of critical thinking skills in the survey course.

Daniel Ortiz (he/him/his) is energized by being around students and loves his daily interactions with them. He believes his course, Principles of Biology, may be the last chance for some of them to fulfill their potential in becoming the capable scientists that he knows they could be. Mr. Ortiz is saddened that some students rarely speak in class, suggesting they don't believe in themselves, so he initiates an assignment for students to track their own academic achievement. Every class period, Daniel makes a point of providing students with verbal encouragement. He spends a great deal of time in his office reviewing student performances and their work products so that he can give positive feedback, especially to those students he suspects have low self-esteem.

Bill Boykin (he/him/his) has been the director of mathematics for his entire career at a prestigious prep school that pulls its student body from around the nation. As the basis of his statistics and data analysis courses, Dr. Boykin teaches students to use their math skills and reasoning abilities to critique the system of meritocracy that might lead students to believe that every one of their classmates has had the same opportunity to excel in mathematics. The culminating assignment for the course is a project titled "Is Zip Code Destiny?" whereby students use various databases to correlate the life trajectories of a series of invented "classmates" to the neighborhoods where they allegedly were born. He assigns students to write letters to their families explaining the project and the mathematics and other skills they enhanced throughout it. Finally, Bill asks students to detail their response to the project question in a written statement and take a position as to whether all students have the same chance of excelling in mathematics.

Ashi Santra (she/her/hers) studied nursing in her home country before moving to the United States at the age of 24. After several years' experience in different hospital units, she earned a doctorate in nursing practice and became faculty at her adopted state's flagship institution. Dr. Santra is quite knowledgeable about her content and sees how critical the progression of courses in the Bachelors of Science in Nursing program is to the production of professional nurses. As she prepared her lecture notes to teach her first cohort of students, Ashi selected 10 to 12 chapters in each text and determined whether she would lecture for 75 minutes once a week or 50 minutes twice a week, using the other time for labs. Dr. Santra couldn't wait to show students the effective note-taking method that she had learned in her doctoral program so that they would be able to quickly absorb the information that she conveyed.

Now that you've read through the scenarios, select the one that best fits how you approach teaching. Of course, you might see yourself in more than one vignette, but select the primary example of how you might teach. What is it about that scenario that resonates?

Each scenario presents a narrative associated with dominance in one of the following five teaching perspectives from Pratt and Collins' work (2011). We encourage you to take the Teaching Perspectives Inventory (TPI; http://www.teachingperspectives.com/tpi/) to learn more about this process and each perspective.

- Apprenticeship—teaching requires learners to perform authentic tasks that challenge them to apply their knowledge (Niko Jackson).
- Developmental—teaching should be planned with the students' development in mind moving from simple to complex concepts as they develop (Margot Rideau).
- Nurturing—teaching comes from the heart and serves to develop students' self-esteem, work ethic, and persistence (Daniel Ortiz).
- Social reform—the aim of teaching is to develop a collective of students toward challenging the status quo and examining the world for power imbalances to address inequities (Bill Boykin).
- Transmission—teaching is effective when experts have a strong command of the subject matter so as to present the content accurately and efficiently (Ashi Santra).

You may wonder which one of these perspectives is the best way to teach. The answer is all of them. These are stances—viewpoints—that we all bring to teaching. Because we come from different backgrounds and experiences, have been trained in different disciplines, and hold different values and identities, none of these perspectives is wrong—just as none of them is "right." The perspectives simply are and describe what we as individuals and educators deem important.

Exploring all these perspectives and adopting pieces of each can help you become stronger, more fluid, and more improvisational in your teaching practice. A blended approach, combining aspects from multiple perspectives, can improve your teaching, help you connect with more students, and help you adapt to different contexts. Moreover, you'll be able to understand and appreciate colleagues who see things differently. Imagine creating an assignment with a colleague who holds the transmission perspective while you are a nurturer. By applying ideas from both perspectives, you can collaboratively develop an assignment that requires extensive preparation and also engages students in metacognitive reflection. This type of teamwork assists students in achieving deeper learning than they might have had only one approach been present, and the assignment offers students multiple ways of demonstrating success. Over the course of reading this book, your dominant perspective may change, or you may see yourself reflected in more than one perspective. We encourage you to take this opportunity to cultivate your own flexibility and change, add, or discard pieces that no longer fit. Just as we believe transformative education can change students, we also believe that becoming a transformative educator nourishes growth and metamorphosis.

> **Reflect to Learn:** Consider the five teaching perspectives discussed in the activity. What are some of the strengths associated with the perspective you selected? Are there elements of the other perspectives that might extend your teaching range?

As we have taken more risks in our courses and challenged ourselves to design courses for students rather than for younger versions of ourselves, the following concepts and theories have become our anchors. Throughout this book, and in all the courses we teach, we build on a foundation of equity, learning theories, student engagement, and motivational theory. As we introduce you to these anchor concepts, consider how they integrate with your own teaching perspective.

Anchor Concept I: Teach Toward Equity

As four White, cis women who walk with immense privilege, we are committed to taking actionable steps toward teaching for equity, knowing we will take missteps. Acknowledging that these mistakes will happen does not let us off the hook when they happen, and we will own those mistakes. The risk of mistakes cannot be used as an excuse to not commit to this important work. Too often, the work and effort done by Black, Indigenous, and people of color (BIPOC) are used by non-BIPOC individuals without adequate reference, and then the non-BIPOC receives the credit and praise. We are not the creators of this equity work, and we have endeavored to acknowledge the original idea generators.

Critical theorists who are making advances in the scholarship of decolonizing, queer, feminist, antiracist, or culturally sustaining pedagogies certainly operate from distinct perspectives that reveal subtle differences in their fields. However, the pedagogies that have emerged from this scholarship have much in common as they all aim to decenter the Western heterosexual cisgendered White male experience so that it is no longer considered the "normal"—a perspective that is commonly the default in college courses (Blackwell, 2010; Ellsworth, 1989; Gay, 2018; Haltinner, 2014; Jenkins, 2018; Kishimoto, 2018; Ladson-Billings, 1995; Morrison, 2017; Smith et al., 2008; Tejeda et al., 2003; Zacko-Smith & Smith, 2010). While the overall philosophies and aims of these bodies of research are different, when we focus on the pedagogies, the methods and practices of teaching, we see meaningful overlap.

These decentering pedagogies invite students and faculty to join together in learning communities. To accomplish this, students need to seek and discover for themselves and to co-create knowledge alongside professors and peers. Entering into relationships in which students and faculty are co-creators may seem odd, but it is more a shift in control than it is in style. Social learning theory related to participation in a community of practice (Lave & Wenger, 1991) explains that by interacting with regularity in a shared activity, members of the community are together constructing "what counts" as knowledge. You'll know you are getting this shift right when you realize that you are experiencing, and not merely delivering, important learning from students. Learning from and with students dismantles the hierarchy that typically puts the professor in control at the head of the class and the students at a lower level. Unfortunately, for many learners, the experience of being "lesser than" is difficult to shake, which obstructs their development and fulfillment of human potential.

In beginning to decenter, one area that demands examination is the "hidden curriculum." As opposed to the formal curriculum that is intentionally taught, hidden curriculum refers to the unintended and unarticulated lessons, values, and perspectives that students learn in school. When young people are praised for being quiet and punished for talking "out of turn" students learn to keep potentially contentious concerns to themselves. When the textbook covers American history predominantly from the standpoint of White citizens, a certain exclusive story is told. Because potent messages are implicitly communicated to students, they become normalized as "the right way to do things" and often disallow other interpretations, values, or perspectives. For learners who do not see their own cultural values reflected in those being transmitted, for those who do not easily pick up lessons from the hidden curriculum, and for those who are learning to think critically, the hidden curriculum should be made explicit and subject to critique. It is not possible to eradicate a hidden curriculum, but exposure can defang its potential to do harm. Bringing to light lessons being learned and making visible the monopoly of uncontested messages can be one way to teach toward equity.

Reflect to Learn: In your teaching experience, when have you felt you were learning as much from students as they were learning from you and in which the class engaged in a co-construction of knowledge?

Decolonizing, queer, feminist, antiracist, or culturally sustaining pedagogies value experience as a form of knowing and recognize that all students come to our classes with a rich, lived experience. Rather than viewing students within a deficit framework, whereby professors need to "fix" and "fill up" their deficits (with the knowledge they have), instead consider the assets, the cultural knowledge, experiences, practices, and perspectives that students bring to the course (Gay, 2018; González et al., 2005; Morrison, 2017; Zhao, 2016). This means valuing the diversity in those experiences and perspectives and not defaulting to centering the White, cis, heterosexual, neurotypical male experience. For some, ourselves included, this requires focus and effort because our upbringings and experiences have taught us to do the opposite. Those who may have been damaged or sidelined by normative, oppressive, exclusive, unquestioned educational practices may feel disoriented by our attempts to decenter our own privilege. We acknowledge that the privileges we hold interfere with our understanding of your experience. Yet we feel that if we were to stand by and continue to let harm occur and do nothing, we would be making the wrong choice. In this decision, we are guided by what we hold to be our responsibility to act to address injustice, to ensure fairness, and to right wrongs, however clumsy these efforts may be.

Beginning to Decenter

Ibram X. Kendi (2019b) writes, "There is no such thing as a 'not-racist' policy, idea or person. Just an old-fashioned racist in a newfound denial. All policies, ideas and people are either being racist or antiracist" (para. 15). The same can be said of pedagogies—they are either racist or antiracist. If we don't adopt explicitly antiracist teaching practices, then we risk perpetuating the same White supremacy that permeates and poisons our institutions and our society. Higher education was designed to be exclusive and support the success of White rich men (Delbanco, 2012; McNair et al., 2016), so it is not surprising that many of the policies and teaching methods commonly utilized in colleges and universities continue to exclude, dehumanize, and even crush students who don't fit into society's collective idea of what a "college student" is.

If you identify as White, you may have cringed at our use of "White supremacy"; that may be understandable but something that we believe that you will need to overcome. White supremacy is not a label only for evil neo-Nazi groups or skinheads. In their workbook, *Dismantling Racism Works* (dRworks, n.d.) defines White supremacy culture as "the idea (ideology) that white people and the ideas, thoughts, beliefs, and actions of white people are superior to those of People of Color" (para 9). White supremacy culture dehumanizes students of color, widens the opportunity gap, and hurts all of us.

Activity: Interrogating White Supremacy in Your Classes

We created the following list by reflecting on the characteristics of White supremacy culture in Jones and Okun's (2001) *Dismantling Racism* workbook. We then considered how these characteristics have been left unquestioned to become the norm in centers of learning.

Review this list. What statements make you uncomfortable? What could you add?

White supremacy in our classrooms occurs when we do the following:

- View failure as an indication that someone doesn't belong in our course (or institution) rather than as an opportunity for learning.
- Create learning environments that normalize White behavior and expect everyone else to assimilate.
- Don't provide time to learn from mistakes.

- Spend more time and energy identifying what is wrong (with students and their work) rather than what is right.
- Communicate that we always know what's best for the group.
- Are uncomfortable with emotions or feelings in the classroom, acting as if knowledge and understanding are separate from emotion.
- Equate certain styles of written communication with higher intelligence.
- React defensively when students suggest changes.
- Encourage competition among students rather than cooperation.
- Value linear thinking and devalue nonlinear thinking or show impatience with students who do not follow our way of thinking or doing.

Most of us don't intend to be racist. Nevertheless, not intending to harm doesn't absolve us of the responsibility to identify how our pedagogies may produce harmful outcomes for students. Once we identify them, we must then act to extricate damaging pedagogies from our practice. We have a moral and ethical imperative to close opportunity gaps by changing the culture of our courses to support all students.

The following are steps to becoming a more equitable educator:

1. Educate yourself—there are great resources listed at the end of this chapter.
2. Evaluate the authors, examples, stories, voices, and role models you include in your curriculum. Intentionally include non-White scholars and non-Western methodologies. Use inclusive examples that center individuals from diverse backgrounds and identities.
3. Critically examine your course policies, syllabus, and activities against the list in the previous activity. We provide more methods and examples of what your new, equitable course might look like throughout the book.
4. Consider how you teach about race/racism, sex/gender/sexism, and power in your course, even if these are not topics that you would traditionally address. Most of our disciplines were built, intentionally or unintentionally, through the lens of White supremacy. Consider who historically or currently decided what counted as knowledge in your field. Who was left out? Who was harmed or exploited to gain knowledge? Whose bodies or minds were considered "typical" and worth studying, whose were left unexamined, and whose were exploited? Who were able to be professional creators and whose creations were never even witnessed by mainstream society?

5. Use current events as teaching tools. If a noteworthy racist or sexist incident happens on your campus, in your state, in your country, or in the world, then address this in class to show that you believe this is wrong and should not be tolerated or ignored. Students, especially those who are part of the group that experienced the incident, will be affected, and your silence on the issue can be interpreted as support for oppression.

6. Ask a trusted colleague to observe a discussion in your classroom and perform an audit noticing who speaks, who is interrupted, who is deferred to, and who is ignored.

Remember at the end of Chapter 1, we encouraged you to take time for reflection and not rush through each chapter? Now might be a good time to put the book down and consider what you just learned.

Anchor Concept II: Construct and Connect

Now we're going to examine foundational learning theories that we have found to be important in our understanding of how people learn. In the 20th century, a great deal of work was done by researchers such as Piaget (1936) and Vygotsky (1978) that examined how individuals, working independently and in groups, construct knowledge. These explanations are grouped today under a learning theory known as constructivism. Constructivism has two main premises: (1) All learners come with previous knowledge—although this knowledge varies across learners' experiences—so they never hold precisely the same understandings, and (2) learners engage to make meaning of experiences and thus are actively building on their previous knowledge. Often, constructivist learning is augmented by participating with others. Within a constructivist approach, learners are not passive receptors with teachers acting as experts who transfer information to students. Instead, learning is best explained as an active construction process that is enhanced by the resources the learner and others bring to the process. In other words, learning is social and builds on prior knowledge. Orchestrating meaningful experiences occurs in communities of learners because each person's experiences from the various cultures to which they belong affect learning, perception, and cognition. In response, more emphasis has been placed on students working collaboratively before completing individual assignments, and dialogue and discussion are now considered as central, even necessary, course features (Barkley et al., 2014; Kuh, 2008).

Constructivist and social constructivist approaches are (too slowly) replacing the outdated model of one smart teacher dispensing knowledge from the front of a classroom while students of similar ages and backgrounds listen passively in quiet rows. The assumption that this unidirectional transfer of information was equated with learning went unquestioned for generations. Although seemingly efficient, linear frameworks for teaching and learning began to break down because they didn't take into account learner differences, varying learning contexts, and the role of human interaction (National Academies of Sciences, Engineering, and Medicine, 2018). Mass-production learning models have dominated the international landscape for centuries, wherein isolated learners were tasked with independently stockpiling information in their heads that originated from that fixed point, the teacher. In contrast, constructivist approaches are being embraced by cultures around the world bringing the promise to foster the innovation, creativity, and equity for students that teacher-centered pedagogies obstruct (Pham, 2016).

Fast-forward to the present where teachers and students encounter dizzying degrees of innovation due to rapidly proliferating technologies. For the foreseeable future, students will be expected to be savvy about internet tools and to develop their digital fluency and creativity. Some researchers now propose that the internet has changed the nature of learning. They theorize that it is the collective connections among all the junctions in a network that result in new forms of knowledge (Downes, 2010; Siemens, 2005). Known as *connectivism*, this still controversial theory recognizes that knowledge is dynamic and proposes that learning can happen outside of individuals. Two principles of connectivism that we want to highlight as especially relevant to transformative teaching are "the capacity to know more is more critical than what is currently known" and "nurturing and maintaining connections is needed to facilitate continual learning" (Siemens, 2005, "Principles of Connectivism"). When we talk of students becoming lifelong learners, we are acknowledging that the ability to identify a problem and take steps to solve it is more valuable than specific content knowledge. Our ability to build and maintain relationships, whether in face-to-face or virtual environments, supports psychological relatedness and promotes learning. In other words, we ascribe to a social learning view that emphasizes the active building of knowledge through reflection and relationship development.

Activity: Learning Theories Concept Map

A concept map is a drawing or diagram showing connections between ideas or concepts. It is a way to organize knowledge. Typically, the concepts are enclosed in boxes or circles, and linking words are written on lines connecting the boxes that describe how the concepts are related. A concept map focuses attention on the mental maps we use to organize information. If you've never created a concept map before, a quick web search will yield an abundance of examples.

Write "Learning theories" in a box or circle in the center of a blank piece of paper (or a screen). Write the terms *constructivism, connectivism, learning, teaching, students*, and *professor* on the paper. Draw lines between terms that you feel are connected and label them to elaborate the connections. Review the previous section and add more terms or phrases to your concept map.

Compare and discuss your concept map with your partner or group. Share a photo of your map with the hashtag #learningthatmatters.

Anchor Concept III: Engage Students Actively

We all want students to be engaged and excited about learning our subject. That engagement is not automatic, and it is both the responsibility and privilege of the instructor to build a learning environment that fosters rich engagement with ideas and people. Many of us were fortunate to encounter a teacher or situation that provided this spark, and now we need to create those same experiences for the students who look to us as teachers. We also need to keep in mind that the students we teach are not *us*, and some even actively resist learning (Kohl & Kozol, 1995), so there is no reason to expect that the same ideas or activities that first engaged us will work for today's learners.

Caralyn's Experience

Engagement looks like students talking to each other, puzzling over challenging questions that allow them to apply concepts in novel ways. If it's one of my large lecture classes, it sounds like a dull roar. The students don't look at me, rather they are engrossed in talking with partners. I walk around, answer questions, provide "just in time" announcements, and try to keep a running average of how far along everyone is. I spent hours beforehand creating the questions and providing the background material, and now I take a back seat to these students having crafted a lesson so they would have the time and brainspace to think, get frustrated, figure it out, and learn.

Reflect to Learn: What is generally happening in your classroom when students are most engaged with learning course material? What are students doing? What are you doing? How do you feel when this happens?

In her book *Student Engagement Techniques*, Elizabeth Barkley (2009) defines student engagement as "a process and a product that is experienced on a continuum and results from the synergistic interaction between motivation and active learning" (p. 8). She is a professor of music, and she shows her ability to make interdisciplinary connections by using DNA as a model to describe how student engagement bridges motivation and active learning. She paints the analogy using a strand of DNA, a double helix rising like a spiral staircase. While one twirled banister represents "student motivation" and the opposite yet equivalent curve is "active learning," the ascendant stair steps that yoke the two are represented as "student engagement." Because both are equally important for student engagement, we explore both in more detail.

We use the definition of *active learning* from Freeman et al. (2014) in their meta-analysis of active learning in STEM (science, technology, engineering, mathematics) courses: "Active learning engages students in the process of learning through activities and/or discussion in class, as opposed to passively listening to an expert. It emphasizes higher-order thinking and often involves group work" (p. 8413). This approach draws from social constructivism and is contrasted with a more didactic or lecture-based approach whereby students mainly take notes and occasionally interrupt the proceedings with a question.

One easy-to-implement, active-learning technique you may be familiar with is *think–pair–share*:

Think–Pair–Share

What: A quick and easy method for increasing student engagement and participation.

How: Pose a question to students. Instruct them to first respond to the question through individual thinking or writing. Then, invite students to share their responses with a partner. Finally, ask students to share their own or their partner's responses with the class.

When: Whenever you want students to stop and process learning. This is a great technique to use in any class, any time.

Why: Students have the opportunity to develop their own thinking and check in with a peer before sharing. The intimidation or hesitancy some students have about speaking in class is countered by providing low-stakes opportunities to form ideas and practice articulating them. Also, it gets everyone involved learning immediately.

Activity: Think–Pair–Share

THINK: What are the benefits, to you and students, of using teaching methods that actively involve students in their learning?
PAIR: Discuss your answer with a partner.
SHARE: Communicate your answers with a larger group or start a virtual conversation at #learningthatmatters.

If you've ever graded an exam or an essay and thought to yourself, "I said this multiple times in class, why do so many students have it wrong?" then you've highlighted an instance where you likely need more active learning. Stating something in class, even repeated several times, does not translate to learning for many students. Listening, while an important and critical first step in learning, is passive. The missing ingredient is built-in opportunities for processing. Cognitive processing moves sensory material into long-term memory. That's why no matter how captivating and entertaining a lecture is, if the audience is not using and applying the material, then many won't learn it deeply enough to retain it.

Have you ever listened to a TED Talk on a topic outside of your area of expertise? The speaker begins with an interesting narrative, shows research and evidence, and clearly explains a complex concept using everyday language and examples. However, when you go to describe that TED Talk to someone, you have difficulty relaying the particulars and find holes in what you're able to recall. You may have been entertained, but because you were listening rather than connecting the ideas, you forgot the key points and, of course, couldn't convey the ideas to others.

We don't know about you, but most of our lectures are not as polished as a TED Talk. Does it make sense to devote effort toward being more polished when you can have greater dividends by supporting students to learn to engage more fully? Your efforts are better spent helping students become a part of the experience by providing multiple opportunities for processing and solidifying understanding. When professors ask students to sit passively or frantically scribble notes, they are missing an opportunity to deepen learning. Including active learning techniques that invite learners to be deeply engaged creates those opportunities. We present active-learning techniques for you to use throughout this book, like the concept map and think–pair–share activities introduced earlier, and Chapter 8 provides a buffet of different strategies.

Multiple studies have shown that active learning leads to improved student performance for all students and reduces grade disparities between overrepresented and underrepresented students (Freeman et al., 2014; Theobald et al., 2020). Importantly, the amount and type of active learning matter—just having a few multiple-choice questions sprinkled throughout a 50-minute lecture is not sufficient. Instead, offering thought-provoking activities in which students work together to practice questions, receive feedback, and integrate the feedback through additional practice is an effective strategy (Theobald et al., 2020). Many students perceive they learn less in active learning classrooms, partly because the increased cognitive load required in active learning is demanding and makes them feel uncomfortable—and that sometimes presents as student resistance. However, Deslauriers and colleagues (2019) found that context affects how well students are able to judge their learning and that achievement in active learning classrooms is actually increased. Just as you felt you were learning in that TED Talk, students perceive that when they listen, they are successfully learning, even when they are not. The missing link is how engaged they are in processing and the effort they're expending to make sense of ideas. Many students who are compliant have had little experience in intentionally making sense and connecting ideas during lectures. When first adopting active learning techniques in the classroom, you should anticipate pushback from some students who believe you've changed "the rules of the game" or who do not yet have the capacity to reflect in the moment. Such a response is a normal part of learning. That is why it is important to understand how motivation influences learning so you can design courses that build motivation and help to overcome this resistance.

Reflect to Learn:

1. Active learning shifts some of the power away from the teacher by transferring more responsibility for learning to learners. Have you given thought to what you believe about teacher power and control? If not, consider whether there is a finite amount of power or whether power and control expand when shared by professors and learners. If power is a finite commodity, how much should students be given?
2. Considering the teacher perspective you pinpointed earlier, how comfortable are you with the unplanned turns and spontaneous insights that active learning can lead to? If this is a growth area for you, what might you do to increase your flexibility in this regard?

Anchor Concept IV: Motivation Matters

Motivation is central to active learning; without it, the double helix collapses because engagement alone is not enough to support active learning. You have probably noted that when people are motivated, almost nothing can stop them. When someone is unmotivated (think of yourself with a dreaded chore), it can be very difficult to even get started. Next we share a condensed primer on motivation theory from the burgeoning research. While designing courses with motivation in mind may not have been expected of professors previously, in the 21st century, this understanding is squarely our professional responsibility.

There are two basic sources of motivation—intrinsic and extrinsic. Intrinsic motivation is behavior driven by internal states of satisfaction. So, for example, if you use your commuting time trying to learn a second language, then you are likely intrinsically motivated to do so. With intrinsic motivation, no one is incentivizing the behavior by agreeing to pay you or holding out a threatened punishment should you fail. Extrinsic motivation is the opposite: If you are so fearful of the prospect of an audit by the Internal Revenue Service that you file your income taxes every year, then you are externally motivated to do this. Extrinsic motivation can also be in the form of external rewards. You complete your timesheet at work because you seek the reward of being paid. Take a look at a few syllabi and you'll see that many college courses are premised on the misunderstanding that extrinsic factors can motivate student learning. Pages of syllabi, utilizing a mix of bold, italics, and underlining, carefully communicate how many points will be lost for this or earned for that.

However, transformative learning requires intrinsic motivation, which can be obstructed by a focus on extrinsic motivation. The kind of learning that is internalized occurs when students are intrinsically motivated and actively work to integrate new material with their previous knowledge, resulting in greater student engagement and achievement.

Reflect to Learn:

1. Consider a professional and personal accomplishment you've had in the past week. What motivated this accomplishment? Were your motivations intrinsic or extrinsic? Do you associate that experience with joy?
2. Consider a time when you have been so engaged in a project that you lost track of time. What were the forces motivating you to complete this project? How might this explain why intrinsic motivation is stronger than extrinsic?

Self-Determination Theory

Self-determination theory (SDT), developed by researchers Deci and Ryan (1985), has evolved into a social psychological explanation of human behavior that understands all human beings to have a natural drive to guide their own lives and to make choices without being compelled to do so. SDT applies to your teaching practice because it makes clear that all learners have three needs—*competence, autonomy, and psychological relatedness*—and that when these needs are met, learners will be motivated to change and develop. The more you can support students' need for choice, mastery, and human relationships within the learning context, then the more engaged and attentive they will be.

There is now a large body of research that indicates that humans generally want to develop their capabilities and are demotivated when they lack control over their own learning (Bartholomew et al., 2018; Deci & Ryan, 1985; Vansteenkiste et al., 2019). In other words, by helping students feel competent, providing choices, and allowing students to work with classmates to build their connection to one another, you create a sure-footed pathway toward learning success.

All people want to develop themselves, and they seek competency, autonomy, and relatedness to do so. Use this perspective as you analyze course assignments and activities, checking to ensure that at least one of the three components is present:

1. Competency/Mastery—Is there an opportunity for learners to work with the material or practice skills and to become aware of their progress?

2. Autonomy—Is there an opportunity for students to make decisions about the assignment, such as the topic, the process for completing it, or the presentation format of the product?

3. Psychological relatedness—Are students able to have peer interaction throughout the learning process that can offer them a sense of relatedness?

If these elements are incorporated in your course, chances are good that students will respond with greater intrinsic motivation toward achievement.

> **Reflect to Learn:** Consider the following scenario. Aaron notices that his evaluation system doesn't seem to be motivating students to earn high grades. He awards 25% of the course grade for out-of-class individual homework and 75% for three in-class exams. Some students don't do well on the homework yet perform well on the exams. Others, the opposite. Using self-determination theory, what tweaks could you suggest to Aaron to make his grading practices encourage competence, autonomy, or relatedness? How would he know if those changes were working to foster intrinsic motivation?

Goal Achievement

We briefly want to explain another motivation theory: goal achievement. Having goals is motivating because goals direct behavior toward a desired outcome. For instance, most students have the goal of attaining a diploma or college degree; thus, they are motivated to go to class, complete homework, study for tests, and the like. Even if they do not necessarily enjoy all of those tasks, goals can help students stay focused and persist despite setbacks.

We are going to explore goals along a continuum of performance to mastery orientations (Elliot & McGregor, 2001; Kaplan & Maehr, 2007; Pintrich & Schunk, 2002). Mastery-oriented learning tends to be on the intrinsically motivated end of the continuum while performance orientations align with the extrinsic. Those with a mastery orientation are interested in the development that comes with striving to reach the goal. They enjoy a challenge and often persist when tasks become difficult. Students with mastery orientations will learn for the sheer love of learning. They may be motivated by thinking, "When I finish this Spanish class, I'll be able to study abroad and have conversations with my host family." Mastery-related behaviors tend to be undertaken by self-directed learners who find satisfaction in the process and the progress they make toward goals.

On the other end of the continuum are the performance orientations: performance approach and performance avoidance. Individuals who have a performance approach tend to prefer a competitive environment where their achievements can be on display, and in many circumstances, they perform well (Senko et al., 2011). These learners may be the ones who are first to turn to classmates, asking, "How did you do on the test?" because they want to know whether they scored the highest. Schools have traditionally been set up to draw on this type of motivation, providing many opportunities for students to be compared. One of us, Karynne, was once a student in a Spanish class where students were seated in rows according to their course averages. Presumably, the teacher believed that this would motivate students to try harder to literally move up in the classroom. (Note: Karynne never moved up.) We think anyone can imagine how it felt for those students who were seated in the last desks.

Unfortunately, those students who are not likely to be "the best" in a competitive environment develop the other orientation, performance avoidance. Students with performance-avoidance goals attempt to escape being judged as failures in front of others. These students may be ones who never volunteer to respond to a question or may not regularly complete assignments. This is not to say that all students who are reluctant to participate are motivated by performance-avoidance goals. However, it is something you should pay attention to, especially if the classroom culture is characterized by comparison and competition. Note that both types of performance orientations use extrinsic motivators to encourage students to comply.

To help shift students' attitudes about learning in your course from extrinsic to intrinsic motivation and from performance to mastery orientations, we suggest that you do the following:

- Get to know the students in your class and provide a means for them to get to know each other. Students who feel seen and welcomed as whole people and not just names on rosters are more likely to take risks, share ideas, and learn. If you have a class that is too large to get to know everyone, organize students in groups to build relationships.

- Avoid grading on a curve, as it encourages competition and comparison, rather than collaboration and deep learning. Better yet, develop a grading system that intentionally connects the grade earned to the competencies demonstrated by the student.

- Design evaluations that provide multiple opportunities for feedback and improvement. Having one bad exam grade determine most of their final grade is demotivating. You'll have more opportunities to consider approaches to grading in Chapter 6.

- Set and convey high expectations and share that you've designed your course so that everyone, with effort, will have the opportunity to meet those expectations.
- Situate yourself as a resource, not just a source of criticism and negative feedback.
- Foster autonomy by encouraging students to select their own topics, grading schemes, deadlines, or types of assignments.
- Write a course description or prepare an infographic that is framed around *why* your course covers the specific topics, ideas, skills, and dispositions rather than one that lists the topic.
- Check in with students regarding how motivated they feel about your course, in general, or a topic, in particular. We've included a motivation class survey on our website that you can modify for your own class.

We encourage you to share with students that you have designed the course with knowledge of motivational theories. Showing them the ways they can reframe their notion of achievement and sharing your expectations for them to (learn to) control their learning by opening up decision-making for their control makes your efforts visible and helps to build a more trusting environment for student success.

Activity: Building Your Foundation

In this chapter, we've introduced you to the concepts that will anchor the course design process that begins in Chapter 3. We recognize that there is a lot of material here and we invite you to spend some time constructing knowledge by seeking connections among the anchor concepts and your own prior learning. Once you've had a chance to complete the first four columns of Table 2.1, discuss your answers with colleagues to co-create a shared understanding of how these concepts are connected. As you read the remaining chapters, periodically return to the chart to fill in the final column as you build on this foundational knowledge.

Wonderful Resources to Extend Learning

The Teaching Perspectives Inventory or ***TPI*** (http://www.teachingperspectives.com/tpi/) developed by **Daniel Pratt and John Collins** (2020) is an online resource where you can complete the TPI to better understand how you express the perspectives through your own beliefs, intentions, and actions and further reflect on your approaches to teaching.

Student Engagement Techniques **by Elizabeth Barkley** (2009) is a gold mine of great teaching strategies, but the introductory chapters are also worthwhile for exploring student engagement.

Drive: The Surprising Truth About What Motivates Us **by Daniel Pink** (2009) pulls together a vast amount of social science research around what motivates adults in this entertaining book.

How to Be an Antiracist **by Ibram X. Kendi** (2019a) includes actions individuals can take to counter systemic racism and build a just society for all.

The **National Museum of African American History and Culture's "Being antiracist" website** (https://nmaahc.si.edu/learn/talking-about-race/topics/being-antiracist) presents definitions, examples, and strategies for those interested in committing to antiracist practices in their courses and daily lives.

Kimberly Tanner's (2013) open-access article **"Structure Matters: Twenty-One Teaching Strategies to Promote Student Engagement and Cultivate Classroom Equity"** lists concrete steps you can take to improve inclusivity and equity in any course.

Dismantling Racism Works (dRworks: https://www.dismantlingracism.org/) offers resources and a web-based workbook for individuals, groups, and organizations aimed at the continuous process of ensuring justice for all.

The ***Inclusion by Design*** **tool by Ed Brantmeier and colleagues** (http://bit.ly/inclusionbydesign) can be used to explore inclusion in your syllabus and course design.

Table 2.1: *Drawing Connections Among the Anchor Concepts and Your Own Teaching*

Topic	2 or 3 most important things you learned.	What questions do you have?	How are these topics conneced to one another? How will you apply these concepts in your course?	As you work through the book, notice where you find this anchor concept and note it here.
Equity				
Learning theories (Constructivism & Connectivism)				
Student engagement and active learning				

References

Barkley, E. F. (2009). *Student engagement techniques: A handbook for college faculty.* Jossey-Bass.

Barkley, E. F., Cross, K. P., & Major, H. C. (2014). *Collaborative learning techniques: A handbook for college faculty.* John Wiley & Sons.

Bartholomew, K. J., Ntoumanis, N., Mouratidis, A., Katartzi, E., Thøgersen-Ntoumani, C., & Vlachopoulos, S. (2018). Beware of your teaching style: A school-year long investigation of controlling teaching and student motivational experiences. *Learning and Instruction, 53*, 50–63. https://doi.org/10.1016/j.learninstruc.2017.07.006

Blackwell, D. M. (2010). Sidelines and separate spaces: Making education anti-racist for students of color. *Race Ethnicity and Education, 13*(4), 473–494. https://doi.org/10.1080/13613324.2010.492135

Collins, J. B., & Pratt, D. D. (2011). The teaching perspectives inventory at 10 years and 100,000 respondents. *Adult Education Quarterly, 61*(4), 358–375. https://doi.org/ 10.1177/0741713610392763

Deci, E. L., & Ryan, R. (1985). *Intrinsic motivation and self-determination in human behavior.* Plenum.

Delbanco, A. (2012). *College: What it was, is, and should be.* Princeton University Press.

Deslauriers, L., McCarty, L. S., Miller, K., Callaghan, K., & Kestin, G. (2019). Measuring actual learning versus feeling of learning in response to being actively engaged in the classroom. *Proceedings of the National Academy of Sciences, 116*(39), 19251–19257. https://doi.org/10.1073/pnas.1821936116

Downes, S. (2010). Learning networks and connective knowledge. In S. C-Y. Yuen & H. H. Yang (Eds.), *Collective intelligence and e-learning 2.0: Implications of web-based communities and networking* (pp. 1–26). IGI Global.

dRworks. (n.d.). *Dismantling racism works web workbook.* https://www.dismantlingracism.org/

Elliot, A. J., & McGregor, H. A. (2001). A 2x2 achievement goal framework. *Journal of Personality and Social Psychology, 80*(3), 501–519.

Ellsworth, E. (1989). Why doesn't this feel empowering? Working through the repressive myths of critical pedagogy. *Harvard Educational Review, 59*(3), 297–325. https://doi.org/10.17763/haer.59.3.058342114k266250

Falk, D. (1995). Preflection: A strategy for enhancing reflection. *NSEE Quarterly*, 13.

Freeman, S., Eddy, S. L., McDonough, M., Smith, M. K., Okoroafor, N., Jordt, H., & Wenderoth, M. P. (2014). Active learning increases student performance in science, engineering, and mathematics. *Proceedings of the National Academy of Sciences of the United States of America, 111*(23), 8410–8415. https://doi.org/10.1073/pnas. 1319030111

Gay, G. (2018). *Culturally responsive teaching: Theory, research, and practice.* Teachers College Press.

González, N., Moll, L., & Amanti, C. (2005). Introduction: Theorizing practices. In N. Gonzalez, L. C. Moll, & C. Amanti (Eds.), *Funds of knowledge: Theorizing practices in households, communities, and classrooms* (pp. 1–24). Erlbaum.

Haltinner, K. (2014). *Teaching race and anti-racism in contemporary America.* Springer Publishing.

Jenkins, C. (2018). Educators, question your level of cultural tesponsiveness. *Journal on Empowering Teaching Excellence, 2*(2), Article 4. https://doi.org/https://doi.org/10.26 077/kttj-v296

Jones, K., & Okun, T. (2001). *Dismantling racism: A workbook for social change groups.* Changework.

Kaplan, A., & Maehr, M. L. (2007). The contributions and prospects of goal orientation theory. *Educational Psychology Review, 19*(2), 141–184. https://doi.org/10.1007/s106 48-006-9012-5

Kendi, I. X. (2019a). *How to be an antiracist.* One World.

Kendi, I. X. (2019b, December 6). This is what an antiracist America would look like. How do we get there? *The Guardian.* https://www.theguardian.com/commentisfree/2018/dec/06/antiracism-and-america-white-nationalism

Kishimoto, K. (2018). Anti-racist pedagogy: From faculty's self-reflection to organizing within and beyond the classroom. *Race Ethnicity and Education, 21*(4), 540–554. https://doi.org/10.1080/13613324.2016.1248824

Kohl, H., & Kozol, J. (1995). *"I won't learn from you" And other thoughts on creative maladjustment.* The New Press.

Kuh, G. D. (2008). Excerpt from high-impact educational practices: What they are, who has access to them, and why they matter. *Association of American Colleges and Universities, 14*(3), 28–29.

Ladson-Billings, G. (1995). But that's just good teaching! the case for culturally relevant pedagogy. *Theory Into Practice, 34*(3), 159–165. https://doi.org/10.1080/00405849509543675

Lave, J., & Wenger, E. (1991). *Situated learning: Legitimate peripheral participation.* Cambridge University Press.

McNair, T. B., Albertine, S. L., Cooper, M. A., McDonald, N. L., & Major, T. (2016). *Becoming a student-ready college: A new culture of leadership for student success.* John Wiley & Sons.

Morrison, K. L. (2017). Informed asset-based pedagogy: Coming correct, counter-stories from an information literacy classroom. *Library Trends, 66*(2), 176–218. https://doi.org/10.1353/lib.2017.0034

National Academies of Sciences, Engineering, and Medicine. (2018). *How people learn II: Learners, contexts, and cultures.* National Academies Press.

Palmer, P. J. (2017). *The courage to teach: Exploring the inner landscape of a teacher's life.* John Wiley & Sons.

Pham, T. H. T. (2016). A theoretical framework to enhance constructivist learning reforms in Confucian heritage culture classrooms. *International Journal of Educational Reform, 25*(3), 284–298.

Piaget, J. (1936). *Origins of intelligence in the child.* Routledge & Kegan Paul.

Pink, D. H. (2009). *Drive: The surprising truth about what motivates us.* Riverhead Books.

Pintrich, P. R., & Schunk, D. H. (2002). *Motivation in education: Theory, research, and applications* (4th ed.). Pearson Higher Education.

Pratt, D. D., Collins, J., & Jarvis-Selinger, S. (2001, April). *Development and use of the Teaching Perspectives Inventory (TPI)* [Paper Presentation]. Annual Meeting of the American Educational Research Association, Seattle, Washington, United States.

Pratt, D. D., & Collins, J. (2020). *The Teaching Perspectives Inventory.* http://www.teaching perspectives.com/tpi/

Sawyer, R. K. (2011). *Structure and improvisation in creative teaching.* Cambridge University Press.

Senko, C., Hulleman, C. S., & Harackiewicz, J. M. (2011). Achievement goal theory at the crossroads: Old controversies, current challenges, and new directions. *Educational Psychologist, 46*(1), 26–47. https://doi.org/10.1080/00461520.2011.538646

Siemens, G. (2005). Connectivism: A learning theory for the digital age. *International Journal of Instructional Technology and Distance Learning, 2*(1), Article 1. http://www.itdl.org/Journal/Jan_05/article01.htm

Smith, M. K., Wood, W. B., & Knight, J. K. (2008). The genetics concept assessment: A new concept iventory for gauging student understanding of genetics. *CBE Life Sciences Education, 7*, 422–430. https://doi.org/10.1187/cbe.08-08-0045

Tanner, K. D. (2013). Structure matters: Twenty-one teaching strategies to promote student engagement and cultivate classroom equity. *CBE Life Sciences Education, 12*(3), 322–331. https://doi.org/10.1187/cbe.13-06-0115

Tejeda, C., Espinoza, M., & Gutierrez, K. (2003). Toward a decolonizing pedagogy: Social justice reconsidered. In P. P. Trifonas (Ed.), *Pedagogies of difference: Rethinking education for social change*, (pp. 10–40). RoutledgeFalmer.

Theobald, E. J., Hill, M. J., Tran, E., Agrawal, S., Arroyo, E. N., Behling, S., Chambwe, N.,Cintrón, D. L., Cooper, J. D., Dunster, G., Grummer, J. A., Hennessey, K., Hsiao, J., Iranon, N., Jones II, L., Jordt, H., Keller, M., Lacey, M. E., Littlefield, C. E., . . . Freeman, S. (2020). Active learning narrows achievement gaps for underrepresented students in undergraduate science, technology, engineering, and math. *Proceedings of the National Academy of Sciences of the United States of America, 117*(12), 6476–6483. https://doi.org/10.1073/pnas.1916903117

Vansteenkiste, M., Aelterman, N., Haerens, L., & Soenens, B. (2019). Seeking stability in stormy educational times: A need-based perspective on (de)motivating teaching grounded in self-determination theory. In S. Karabenick & T. C. Urdan (Eds.), *Advances in Motivation and Achievement* (Vol. 20, pp. 53–80). Emerald Group Publishing. https://doi.org/10.1108/S0749-742320190000020004

Vygotsky, L. S. (1978). *Mind in society: The development of higher psychological processes.* Harvard University Press.

Zacko-Smith, J. D., & Smith, G. P. (2010). Recognizing and utilizing queer pedagogy: A call for teacher education to reconsider the knowledge base on sexual orientation for teacher education programs. *Multicultural Education, 18*(1), 2–9.

Zhao, Y. (2016). From deficiency to strength: Shifting the mindset about education inequality. *Journal of Social Issues, 72*(4), 720–739. https://doi.org/10.1111/josi.12191

CHAPTER THREE

Design Matters

> *Preflection*
>
> Imagine you've been tasked with teaching a new course or are preparing a unit on a topic that you've not taught before. You've cleared your schedule of distractions and are sitting at your desk ready to start planning. What is the first thing that comes to mind? What do you do first? What do you need? Where do you turn for support?

As you read this chapter, reflect on it, and engage with the activities both independently and with fellow readers, note that it has been designed to support you in the following:

- Evaluating how using design to guide your course planning can support student success in your course
- Exploring three complementary approaches to design: design thinking, backward design, and Universal Design for Learning
- Beginning the process of applying the principles of intentional design to your course

It is a human urge to try to anticipate the future, and there are so many historical feats that we can recount to demonstrate that people are great planners. It isn't only the pyramids of Giza that show tremendous attention to detail; on a more day-to-day level, think about how fast-food restaurant managers prepare for their rush hours by bringing in personnel for short shifts and cooking ahead or how the Red Cross is able to respond to disasters on several continents simultaneously. Thinking ahead and imagining a procedure for completing a task takes much forethought, but planning and thoughtful design are skills that can be developed.

Design has long been the domain of those who make things—like engineers and architects. More recently, educators have applied the principles of design to learning experiences. Design matters in teaching because the decisions you make when planning your course can result in students experiencing learning as an invitation to engage or a barrier to being successful. A design approach to planning can bring intentionality and clarity to your decision-making. Using design thinking to guide your teaching and course planning is a mindset you must develop, but it is a game-changing outlook to embrace. (Side note: If you have instructional designers on your campus, invite them to a conversation about course design. They have much to offer.)

In this chapter, we hope to convince you that using design to guide course planning can bring benefits to you and students. We do this by exploring three variations on design that offer you some options for becoming a course design superstar. These design approaches are complementary but not equivalent—each brings a unique stance. You may find a stronger affinity with one approach over the others.

Design Thinking: Create With the Learner in Mind

As you thought about how you might begin planning a new course in the preflection, you might have experienced a creative burst of ideas or you may have struggled to find a single good idea. We often fall into a trap of thinking that creativity is a mystical entity that can't be harnessed or taught. In fields like design and architecture, where creative problem-solving is integral to success, much attention has been paid to cultivating creative thinking and innovation. Design thinking offers a human-centered protocol for innovation through a process-oriented methodology that cultivates expansive thinking and directs it toward a purpose. Essentially, the design-thinking process consists of three stages: (1) taking a human-centered approach to understanding the problem, (2) generating creative, bold ideas, and (3) testing multiple prototypes (Brown, 2008).

Stage 1: Human-Centered Problem Definition

Klang and Suter (2017) describe design thinking as a user-centered innovation because the process deliberately centers the user in the planning. The design-thinking process begins by using empathy to concentrate on the human experience by understanding as much as one can about the individuals who will use the innovation. In course design, the users are students and the innovations are the courses intentionally designed to support learning. Mechanisms for centering these learners in your process include conducting interviews or focus groups with students to understand their goals, hopes, and concerns. Assembling the user's perspective from firsthand information is always preferable but isn't always possible. Often, we don't have access to students before the course begins, which means we must rely on less direct sources of information when we design. The empathy map activity that follows is a tactic for centering students in the design process by building narratives that describe their diverse experiences and perspectives. We encourage you to learn more about the students likely to enroll in your courses by seeking information from areas outside your department or division. For example, colleagues in institutional research and assessment offices are keepers of a wealth of valuable data that describe how students are progressing and achieving. Student affairs and residence life professionals work closely with students and can help you understand the social and emotional environment of students in your classes. You might be surprised by how excited these individuals will be to have this conversation.

Activity: Build an Empathy Map

An empathy map is a creative approach to articulating student perspectives.

Start by imagining the students who will be taking your course. Who are they? What backgrounds do they come from? What talents do they bring? What are their goals? Why have they enrolled in your course? What futures are they seeking? What does success mean for them?

Now, divide a piece of paper into four quadrants. Use each quadrant to probe student perspectives with respect to school, learning, and your course.

Table 3.1: *Empathy Map*

Quadrant 1: Think and Feel What might students think and feel? What worries them? What gets in their way? What do they need? What do they plan to do with their lives?	Quadrant 2: Do and Say What are students' actions and behaviors? What motivates them? What might they say when asked about the future? What are some quotes and defining words students might say?
Quadrant 3: Hear What might students hear? From other students? From other teachers? From advisors and career counselors? From the media? From their families?	Quadrant 4: See What do students encounter in their environment? What kinds of things are they surrounded by? What implicit or explicit expectations do they experience?

Once you've completed the quadrants, take a moment to list the opportunities available to students and barriers they might encounter in your course. For example, while completing the quadrants, you might identify that a significant portion of the students are working or have family obligations in the evenings. These students might experience a barrier in completing course work without more than a couple days' warning. On the other hand, the experiences these students have in the working environment presents an opportunity to connect with "real-world" applications of your course material.

The empathy map provides a useful protocol for bringing student perspectives into the forefront of your planning, thus countering the impulse to design for a younger version of yourself. As you know from your own experience, students have diverse backgrounds and a wide variety of reasons for seeking a degree. You might have found the empathy map challenging because you aren't sure who the students in your class will be. One technique to represent this diversity in your empathy map is to use composite personas when you don't have access to students for interviews. Be careful here! A composite never substitutes for actual humans, but it can be useful to help instigate human-centered thinking. It is important that your composites are inclusive of the full range of perspectives and experiences that students likely to enroll in your course will bring. The following four composites were developed using institutional data from a small university that places a high value on teaching and serves a significant part-time student population:

> Juawn is an African American male in his late 20s. He currently works as a manager at a call center and serves in the National Guard. He is interested in a degree program that will lead to a job he enjoys. Juawn commutes to campus and needs a schedule that allows him to work three days a week.
>
> Ameena is a queer native person with a passion for activism. They led efforts in their high school to add Black, Indigenous, people of color (BIPOC) authors to the reading list and reduce the school's carbon footprint. Ameena is the first in their family to attend college. They are excited about tapping into a community of students with similar passions. They want to finish college as quickly as possible.
>
> Isabella is a Latina female in her early 20s. She is from a rural community where she earned an associate's degree at the local community college. She is excited about getting her bachelor's degree; however, she has frequently felt that teachers dismiss her ability. She has a needs-based grant that requires her to live on campus. She works part-time to pay outstanding credit card debt and is hoping to find a paid internship as soon as possible.
>
> Jocelyn is a White female in her mid-30s. She is recently divorced and has two children. Her oldest has just started first grade, which gives her time to go back to school and finish her degree. She plans to put her younger child in day care while in class. She completed one year of college when she graduated from high school, where she earned 30 credits of general education. She initially struggled in college until she sought help from student support services, where she was diagnosed with dyslexia. With special software and additional time for long or complex reading, she was able to successfully complete her courses.

These composites can be used to flesh out empathy maps that will help you design for a diverse set of students. You might find that these particular composite profiles don't reflect the students you teach. If that is the case, we encourage you to collaborate with the institutional research and student affairs professionals on your campus to create composites that are more closely aligned with your actual student populations. The goal is to have the diversity of students you are likely to encounter in mind as you design your course so you can avoid relying on biases you might hold about students that will result in less relevant and effective courses.

Reflect to Learn: As you built empathy maps for the composite students (or students you have personally known), what ideas came to mind in terms of designing a course that would be a good fit for them? How has considering the learner first impacted your thinking?

Activity: From Empathy to Vision

Now that you've developed a richer profile for the learners who might enroll in your course, use this newfound understanding to frame a vision statement that you can share with students on the first day of class. A vision statement provides an opportunity for you to imagine the future you want to be true. It draws on your deepest hopes as well as the assets you and students offer.

After reviewing your empathy maps, take a moment to reflect on the following questions. This would be a good moment to engage in freewriting by taking 10 minutes to write everything that comes to mind without editing. Freewriting is an expansive way to unleash creativity and discover ideas that you might not have known you were harboring.

Bring a specific course you teach to mind. If students completing the course were to tell a friend about what they learned in your course in two minutes or less, what would you hope would be a part of that summary? What do you hope students retain after a year or two?

After reflection and freewriting, take these thoughts and draft a concise statement for your course that communicates (in three to five sentences) your course vision. The audience for this statement is future students, and you will likely communicate your vision to them through your syllabus, so keep the language accessible and free of jargon. We encourage you to share your vision with colleagues or post using the hashtag #learningthatmatters.

We've included several vision statements developed by educators like yourself to show you the variety of forms they can take.

Course: Principles of Biology II

Greetings Students,

I am very excited about the beginning of this semester and the work that we will do together. My vision for this course is that you will experience the importance of conceptual learning in Biology and how it applies to biological systems. The course will offer a special emphasis on organ systems and is a continuation of Principles of Biology I, where you learned about the nuts and bolts of Biology. Upon completing the course, you should be able to appreciate, analyze, and synthesize new ideas about how biological systems behave.

Course: Introduction to the Humanities

In this course, you will learn about the most notable monuments of the human imagination, those works of art, architecture, literature, philosophy, and music that have helped shape the world's cultures and ways of thinking. You will also develop an appreciation for the role of individuals whose visions, actions, and decisions have played a significant role in history. While broader economic and social forces place constraints on what individuals may do, those forces do not determine human events. People do. This course will be a grand adventure in your life and the lessons you learn will not be forgotten. This is not a course for the faint-hearted. Application, persistence, intellectual curiosity, and openness are all vital attributes to a successful learning experience.

Course: Toxinology

It is my hope that this course will help you to develop a solid background in toxinology, including understanding toxin diversity and evolutionary trends, to incorporate concepts and tools from various scientific disciplines for the characterization of toxins, to become familiar with resources including laboratory and computer-based informatics techniques for the study of toxins, and to synthesize and communicate this knowledge to others.

Course: Critical Thinking and Communication

"The function of education is to teach one to think intensively and to think critically. Intelligence plus character—that is the goal of true education." —Martin Luther King Jr., 1947

This course encourages learners to become curious thinkers who employ inquiry, analytical analysis, problem-solving, and reasoned, persuasive argumentation as a means to foster fair-minded civic engagement and advocacy in collaboration with others.

> **Reflect to Learn:** As you read these course vision statements, what do you notice? Are there approaches that surprise you? Did reading these lead you to revise your course vision statement?

Stage 2: Creative Idea Generation

Now that you've had the experience of engaging in *human-centered problem definition* through an empathy map and vision statement development, the design-thinking approach turns toward the creative generation of potential solutions—a process often called "ideation" in design thinking. *Ideation* is really another word for brainstorming. This is your opportunity to play with some out-of-the-box thinking by temporarily releasing yourself from pressures such as external mandates, logistics, or resource constraints. It is also a good time to invite others into your creative thinking process—generative thinking is often more possible (and more fun) with a partner. At this point in the process, you need to convince yourself that no idea is too bold!

There are many ways to induce this type of creative exploratory thinking. We've listed a few to get you started.

"How Might We?" Questions

> How might we create a project where students learn through civic action?
>
> How might we create a remote first-year seminar that connects new students to the campus?
>
> How might we design writing activities that support and challenge both English-language learners and students with advanced English writing skills?

"How might we" (HMW) questions are short, provocative questions that launch brainstorms. They provide just enough constraint for creative thinking. The goal is to use these provocative questions to reframe your challenge in ways that encourage you to seek new or unknown solutions.

Brainstorm–Organize–Rank

There are infinite ways to facilitate brainstorming. One of our favorites is simple yet effective:

1. After framing the issue or question, take 10 minutes to generate as many bold ideas as you possibly can. Write each idea on a single sticky note.

2. Put the sticky notes on the wall and start to organize them into categories of similarity.

3. Rank the ideas from most to least promising.

TRIZ

This technique is borrowed from Lipmanowicz and McCandless (2014), who, in turn, adapted it from the Russian engineering approach *teoriya resheniya izobretatelskikh zadatch*, which in English is known as the *theory of inventive problem-solving*. This counterintuitive approach asks you to imagine how you might achieve the worst possible result. For example, you might ask yourself what you would need to do to guarantee that every student in your class would fail or how could you make it possible that certain subsets of students would struggle excessively in your course. Once you've generated a list of actions, very honestly review it and make a second list of anything you are currently doing that *in any way* resembles what you have on the list. Use that second list to decide what steps or actions you can take to avoid unwanted outcomes.

Stage 3: Build and Test Prototypes

The last stage of design thinking uses your newfound, human-centered understanding of students and the product of your creative brainstorming to develop and test prototypes. There are multiple ways to go about building course prototypes. The backward design process first developed by Wiggins and McTighe (2005) is one of the best approaches we've encountered for developing a course design and is the focus of the next section.

Testing prototypes can be a challenge in the context in which many of us teach. After all, isn't teaching a course the ultimate "test" of the design? Teaching a course cannot be considered prototyping. However, many of us do have the opportunity to teach the same course repeatedly. This gives us the opportunity to learn from the experience and continuously refine the course—a process that retains the spirit of prototyping. However, there are other ways to prototype your course before you actually teach it.

Check in With a Novice

An effective strategy for garnering feedback on class activities, assignments, syllabi, or other course materials is to get feedback from a novice. Many people can play the role of a novice: a student, a colleague from a different department, a family member, or a friend. This is a simple strategy, but we've been surprised how often we hear from faculty that it isn't a common practice. Feedback from someone who has a different background from you can help you identify language or assumptions that might present barriers to students. We've borrowed a protocol from the TILT Higher Ed project developed by Mary-Ann Winkelmes (2014) for gathering feedback on assignments, projects, or activities. In this protocol, the novice approaches the assignment from the perspective of a student unfamiliar with the material. After listening to you describe the assignment and reviewing materials, the novice reflects back their understanding to provide a window into how your course materials will be interpreted by students. You will learn very quickly where you may have made assumptions about prior knowledge or if you are using academic language that is not easily understood. Taking time to check in with a novice before you deliver an assignment or share your syllabus can prevent widespread misunderstandings among students and improve their performance.

The Course Fair

When Julia was a student many years ago at The Evergreen State College, students would determine which classes they might like to take by attending a "course fair." At this fair, each faculty member creates and presents a poster, along with other artifacts such as sample assignments, the syllabus, and so on to communicate what their course would be about, what it would be like, and what a student could hope to gain from that course—a kind of "elevator speech" in a graphic format. We've used a version of the course fair to test course design prototypes at workshops. In the workshop scenario, faculty create posters to explain their courses to potential students in a way that simultaneously captures the vision for the course, the student learning outcomes, and what a student can expect. Other workshop participants take on the perspective of prospective students by reading the posters and interviewing the poster's creator as if they were a student considering enrolling in the course. Those reviewing the posters offer feedback from a student's point of view using guiding prompts. This would be useful to use within a department or program to provide feedback to one another while also learning about each other's courses. We've posted protocols for organizing your own course fair on our webpage.

> **Reflect to Learn:** Revisit the three phases of design thinking. How can you imagine incorporating this approach into your own course planning? What elements of the approach do you find challenging?

Design thinking offers an approach to course planning whereby the student experience is a central consideration in design choices, bold idea generation is encouraged, and intentional integration of feedback along the way is used to improve the final design. As with any course planning process, the actual process will be iterative—design thinking simply provides a framework to help guide your choices. Now we shift your attention to a design process, backward design, that focuses on intentionally aligning all elements of the course with the goals you set for students.

Backward Design: Start With the End in Mind

Imagine a friend has called you up to ask for some help planning a party. What would be the best first question to ask? We've asked this question to many people over many years, and there are a lot of common answers: Where will it be? When will it be? Who will be invited? But arguably the best first question is, "What is this party for?" Hopefully the where, when, and who will all follow from that key question. The answers to those other questions would be very different for a child's fifth birthday party than a 50th wedding anniversary party for your parents. It helps to start with figuring out where you want to end up.

Backward design (Wiggins & McTighe, 2005) for learning starts from the same principle—where do you want the learners to end up? Asked in another way, what do you want to be observably true about a student long after a unit, a course, or the degree is over? Once you've answered this seemingly simple question, everything else follows from there. The end point becomes your planning North Star.

When you reflected on planning a new course in the preflection, what was your first thought? Often, we turn to content when planning a new course by asking ourselves, "What topics do I need to cover?" It might feel counterintuitive for someone with expert knowledge to first articulate how students *would use what they learn*, yet that is exactly what backward design asks you to do.

The Three Stages of Backward Design

1. *Goals:* START by deciding how students will use what they learn and what they will be able to do years from now.

2. *Assessments:* THEN ask yourself, "What would be a valid, authentic, and engrossing means of checking to see if students really know and can do what I hope they can?

3. *Everything Else:* FINALLY, choose resources and design learning sequences that will best enable students to meet your objectives and be successful on meaningful, authentic assessments.

Obviously, the planning won't be completely linear, and there will be a good bit of cycling back, but generally following this order allows for spectacular focus and provides a logical structure that can keep you from feeling overwhelmed.

A Story of Before and After

Imagine an introduction to education survey course that is taken by prospective teachers in a middle-grades education program. The topic for the first four-week unit is "The History of Education in the United States." The text has a section of the same title divided into three chapters. Natasha has just been hired in her first college teaching job and is tasked with preparing this unit. She has been provided with the textbook and a sample syllabus, but she doesn't have access to development or other teaching support.

How do you picture Natasha's preparation proceeding? What will her likely basic plan for this unit be? How do you imagine she will plan to evaluate and grade students?

Most of us have been in this predicament before and have a pretty good idea of what Natasha will do. She knows she has four weeks, so she will devote one week to each of the three chapters and then review the fourth week. She will have the students read the associated chapter prior to the week they study it. She will use slides, probably provided by the textbook company, to reinforce key points. At the end of the unit, students will take a multiple-choice test pulled from a bank of questions also provided by the textbook company.

What did these future teachers gain from that perfunctory unit planned by Natasha? To what extent will this unit change who they are as teachers or impact the quality of their teaching? What opportunities did the students have to connect the learning to their own schooling experiences?

Now imagine a more experienced Natasha with some professional learning under her belt teaching the same unit. This time, Natasha's department chair gave her this book.

Natasha starts by pondering what she wants students to gain. After doing some research on the demographics of students she will be teaching, she thinks about what those students will most need from this unit to be successful teachers *and considers concurrently* what is likely to engage them. She writes the following learning goals:

1. Students will trace connections from the historical development of the educational system in the United States through to challenges within the current context.

2. Students will compare points of view of students who did not have privilege or wealth in this history with those who experienced privilege or wealth.

3. Students will propose a possible solution for a current systemic educational issue that has historical roots.

To meet these goals, students will need the key terms, facts, people, dates, and other information that Natasha would have taught as a novice, setting minimal expectations for learning in the first instance. Yet consider how much further this lesson will take these future teachers and how much more rewarding it will be for Natasha to guide them because she is knowledgeable about how people are motivated by challenge and purpose.

After creating her goals, Natasha moves on to designing the main summative assessment for the unit that requires learners to assume the perspectives of those from another time: Imagine that one of your long-deceased relatives experienced one of the marginalizing identities in terms of one of the historic educational issues we studied. Craft your relative's personal profile that includes a photo (or portrait) of your "ancestor" and perhaps other images as well, excerpts from your ancestor's journal, and include your own editorial describing how the same marginalization still occurs today (but perhaps in a different guise). Propose a possible intervention to address the marginalization in the current educational system. If your studies revealed no patterns of marginalization, explain the intervention(s) and how they corrected the unjust practices.

Now that she knows how her students will demonstrate what they know and can do, she is ready for *Step 3: Everything Else*. Natasha begins to design to build the content knowledge and skills the students will need to be successful in this culminating project. She asks herself, "Which activities and resources will lead to students meeting the goals and achieving success on the culminating project? What skills will students need to develop to do so? What content knowledge will they need to learn? What order of activities will scaffold learning over the four weeks of the unit?" Throughout the planning process, she continues to return to her learning goals as a guide. She ultimately decides to break the four weeks into some broad overviews that not only involve the class as a whole but also allow time for students to take individualized deep dives into a variety of historical issues, knowing they will eventually share their discoveries with one another. She finds that the textbook the department uses for the course is too dull to generate the level of student interest that she desires for these projects, so she adds some first-person historical narratives and articles written by individuals who are passionate about specific periods in the history of American education to the reading list.

What do you think these future teachers might gain from this unit? Does the novelty of the assessment and choice Natasha provided for students to demonstrate their learning seem engaging? How might this unit impact how these future teachers teach their students? We expect that you noticed that while the second unit includes the straightforward objectives of the first, it does so in ways that lead toward outcomes such as perspective taking and problem-solving that are portable to future courses, careers, and civic participation.

Reflect to Learn: How was Natasha's planning experience influenced by her lessons in backward design? How do you imagine her teaching experience will be different? What pitfalls or challenges might she encounter with this approach? What joy might the new process bring her?

Backward design seems so simple, and once you put it into practice you might claim that it was hiding in plain sight all along—or perhaps you've been planning this way without knowing it was a thing. We have found that when you use the goals you've envisioned for students to achieve to drive the course design, it is truly revolutionary. Once you make this shift, it is impossible to return to prosaic planning. Obviously, course design is strengthened by setting good outcomes, creating relevant assessments of important skills and knowledge, and incorporating engaging strategies and resources in your designs, but we will be supporting you in learning those in later chapters. Right now, understanding the wisdom of building courses as a design process is a great start.

Universal Design for Learning: Remove Barriers to Learning

The third design approach we present for your consideration is one that puts a high value on recognizing that students in a learning community have a variety of aptitudes and learning histories. Universal Design for Learning (UDL) is a framework that accommodates individual learning differences by intentionally seeking out and removing barriers experienced by diverse students. UDL draws from the architectural concept of universal design—a design philosophy that seeks to make the physical environment accessible to the widest number of users. The idea is to move from "retrofitting" an existing design toward considering the whole range of human diversity during the design process. Consider, for example, a public building designed with ramps and automatic doors at its entrance. These features improve access for a broader set of the population than buildings that don't by offering multiple ways to enter. Not only are those who use wheelchairs and assistive mobile devices able to gain access to the building, but many others also find these features improve their access such as the family with a small child in a stroller or the visitor bringing a case of files to a meeting.

Similarly, the UDL framework reduces barriers for students by considering the cognitive diversity (neurodiversity), physical abilities, and cultural diversity of learners in the classroom. An example of applying UDL is including captions on videos in multiple languages. The captions make the video accessible to those who are deaf or hard-of-hearing *while also* improving understanding for learners who find that reading the dialogue while it is spoken helps their understanding, for those whose primary language is not English, or for those who are watching the video in a noisy environment.

Creating learning environments that are universally accessible might, at first, seem like a daunting task. However, if you've ever received an accommodation request on behalf of a student, you've likely had to apply these principles in a special case. The promise of UDL is designing for diverse learners from the start by creating learning environments that support a broad set of learning aptitudes with the aim of increasing accessibility, inclusivity, and success. However, UDL is not a substitute for meeting individual student accommodations. The office that provides access or disability services on your campus can offer expert support for supporting accommodations and would be a good place to turn as you consider applying UDL to your course.

The Center for Applied Special Technology (CAST; 2018) has developed guidelines meant to support cognitively diverse learners to become "expert learners" by changing the learning environment rather than attempting to change the learner. The guidelines are organized into three broadly defined principles that provide flexibility in the ways (1) students are engaged in learning, (2) information is acquired, and (3) students reach and demonstrate mastery. The descriptions that follow are not comprehensive but rather draw out select elements from each principle to illustrate how you might use them to guide course design. There is much more to learn including useful tools and checklists from the CAST website (http://www.cast.org/).

Principle 1: Provide Multiple Means of Engagement

When encountering new learning, interest in a subject or particular skill will vary among students. Some students will arrive in class activated and excited to study a particular topic; others will need to build interest. Engagement can fade over time, even for those who entered the learning with a keen interest, which necessitates tools to support persistence. Ultimately, students should develop a toolbox of strategies they can use to build and sustain their own engagement. Students can be supported in these efforts by encountering opportunities for choice and autonomy in learning, drawing connections to what is relevant for them in their lives and desired futures, and developing skills in self-reflection and self-motivation. We focus on these in later chapters.

Principle 2: Provide Multiple Means of Representation

In this context, representation refers to the forms through which students acquire the information and knowledge that leads to comprehension—from reading, watching, or listening. Learners differ in their ability to acquire and comprehend the information that we present to them. Choosing and preparing course materials in multiple modalities can reduce barriers experienced by students with sensory disabilities, learning disabilities, language and cultural differences, or other diverse attributes that impact learning.

For example, many courses rely on a combination of reading and in-class discussions or presentations to relay information. This approach to learning can present barriers for some students if they can't reliably read the materials provided or understand what is spoken in the classroom. We can take relatively simple steps toward improving equitable access to information by providing written materials in accessible electronic formats and by providing access to an outline or the slide presentation prior to a lesson. This simple modification allows a student with low visual acuity or dyslexia to use a document reader to listen to the written materials and review the slides. Students who have difficulty hearing or comprehending spoken information can follow along using the outline or slides presentation. You could take one step further toward equity by making recordings of your in-class presentations available.

Making information accessible is important, but it isn't sufficient. The goal is for students to reach comprehension so they can apply new learning and transfer that learning into new contexts. This UDL principle provides guidance in supporting diverse learners' comprehension by encouraging the use of graphic organizers or note-taking techniques that help students organize and make sense of information. For example, consistently guiding students to map their learning using a concept map provides a visual cue of their learning progress over time.

Principle 3: Provide Multiple Means of Action and Expression

Learner diversity includes how students navigate their learning environment and express what they know. Providing students flexibility allows students the opportunity to approach learning tasks and demonstrate what they know in different ways and sometimes at different rates.

It can be challenging to imagine how to implement this type of flexibility, particularly if you are teaching a large lecture course. Luckily, there are some simple approaches. For example, providing opportunities for students to compare responses when given a challenging problem provides an opportunity for students to explain their own thinking and hear an explanation from someone new.

Ask yourself if the projects or activities for your course could take a variety of forms. Could students equivalently demonstrate their learning through writing or an oral presentation? What about a video or poster presentation? You don't need to decide this now! For now, we simply want you to ponder what it might look like if you were to offer students more choice in your course. You will get a chance to revisit these ideas in later chapters.

Reflect to Learn: Imagine that you are teaching a class and after the first exam or major project it becomes clear to you that about a third of the class didn't sufficiently demonstrate comprehension of the material. The next unit builds on this knowledge, so what should you do? You could stop and review the material for the entire class, but then you'd be requiring two thirds of the class to spend time reviewing something they've already mastered. You could move on, but that would mean you'd be leaving a third of the class behind and at a disadvantage moving forward.

Now imagine you have the opportunity to travel back in time and redesign the course. How might you build in flexible pathways for learners who needed more time to gain comprehension?

We've found that the UDL principles are especially useful when you are experiencing a particular challenge in the classroom where students aren't achieving equitably—like in the Reflect to Learn scenario. In this situation, you could use the UDL guidelines as a lens to better understand this teaching puzzle. Consider the following questions to identify how you might use UDL to devise a solution:

- **Engagement:** Are students able to articulate how course content is relevant to their lives or future goals? Do students understand the skills and knowledge they will gain from course activities?

- **Representation:** Is the material accessible? Do documents support screen readers and do all videos have closed captions and transcripts? Have you provided students with what they need to decode complex language or symbols? Is content presented in multiple formats such as text, diagrams, and videos?

- **Action and Expression:** Have you provided flexibility in how students will demonstrate their learning? Are there multiple ways for students to interact with each other, for example, in-class discussions and online forums? Have you demonstrated ways to solve problems using a variety of strategies?

If you want to explore the UDL approach but are feeling a little overwhelmed, then start small. Choose one strategy that appeals to you and play around with it.

Reflect to Learn: Return to the preflection at the beginning of the chapter. Now, when you think about teaching a new course or unit, what do you think your first step will be? What elements of these approaches to course design do you imagine being most useful? Which elements do you want to know more about? What seems challenging?

We hope we've achieved our goal of convincing you that a design approach can support you in planning and teaching your courses. At the very least, we expect that you've learned of some good strategies for organizing and generating ideas when you plan a course. As you move forward in the book, you will notice that we return to many of the elements of design that we've described in this chapter. In particular, we return to the empathy maps you built and the course vision you wrote.

Make It Happen: Communicate a Supportive Vision

Communicating with students, before the course even starts, that their success is your goal *and* you've intentionally designed the course with that in mind sends an empowering and compassionate message.

Return to the vision statement you wrote earlier in this chapter. Imagine you are a student reading it for the first time—or, better yet, share it with someone who doesn't know your course material. What questions does it bring to mind? How do you imagine a novice student responding to the vision statement? Are they excited? Are they nervous? Add a sentence or two to the vision statement that communicates to students how the course is designed to support their success.

Share your supportive vision statement at #learningthatmatters.

Wonderful Resources to Extend Learning

In ***Wicked Problems in Design Thinking***, **Richard Buchanan** (1992) makes a thoughtful and eloquent case for the centrality of design-thinking.

The d.school (https://dschool.stanford.edu/) at Stanford University hosts a wealth of resources on design thinking.

Understanding by Design by **Grant Wiggins and Jay McTighe** (2005) is a workbook with a trove of resources that introduced the concept of backward design to education.

The **UDL On Campus** website (http://udloncampus.cast.org/), developed by **CAST**, hosts an extensive collection of resources for higher education.

Todd Rose's TEDx Talk (2013), ***The Myth of Average***, provides an inspirational and riveting explanation of why designing a course for the "average" student benefits no one.

In their book, ***Engaging Students as Partners in Learning and Teaching: A Guide for Faculty***, **Cook-Sather, Bovill,** and **Felten** (2014) present a multitude of case studies where faculty have involved students in every aspect of the course design process.

References

Brown, T. (2008). Design thinking. *Harvard Business Review, 86*(6), 86–95. https://hbr.org/ 2008/06/design-thinking

Buchanan, R. (1992). Wicked problems in design thinking. *Design Issues, 8*(2), 5–21. http://www.jstor.org/stable/1511637

CAST. (2018). *Universal Design for Learning guidelines version 2.2.* http://udlguidelines.cast.org

Cook-Sather, A., Bovill, C., & Felten, P. (2014). *Engaging students as partners in learning and teaching: A guide for faculty.* Jossey-Bass.

King, M. L. (1947, January). The purpose of education. *Maroon Tiger.*

Klang, C., & Suter, M. (2017). *Learning design: Create amazing learning experiences with design thinking.* CreateSpace Independent Publishing Platform.

Lipmanowicz, H., & McCandless, K. (2014). *The surprising power of liberating structures: Simple rules to unleash a culture of innovation.* Liberating Structures Press.

TEDx Talks. (2013, June 19). *The myth of average: Todd Rose at TEDxSonomaCounty* [Video]. https://www.youtube.com/watch?v=4eBmyttcfU4

Wiggins, G. P., & McTighe, J. (2005). *Understanding by design.* ASCD.

Winkelmes, M. A. (2014). *TILT higher ed.* https://tilthighered.com/

CHAPTER FOUR

Portable Outcomes

> *Preflection*
>
> Draw on your past experience with learning outcomes, which may be thin or thick, to begin to form a stance on the following questions:
>
> - Is articulating anticipated learning for students before they begin a course important? Why or why not?
> - Does all learning need to be defined and measured?
> - Is learning that is not observed less valuable than learning that is?

As you read this chapter, reflect on it, and engage with the activities both independently and with fellow readers, note that it has been designed to support you in the following:

- Developing student-centered, higher order, measurable, inclusive, student learning outcomes that students can carry with them to their next learning experience.

Marisol's Journey

Throughout high school and while completing her general education requirements at a community college in North Carolina, Marisol saw herself giving back to her community by becoming a family physician. As a 19-year-old, she transferred to a small liberal arts college close to her home to pursue a degree in chemistry, which she expected would lead to medical school admission. Although her academic performance was strong, Marisol had doubts about becoming a medical doctor, having particularly enjoyed the fieldwork in her soil science and chemistry course. In the second semester of her junior year, she found herself weighing the pros and cons of her intended path. Upon reflection, she decided that the literal cost of a medical degree was not sensible. Moreover, while she wanted to explore and live outside of North Carolina for a short time, she doubted whether she would be happy living so far away from her family for the time it would take to complete medical school.

After several conversations with a trusted advisor in the chemistry department, Marisol crafted a plan to apply her chemistry degree to improving her rural community in North Carolina as she had always hoped she would do. In the new plan, Marisol decided to pursue a master's degree in public health after a post in the Peace Corps. This allowed her to realize her desire to use science in service of others. The new direction provided her with a fulfilling adventure and the opportunity to return to her family. Marisol was especially pleased to discover that her broad background and experiences prepared her to undertake the varied skills she would need for a public health position.

We present this fictionalized story to contrast measurable outcomes and aspirational goals. Marisol's education could be measured by some tangible outcomes such as her high grade point average (GPA) and admission to graduate school. There were also concrete student learning outcomes that Marisol developed such as intercultural communication, techniques for testing soils, and ethnography methodologies. More important, Marisol was able to fulfill her life goals and transfer the knowledge and skills she gained from college into leading a meaningful life. These long-term aspirational goals may not be measurable, but they are important and worthwhile to pursue even if they are less tangible than a GPA. As you go forward in this chapter on portable outcomes, we want you to be aware that cultivating the aspirational goals you have for students and those they hold for themselves, such as making positive contributions to their communities, is a good use of your time and energy—even though you may rarely be able to see these goals come to fruition.

Your Aspirations Matter

In this field guide, we'll use the term *aspirational goals* to refer to goals that address the big changes in students' demeanor, attitudes, and behavior that will last long after they've forgotten our names. For many of us, the outcomes that matter, or these aspirational goals, are what keep us excited and passionate about teaching. For us, the aspirational goals we have for students is a principal reason that we are enthusiastic about teaching a new cohort of students each new term—even in courses we've taught numerous times. We share two of the aspirations we have for students who leave our classes. As you read through this, notice what comes to mind for you and the goals you might have for students you'll be teaching in the future.

Caralyn: Years after students leave my class, I want them to continue exercising the skills necessary for critical evaluation of complex issues, an understanding of how science is done, and the ability to use evidence to make choices that benefit themselves and others.

Karynne: When preservice teachers complete any course in their teacher preparation program that I teach, I always intend they will be better equipped to make needed changes to the educational system to ensure more equitable outcomes for all learners.

You may have articulated aspirational goals in your teaching philosophy. Don't bury those goals in a job application. Instead, share them with students as a way to be transparent with your intentions as well as to encourage them through examples of your own motivation and intentionality. You made a start at doing this when you wrote your course vision statement.

Student learning outcomes (SLOs), while aligned with your aspirational goals, are more concrete and specific and should be measurable. These learning outcomes are the observable manifestation of what students take with them to the next course or to other aspects of their lives. It's usually a given that students will gain *knowledge*—the content and concepts we teach. Students also develop skills and dispositions as they move through our courses. *Skills* are the technical, verbal, mental, or manual proficiencies that students develop through practice. *Dispositions*, attitudes, and values are the commitments students develop that likely endure for a long while—and are often the outcomes most closely aligned with aspirational goals.

As you read through the following description of an Ancient Egyptian Archaeology course, see if you can identify the three categories of outcomes: knowledge, skills, and dispositions. Students in this course will learn to analyze artifacts from archaeological sites. They will also learn about pyramids, pharaohs, and hieroglyphs. Finally, students will appreciate the rich cultural heritage of ancient Egypt and see the large influence it has on current peoples.

Articulating student learning outcomes that describe the knowledge, skills, and dispositions you intend students to acquire communicates to students what they can expect from a course. Having concrete, specific, measurable learning outcomes doesn't replace aspirational goals. Aspirational goals and student learning outcomes are complementary and can easily exist in harmony with one another.

At first glance, writing student learning outcomes may seem simple, but crafting solid, substantive SLOs that can skillfully guide a course takes time. That's why we've loaded this chapter with plenty of examples and designed a number of activities to help guide you. As you engage, notice the general sequence that is used to create appropriate SLOs that foster student acquisition of outcomes.

Keep in mind that skills, abilities, and attitudes are not acquired as one might gain immunity through a single vaccine shot—only one is needed, and then you're covered for life. Learners need continued practice over time and through multiple courses and experiences to develop mastery. However, even a single course can ignite transformation and have continued impact. Consider how students will have opportunities to engage multiple times with ideas and procedures, but also know that your course has the potential to spark a shift in how students think simply because of this more empowering approach. What students do in your class can reframe their position in relation to others and change their perspective in a fundamental way.

Objectives? Outcomes? Competencies?

We recognize that SLO may not be the term used at your institution. It may be that your department wants you to list "learning objectives" rather than "learning outcomes." Different schools and different disciplines use different jargon. When you are writing your syllabus, use the language of your program. We don't think these semantics are worth haggling over. No matter the name, the important feature for you to remember is that the purpose of outcomes is to communicate the knowledge, skills, and dispositions that are intended for students to demonstrate.

Activity: Head, Heart, Hands

Envision a student that will enroll in a course you will teach next term. Once they successfully complete the course, how will they have changed? What are your aspirational goals for them? How will they use what they learned from your class five or 10 years in the future? What will they know (head)? What will they value or appreciate (heart)? What will they be able to do (hands)?

Describe the intellectual (head), dispositional (heart), and practical skills you hope they will gain (hands). Don't be afraid to think big!

As you consider what students will remember five or 10 years in the future, keep in mind that this will differ for students taking classes in their major compared to general education courses.

Alignment Matters

In our experience, when faculty plan their courses, they often don't pay much mind to how the course "fits" into a curricular structure—an omission that each of us has made in our own teaching practice. When planning courses, it is important to keep in mind that individual courses don't happen in isolation. Students encounter each course as part of an educational path or curriculum. In the majority of our institutions, students move through both a general education *and* a major course of study. The degree to which these two curricula are integrated will vary. However, our colleges and universities generally want students to have cohesive learning experiences that build toward integration. The learning outcomes we develop to guide our course choices have a critical impact on the degree of coherence students experience throughout their degree. In Chapter 2, we presented several theories from the learning sciences that underscore the importance of connection for deep learning. Sometimes that connection may occur by tapping into the student's prior learning (constructivist approaches), or it may be by showing learners the purpose for or value of the knowledge (motivation theory). When connectivity is strengthened and intensified through alignment, deep learning is the consequence.

If we've convinced you that alignment matters, your next question is likely "How?" You might be wondering how to align your outcomes to the curriculum that contains your course. Our first recommendation is to find out if there are prescribed outcomes for your course. These program-level learning outcomes will be broadly defined and will describe where the student will end up once they complete the program. Articulating course-level SLOs that align with program- or degree-level outcomes is an important, and too often overlooked, tool for bringing coherence to the student academic experience.

Before you begin writing your own course SLOs, check with those responsible for managing the curriculum that includes your course. It may be that significant effort has already been devoted to developing learning outcomes for the course you will teach. If that is the case, you will want to start your course planning with these shared outcomes. Shared outcomes are increasingly used to ensure consistency in the curriculum. Shared learning outcomes also help ensure a degree of reliability to course sections taught by multiple instructors. While it might feel confining to have predetermined learning outcomes, we encourage you to view these as a productive constraint. There is still room for you to bring your unique approach to the course.

Regardless of whether you have predetermined SLOs or are starting from scratch, your first step toward alignment is to identify how your course "fits" into the curriculum. The following activity provides a starting point. As you do this thinking, reach out to your colleagues who teach other courses in the curriculum and ask them to weigh in. Through this process, you also gain some insight into the culture and begin to be folded into the community of faculty at your specific institution.

Activity: Where Does Your Course Fit?

Draw a visual representation that depicts where your course fits in students' curricular journey. Use the following guiding questions to locate the information you'll need to construct a detailed map:

1. Does the course build on prior learning from other courses? Does the course serve as a prerequisite or provide essential skills students will use frequently?

2. Where does the course fall in the curricular sequence? An introductory course that acts as a gateway to advanced learning? A broad survey course that serves as students' only exposure to the subject? An upper-level elective?

A capstone or culminating course? Is the course aligned with program-level learning outcomes? Is the course aligned to university-level or general education outcomes?

3. How does the course contribute to students' life and career goals? Is the course an opportunity to synthesize learning from across the curriculum?

Share your drawing with colleagues to check your understanding of the role your course plays in the curriculum. This might just start a rich conversation about the curriculum in your program or department. Consider sharing this map with students on the first day of class to help them understand that the course they are about to embark upon has a meaningful and intentional purpose in the curriculum. Take a moment to share your creative drawings with us at #learningthatmatters.

Writing Substantive SLOs

Now that you've considered where your course fits in at your institution, it's time to move on to writing SLOs. Substantive SLOs should evolve from your aspirational goals. We encourage you to use the stem, "Years from now, students will be able to . . ." We know you won't be able to observe what students can do 10 years after they complete your class, but it's nonsensical to teach skills or concepts that will only exist in students' minds for a few months, if that long. Making this claim in writing in your syllabus sends the message to students that what they are learning is enduring and portable.

Most of your course-level SLOs should be student-centered, measurable, and inclusive. Some of your SLOs should also be focused on portable, higher-order thinking skills. First, we're going to describe what we mean by those terms and examine example SLOs.

Student-Centered

Of course, you want to know where you are headed in terms of instruction, but SLOs indicate what you intend for *the students* to be able to do upon successful completion of the course. Your outcomes should be student- focused, not instructor-focused. Consider the following learning outcome statement:

> This course will introduce students to the fundamental concepts of calculus.

This outcome is *less* student-centered because it places the focus on the course. To ensure that your SLOs put students at the center, you can begin each of your SLO with the stem, "Years from now, students will . . ." Now consider the following ***more*** student-centered version:

> Students will demonstrate their understanding of a fundamental concept of calculus by calculating derivatives. OR Students will calculate derivatives.

Well-crafted SLOs keep students front and center. This ***more*** student-centered learning outcome is specific and does a better job communicating to students the learning they can expect from the course. The following learning outcome gives an additional example of what a ***more*** student-centered learning outcome might look like in a humanities course:

> Students will compose research-informed academic arguments.

Measurable

When writing an SLO, consider if you are able to design an activity, project, or exam question that would allow you to determine to what degree students have met the outcome. You may also hear people refer to measurable outcomes as "assessable," which means the same thing. If you can't imagine a way that a student would demonstrate the learning described in the SLO, then the outcome is likely not measurable. In the calculus example earlier, you can probably picture students calculating derivatives. Consider the following ***less*** measurable SLOs. Can you identify why they would present challenges in measuring the learning?

> Students will learn to think critically.

> Students will know the importance of the authors' stance.

The following revised versions are ***more*** measurable because they clearly indicate how the learning can be demonstrated and observed:

> Students will implement effective search strategies and evaluate sources of information for relevance and authority.

> Students will examine a variety of texts for authors' stance, distinguishing them by degree of racialization.

Be careful with the verbs to *know*, *learn*, and *understand*. As you can see in the earlier examples, these verbs indicate internal mental states that are not automatically observable by outsiders. To meet the criteria of measurable, students must *demonstrate* understanding to make learning visible and assessment possible.

Consider this consequential outcome you might be able to adopt for your own course:

> By the end of this course, students will develop into lifelong learners.

The outcome is ***less*** measurable. It could be possible to determine if someone has become a lifelong learner but not for years. Now, consider the following learning outcome, which is a ***more*** measurable version.

> By the end of this course, students will define what they don't know about an issue and examine reliable sources on the topic to bridge their information gap to solve a problem.

The ***more*** measurable version identifies characteristics of a lifelong learner that could be developed and observed in a single course. You will still have the aspirational goal that students will develop into lifelong learners, and you will still tell students that that is what you are working toward, but it wouldn't be an official course SLO.

Interlude: Dispositional Outcomes

We want to take a moment now to discuss dispositional outcomes, or outcomes that measure learning in the affective domain (Krathwohl et al., 1964). The examples listed so far in this chapter, and likely the SLOs you're most familiar with, are generally outcomes for learning in the cognitive domain. The affective domain includes our feelings, emotions, values, and attitudes. Dispositional or affective outcomes are those things we intend for students to care about or act on as a result of having completed the course.

Dispositional outcomes are associated with the heart in the first activity in this chapter. While such outcomes are often overlooked and may even make some instructors uncomfortable, emotions matter for learning (Cavanagh, 2016; Immordino-Yang & Damasio, 2007). We think deeply about ideas and topics that we care about, meaning that an emotional connection is required for transformative learning. When we truly reflect on our teaching, we often have unstated dispositional outcomes for our students—often these are connected to those lofty, aspirational goals we hold for students. We challenge you to be forthright with students, include those outcomes on your syllabus, and refer to them throughout your course (as you would any of your SLOs).

Activity: Dispositional Outcomes

For each of the dispositions in Table 4.1, first select the measurable outcome from the middle column; then create one or more activities that students could complete to show they had met the outcome. Once you've completed the activity on your own, get together with a partner or group, and explain your choices. What do you notice?

Don't have a group to work with? Ask the virtual faculty learning community at #learningthatmatters.

Table 4.1: *Dispositional Outcomes*

Disposition	**Outcomes - select the one that is measurable.**	**Activity that demonstrates the outcome has been met.**
Sustainability	Students will show that they appreciate the environment by describing how they benefit economically, socially, and psychologically from the natural environment. Students will respect the many important economic, social, and psychological benefits the environment provides.	Journal entries in response to a prompt about how they benefit from a clean environment. Groups create posters or murals demonstrating the economic, social, and psychological benefits of creating greenspaces in urban areas. Groups create activities that examine "ecosystem services" and bring these activities to a local elementary school's Earth Day celebration. Create your own:
Values technology	Students will value technology. Students will describe useful applications of technology in their daily lives.	Create your own:
Interpersonal communication	Students will appreciate multiple perspectives and value individual differences in discussions. Students will actively listen in discussions and validate the feelings, opinions, and contributions of others.	Create your own:
Scientific reasoning	Students will value scientific expertise in decision making and demonstrate this by using accurate evidence. Students will appreciate scientific expertise in public discourse.	Create your own:
Art appreciation	Students will see the benefits of public art exhibits. Students will describe psychological, social, and intellectual reasons for why people attend art exhibits.	Create your own:

Inclusive

When you write SLOs to describe the learning students will attain, consider the cognitive, cultural, and identity diversities of students. Writing inclusive learning outcomes is the gateway to creating a course that supports equitable student success. Because we are human, sometimes the outcomes we write contain implicit biases or don't adequately consider how all students might be supported to attain the outcome. We are still learning how to do this and hope that the advice and guidance we provide here helps you do the same.

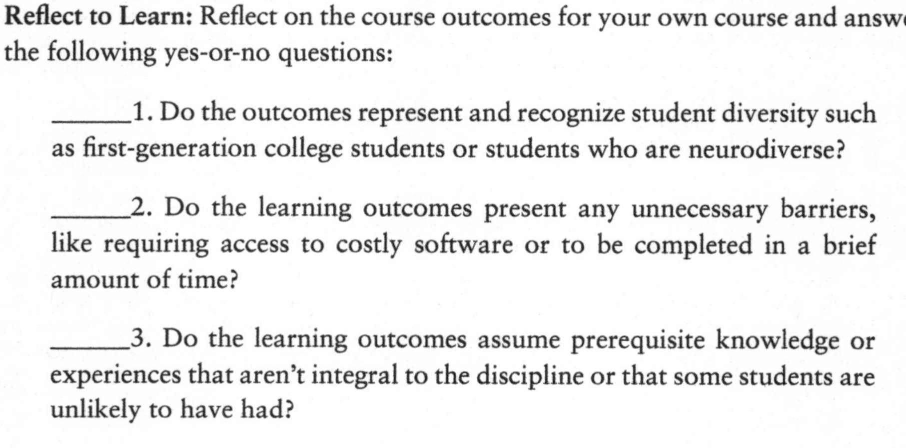

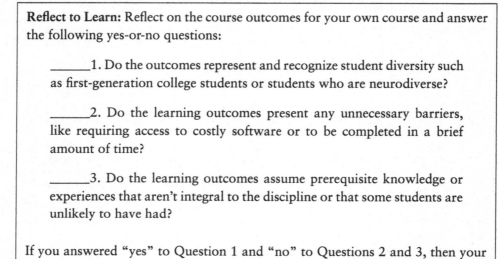

Reflect to Learn: Reflect on the course outcomes for your own course and answer the following yes-or-no questions:

______1. Do the outcomes represent and recognize student diversity such as first-generation college students or students who are neurodiverse?

______2. Do the learning outcomes present any unnecessary barriers, like requiring access to costly software or to be completed in a brief amount of time?

______3. Do the learning outcomes assume prerequisite knowledge or experiences that aren't integral to the discipline or that some students are unlikely to have had?

If you answered "yes" to Question 1 and "no" to Questions 2 and 3, then your outcomes are well on their way to being inclusive. If you answered otherwise, then your outcomes may not be inclusive *yet*, but they will be soon.

Remember in Chapter 3 when we introduced the Universal Design for Learning (UDL) principle to *provide multiple means of action and expression* and asked you to consider if students could demonstrate learning in multiple modalities or formats? Examine your SLOs and determine if they restrict students to only one method of achieving the outcome. Sometimes, linking the outcome to the means of achievement is intentional. For example, using a persuasive essay as the means of achievement in a composition course makes sense. In other cases, tying demonstration of learning to a particular format can create unnecessary barriers for students. For example, consider the following SLO:

> Students will present the ethical dimensions of international management in the public and private sectors of society through an oral presentation.

This SLO is *less* inclusive because it requires an oral presentation. Now, it may be that the oral presentation is intentional because oral communication is a desired outcome of the course. However, if that is not the case, the outcome can be made ***more*** inclusive by simply separating the outcome from what students will produce to demonstrate it, as has been done in the following revision:

> Students will articulate the ethical dimensions of international management in the public and private sectors of society.

Revising the SLO from "orally present" to "articulate" allows students to express their knowledge using a variety of formats—for example, an oral presentation, a formal report, or a poster presentation. Students might be given a choice as to what type of final product they will produce, which is good for motivation, as you learned in Chapter 2. Cognitive science explains that when learners grapple with content through more than one modality, the information is retained and understanding is enhanced (Jaipal, 2009). The more inclusive SLO also gives the instructor more freedom to design a variety of assessments that measure this outcome rather than being limited.

In addition to offering flexibility and choice, inclusive outcomes are also culturally affirming, meaning that outcomes are not written in ways that deny or devalue some students' cultural backgrounds and identities. Montenegro and Jankowski (2017) indicate that developing learning outcome statements using a cultural lens requires involving students in the process. Involving students is a dependable method for producing statements that are clear and meaningful. Consider the following ***less*** inclusive SLO:

> Students will trace their own family migration to the United States by exploring family primary documents.

At first glance, this seems like an interesting project that would bring relevance to learning about migration by connecting with students' histories. However, there are some worrying assumptions here. The SLO is clearly ***not*** inclusive of Indigenous peoples because it assumes all students come from families that migrated to the United States. Additionally, the outcome requires students have access to the histories of their own families through primary sources, such as family photo albums, diaries, and records. Students might not have access to these types of documents for myriad reasons. Furthermore, the learning outcome assumes that investigating family history is a harmless activity. This particular learning outcome could put students in the position of revealing their own or family members' citizenship status to fellow classmates. This rewrite is ***more*** inclusive because it removes the personal exploration but still achieves the desired learning:

> Students will trace patterns of migration in the United States through primary documents.

In addition to offering flexibility for diverse learners and affirming students' cultural identities, inclusive outcomes increase transparency for students and make the hidden curriculum explicit. The hidden curriculum, which you may remember from Chapter 2, includes unspoken norms about interactions and means of expression—these are often understood by students as the "hoops" they have to jump through to be successful. For example, consider the following ***less*** inclusive outcome from one of Julia's old general chemistry syllabi:

> Students will maintain professionalism in their laboratory work.

When Julia wrote this outcome, she had a mental image of what "professionalism" meant that had been cultivated through her years in graduate school and the time she spent working in laboratory settings. It is likely that any student who comes from an upper middle-class background can conjure up the outlines of a similar mental image, which makes the learning outcome transparent to some and opaque to others depending on their cultural and educational experiences. The following rewrite of the outcome is ***more*** inclusive because it makes explicit what Julia means by professionalism:

> Students will adhere to the American Chemical Society Academic Professional Guidelines by following and enforcing safe laboratory practices; maintaining high standards of honesty, integrity, and ethics; treating lab partners with respect; and documenting work in a laboratory notebook.

We deliberately included this example on professionalism because norms of professionalism, especially norms that dictate how a person should dress and communicate, may be problematic (Gray, 2019; Tobia, 2017). Many courses include elements of career readiness and professional standards, which can perpetuate harmful norms by presuming that some individual's physical appearance or dialect is not professional. However, we recognize the tension between the need to exterminate these barriers and our desire to equip students with the means to be hired for a job that leads to a career. If your course teaches professionalism, be sure to interrogate what this means with students and employers. Together you might brainstorm ways to maintain identities while navigating the demands of an unfamiliar field. If you have access to professional standards through your professional association, they may be a useful place to start a conversation with students. Recognize that professionalism norms can send the message that students cannot be their true selves and professionals simultaneously.

Reflect to Learn: A student who identifies as genderqueer asks you what they should wear to an upcoming job fair where they will be meeting potential employers. What advice do you give? What would your discussion be like?

Higher Order—and Working Toward Portable

Many of our students, and many of us, are masters at memorizing and cramming information into our brains for a short time, taking the exam, and then quickly forgetting what we just "learned." The fleeting nature of information retention indicates that there is nothing transformative about that experience! We all want the learning that occurs in our classes to last beyond final exams. For that to occur, we need to move beyond lower order (list, identify, classify) toward cultivating learners' higher order thinking (predict, analyze, develop, evaluate). Research shows that students will acquire the foundational skills as they move toward achieving the higher order outcomes, so it makes sense to spend the valuable time we have directed toward these loftier aims (Agarwal, 2019; Jensen et al., 2014; Lucariello et al., 2016; Nevid et al., 2017). Of course, movement toward the elevated objectives may require what is known as "scaffolding." Scaffolds refer to the supports that the instructor puts into place so that the learner can reach a higher, deeper, or more complex understanding. The scaffolds are removed as learners progress.

You may be familiar with Bloom's taxonomy, which uses verbs to classify types of learning based on the complexity within a domain required in the task (Krathwohl, 2002). Although well established and updated, Bloom's is not the only learning taxonomy out there. Some other useful taxonomies include Fink's Taxonomy of Significant Learning (2013), Six Facets of Understanding (Wiggins & McTighe, 2005), the Building Equity Taxonomy (Smith et al., 2017), the Structure of Observed Learning Outcomes (SOLO) Taxonomy (Biggs & Collis, 2014), Marzano's (2001) taxonomy, and the Depth of Knowledge model (Webb, 1999). It is less important which of these you consult but rather that you are able to distinguish the differences among the learning levels in the taxonomy. With Bloom's taxonomy, the main idea is that we're contrasting lower order or foundational thinking, which is recalling, remembering, or reproducing something, and higher order thinking, which is strategic and complex, requiring analysis, interpretation, or evaluation.

One of the most useful ways of applying Bloom's taxonomy to the development of SLOs is using the taxonomy to choose action verbs. You can find dozens of tables and charts that do this online. Table 4.2 provides a succinct version that describes the processes associated with the different levels of Bloom's Revised Taxonomy (Anderson et al., 2001). Once you've decided on the appropriate taxonomy level, use the table to select a verb for your SLO from the column labeled "Action Verbs." The far-right column describes activities that are appropriate for that level of learning.

You will notice that the main distinction along the continuum is the degree of unsupported complexity the learner engages in. Foundational tasks are not necessarily easy, but they are straightforward. For example, expecting students to "correctly identify all the bones in the human skeletal system" may be a foundational skill, but it is definitely not easy. As you move up the taxonomy, the mental processes required become increasingly complex, and these more challenging, complex, mental processes at the upper end of Bloom's are associated with enduring learning.

Table 4.2: *Action Verbs and Assessments Aligned With Different Levels of Bloom's Revised Taxonomy (Anderson et al., 2001)*

	Taxonomy Level	Action Verbs	Assessment or Activity
Higher-Order Learning	**Create (produce new or original works)**	arrange, compose, construct, create, design, develop, invent, produce	Song, painting, theater production Computer code Blueprints
	Evaluate (use criteria to judge an outcome or a decision)	appraise, assess, choose, conclude, convince, critique, defend, distinguish, editorialize, evaluate, grade, judge, justify, recommend, persuade	Position papers Oral arguments Editorials
	Analyze (take something apart or draw connections among ideas)	analyze, differentiate, distinguish, infer, interpret, prioritize	Lab reports Market analysis Art interpretation Statistics Literary review
Application Learning	**Apply (use information in new situations)**	apply, calculate, chart, compute, construct, develop, dramatize, illustrate, manipulate, operate, predict, solve, write	Essays Oral presentations Computer code output
Foundational Learning	**Understand (explains ideas or concepts)**	categorize, classify, compare, contrast, convert, demonstrate, describe, differentiate, discuss, distinguish, estimate, explain, express, generalize, give examples, paraphrase, summarize, translate	Class discussions Summary sentences Analogies Paraphrased answers Answers from short answer or essay questions Pictures, diagrams, or concept maps Oral presentations
	Remember (recall facts and basic concepts)	define, group, identify, label, list, locate, match, memorize, name, quote, recall, recite, recognize, reproduce, select, state	Matching terms to definitions A picture with labeled parts Answers from multiple choice or matching questions

Now, for an example of a ***less*** higher order SLO:

> Students will identify the reactants and products in all the reactions of photosynthesis.

The action in this SLO is identification, which, as you can see from Table 4.2, is a verb associated with foundational learning. Now, contrast that with the following amended SLO:

> Students will predict outcomes when changes are made to the reactions of photosynthesis.

Changing the action the student will take from identifying to predicting moves the action verb from foundational learning to application and requires ***more*** higher order thinking. Furthermore, if students can demonstrate their ability to predict outcomes when changes are made in the reactions, they will certainly be capable of identifying elements of the reaction.

Activity: Practice Evaluating SLOs

For each of the following SLOs, determine if it is student-centered, measurable, inclusive, and higher order. Take a stab at writing revisions for a few to better meet the criteria. Visit our website for our evaluation of these outcomes:

1. This course will introduce students to the major developments in the history of Western civilization.
2. Students will collaborate with classmates by providing useful peer review and feedback.
3. This accounting class will introduce merchandising operations and related inventory methods.
4. Students will examine the cultural significance of photography.
5. Students will use model-based reasoning to solve problems.
6. Students will demonstrate critical thinking skills by articulating arguments that use logic and evidence.
7. Students will demonstrate an understanding of dance technique, classroom etiquette, dress, and process.
8. Students will interrogate the underlying mechanisms that perpetuate Asian women's marginality and subordination.
9. This course focuses on the development of basic reading comprehension skills in Italian.
10. By the end of this course, students will appreciate rocks and minerals.

Finally, Becoming Portable

Portability means students will take their learning with them to the next class, through graduation, into their careers, and onto a lifetime of learning. Portable outcomes are generally the broad skills that we hope students attain by graduation, such as teamwork, creative thinking, and ethical decision-making. However, students are unlikely to build these skills at a significant level unless we explicitly teach those skills and devote time to developing them.

Portable learning is antithetical to cramming for the final exam or earning an A but forgetting everything before the start of the next term. Portable learning is transformative. Student attainment of portable, transferable outcomes signifies education at its best and is the rare condition that more educators, colleges, and schools should be striving to achieve.

Teaching portable outcomes means taking a big step back from your course and being brave enough to distill it down to its most critical elements, thinking about the most important things that students need from your courses. It means letting go of the slides bursting with interesting information. It means letting go of the security that you might find in presenting dates, authors, or equations without developing students' capacity to use this knowledge meaningfully. By necessity, the list of portable outcomes in any one course is a short list, but that doesn't mean that it will be easy to design learning experiences that lead to that kind of learning.

Activity: Portable Outcomes

The purpose of this activity is to begin building portable outcomes. Consider one or more of the following learning outcomes and describe how your course helps students achieve these (your course need not align with all or even most of these outcomes). For the outcomes that are aligned with your class, consider how you might write a revision that is specific to your course. A few examples are given next, and we've posted more examples on our website. Share your portable outcomes with us at #learningthatmatters.

Communication: Students will be able to communicate persuasively and effectively, both orally and in writing.

Course-level sample: Students will effectively communicate in writing for a wide variety of purposes and audiences.

Critical thinking: Students will synthesize information, explain issues, analyze concepts and evidence, assess assumptions, define their own perspectives and positions, and evaluate the implications and consequences of their conclusions. (Hawai‘i Pacific University)

Course-level sample: Students will demonstrate critical thinking skills by writing analyses that utilize high-quality evidence and argumentation.

Diversity, Equity, and Inclusion: Students will demonstrate critical awareness of how individual perspectives and biases influence ways of seeing the world. (University of Massachusetts Amherst)

Information literacy: The ability to know when there is a need for information, to be able to identify, locate, evaluate, and effectively use that information for the issue or problem at hand. (National Forum on Information Literacy)

Make It Happen: Write Your SLOs

Now it's time for you to apply the information from this chapter and practice developing the skill of SLO writing. Write three to seven SLOs for your course and make at least one portable. Start by referring to your notes from the Head, Heart, Hand activity earlier in the chapter. Once you've prepared your first draft of SLOs, return to the empathy maps you developed in Chapter 3—if any of your SLOs present barriers to students, revise them to make them more inclusive. Once you've written your SLOs,

- share your SLOs with others, ideally someone outside of your discipline or students familiar with the course, for feedback.
- if you can, write your course title on a whiteboard and post your SLOs on a large sticky note underneath. Allow others to read and provide feedback.
- revise SLOs based on feedback.

Now evaluate your outcomes:

- Are they student-centered?
- Are they measurable?
- Are they inclusive?
- Are they higher order?
- Is at least one portable?

Activity: Pin the Outcome on the Taxonomy (group activity)

Sometimes we write SLOs that we think describe learning that is more complex than it actually is. It can be helpful for a fresh set of eyes to read the SLO and evaluate the level of learning.

Step 1: Divide a whiteboard or wall space vertically into three sections and label them as follows:

- Higher Order Learning: Analyze, Evaluate, Create
- Application Learning: Apply
- Foundational Learning: Remember and Understand

Step 2: Write each SLO on a small sticky note or strip of paper—one outcome per note.

Step 3: Shuffle the outcome notes. Each person selects outcomes that are not their own and sticks them to the section where they think they belong.

Step 4: Each person walks up to the board one at a time to retrieve their outcomes. Before they pull it off the wall, they indicate if they agree or disagree with its placement. If there isn't agreement, the group discusses rewording the outcome to meet the level of learning desired.

Field Notes From Cynthia: From Course SLOs to Lesson Objectives

OK—now you have excellent SLOs, but what about when you're planning for a specific lesson? How do you get from course-level SLOs to unit/module-level outcomes to daily lesson objectives (Table 4.3)?

Table 4.3: *Relationship Among Course-, Module-, and Lesson-Level Objectives*

Course-level outcomes: Addressed throughout the span of the term
Module-level outcomes: The anticipated student learning outcomes from a module within the course. Courses can have several modules.
Lesson objectives: The objectives you use to plan a single lesson or addressed within a class period

Writing outcomes for each level comes back to backward design (Chapter 3) again, starting with where you want to end up and considering what it would take for students to get there.

In a course on "The American Novel," the following might be an SLO: "Years from now, you should be able to explain the choices authors make that bring their novels alive for the reader." In other words, I want students to recognize that authors make conscious choices that can make or break a novel. I want students to be able to recognize those choices and explain the effect those choices have. To turn that SLO into a module-level outcome, I would need to ask myself, "If the target goal is *x*, what knowledge, skills, or dispositions would students need to learn that would eventually add up to them being able to do *x*?" In this case, students would need to discover that authors' choices fall into categories such as setting, character, and point of view—each could be a module-level outcome (Table 4.4). For point of view, consider the following:

> Students will explain the effect the author's choice of a specific point of view has on a novel.
>
> Students will analyze how an author develops the point of view of the narrator in a novel.

I can't teach students to do either of those in a single class period, but students could learn to do them over several days or a few weeks. I need to break these down further and again use the question, "If the target objective is *x*, what knowledge, skills, or dispositions would students need to learn that would eventually add up to *x*?" But this time, I'm going to break those into chunks that students could learn in a class period or two, and I am going to put them in order from simpler to more complex (Table 4.4). Bloom's taxonomy can be useful for doing this.

Table 4.4: *Table 4.4 Example of Sequential Analysis in Moving From Outcomes to Objectives*

Course-Level Outcomes:
Years from now, you should be able to explain **the choices authors make** that bring their novels alive for the reader.
Module-Level Outcomes:
Students will explain the effect the **author's choice of a specific point of view** has on a novel. Students will analyze how an **author develops the point of view** of the narrator or speaker in a novel.
Lesson Objectives:
By the end of the period today, you will 1. define point of view. 2. determine the **point of view** of a narrator. 3. recognize specific strategies the author uses to develop **point of view** (e.g., character actions and thoughts, dialogue, reactions and thoughts of other characters). 4. identify examples in a text where the author develops the **point of view.** 5. explain how the author uses the narrator to develop the **point of view.** 6. analyze how the author develops the **point of view.**

The lesson objectives are what students would learn about/meet over a class period or two. If you are transparent about how the lesson objectives build to module-level outcomes, and the module-level outcomes build to course-level outcomes, then you can help students get that sense they are gradually mastering a complex idea, which can be very motivating. Additionally, breaking SLOs down in this way provides you with a clear sense of how learning will be scaffolded from foundational to higher order, which can help illuminate potential gaps that might keep students from progressing.

Make It Happen: Module-Level Outcomes

Select one of your SLOs and imagine an aligned module-level outcome. Just as you did for your SLOs, be sure to ask yourself whether the module-level outcome meets the criteria of being student-centered? Measurable? Higher order? Inclusive?

Once you're satisfied that you've created a substantive module-level outcome, further break it into several objectives that could be used to guide a single lesson.

Finally, build a table or graphic organizer similar to Cynthia's (Table 4.4) that shows the connections between the course-level outcome, the module-level outcome, and the lesson-level objectives.

Wonderful Resources to Extend Learning

In the book ***Creating Significant Learning Experiences: An Integrated Approach to Designing College Courses***, **L. Dee Fink** (2013) adapts backward design to the college classroom.

While this book is intended for K–12 teachers, ***Where Great Teaching Begins: Planning for Student Thinking and Learning***, **Anne Reeves** (2011) does an excellent job of explaining the process of writing high-quality outcomes.

In **"Toward a Theory of Culturally Relevant Pedagogy," Gloria Ladson-Billings** (1995) explains the components of culturally relevant pedagogy and examines the intersectionality of culture and teaching.

Anton Tolman (2014) revises Bloom's pyramid in a **Bloom's Taxonomy for Course Design and Teaching** diagram. This reframing shows the interdependence of analysis, creation, and evaluation in critical thinking and application acts as a bridge between foundational knowledge and critical thinking.

References

Agarwal, P. K. (2019). Retrieval practice & Bloom's taxonomy: Do students need fact knowledge before higher order learning? *Journal of Educational Psychology, 111*(2), 189–209. https://doi.org/10.1037/edu0000282

Anderson, L. W., & Bloom, B. S. (2001). A taxonomy for learning, teaching, and assessing: A revision of Bloom's taxonomy of educational objectives. Longman.

Biggs, J. B., & Collis, K. F. (2014). *Evaluating the quality of learning: The SOLO taxonomy (structure of the observed learning outcome).* Academic Press.

Cavanagh, S. R. (2016). *The spark of learning: Energizing the college classroom with the science of emotion.* West Virginia University Press. https://muse.jhu.edu/book/47958

Fink, L. D. (2013). *Creating significant learning experiences: An integrated approach to designing college courses.* John Wiley & Sons.

Gray, A. (2019, June 4). The bias of 'professionalism' standards. *Stanford Social Innovation Review.* https://ssir.org/articles/entry/the_bias_of_professionalism_standards

Immordino-Yang, M. H., & Damasio, A. (2007). We feel, therefore we learn: The relevance of affective and social neuroscience to education. *Mind, Brain, and Education, 1*(1), 3–10. https://doi.org/10.1111/j.1751-228x.2007.00004.x

Jaipal, K. (2009). Meaning making through multiple modalities in a biology classroom: A multimodal semiotics discourse analysis. *Science Education, 94*(1), 48–72. https://doi.org/10.1002/sce.20359

Jensen, J. L., McDaniel, M. A., Woodard, S. M., & Kummer, T. A. (2014). Teaching to the test . . . or testing to teach: Exams requiring higher order thinking skills encourage greater conceptual understanding. *Educational Psychology Review, 26*(2), 307–329. https://doi.org/10.1007/s10648-013-9248-9

Krathwohl, D. R., (2002). A revision of Bloom's taxonomy: An overview. *Theory Into Practice, 41*(4), 212–218.

Krathwohl, D. R., Bloom, B. S., & Masia, B. B. (1964). *Taxonomy of educational objectives: Handbook 2. Affective domain.* David McKay.

Ladson-Billings, G. (1995). Toward a theory of culturally relevant pedagogy. *American Educational Research Journal, 32*(3), 465–491. https://doi.org/10.3102/00028312032003465

Lucariello, J. M., Nastasi, B. K., Dwyer, C., Skiba, R., DeMarie, D., & Anderman, E. M. (2016). Top 20 psychological principles for PK–12 education. *Theory Into Practice, 55*(2), 86–93. https://doi.org/10.1080/00405841.2016.1152107

Marzano, R. J. (2001). *Designing a new taxonomy of educational objectives: Experts in assessment.* Corwin. https://eric.ed.gov/?id=ED447161

Montenegro, E., & Jankowski, N. A. (2017). *Equity and assessment: Moving towards culturally responsive assessment.* www.learningoutcomesassessment.org

Nevid, J. S., Ambrose, M. A., & Pyun, Y. S. (2017). Effects of higher and lower level writing-to-learn assignments on higher and lower level examination questions. *Teaching of Psychology, 44*(4), 324–329. https://doi.org/10.1177/0098628317727645

Reeves, A. R. (2011). *Where great teaching begins: Planning for student thinking and learning.* ASCD. http://www.ascd.org/Publications/Books/Overview/Where-Great-Teaching-Begins.aspx

Smith, D., Frey, N., Pumpian, I., & Fisher, D. (2017). *Building equity: Policies and practices to empower all learners.* ASCD. http://www.ascd.org/publications/books/117031.aspx

Tobia, J. (2017). *Why I'm genderqueer, professional and unafraid.* HuffPost. https://www.huffpost.com/entry/genderqueer-professional-_b_5476239?guccounter=1

Tolman, A. O. (2014). *Bloom's taxonomy for course design and teaching.* Wikimedia Commons. https://commons.wikimedia.org/wiki/File:Bloom%27s_Taxonomy_for_Course_Design_and_Teaching.pdf

Webb, N. L. (1999). *Alignment of science and mathematics standards and assessments in four states* (Research Monograph No. 18). National Institute for Science Education & Council of Chief State School Officers.

Wiggins, G. P., & McTighe, J. (2005). *Understanding by design* (Expanded 2nd ed.). ASCD.

CHAPTER FIVE

The Dilemma, Issue, or Question Approach

Preflection

What are some of the questions that have fascinated you for years? What issues in local, national, and global news are particularly interesting to you?

As you read this chapter, reflect on it, and engage with the activities both independently and with fellow readers, note that it has been designed to support you in the following:

- Applying the Dilemma, Issue, or Question (DIQ) approach to enhance student learning
- Identifying intersections of course content with multifaceted, problematic questions facing society
- Evaluating and selecting a DIQ for your course

Imagine you are a student. It's the second day of class, and instead of presenting a lecture on the first chapter of the assigned textbook, your instructor presents you with a prompt like one of the following:

- **Nursing course:** Have systemic racism in our health care systems and social inequities put some communities at higher risk of getting sick and dying from COVID-19?
- **Music education course:** This week, the top three songs on Billboard's Hot 100 chart are by DaBaby, Jack Harlow, and DJ Khaled. Analyze the lyrics for references to gender. What do you notice? How similar are the gender views expressed by each?

- **General education art course:** According to the dictionary, graffiti is "usually unauthorized writing or drawing on a public surface" (https://www.merriam-webster.com/dictionary/graffiti.) Who creates graffiti, and who gets to decide if it is vandalism or art? Can it be both at the same time?

The professor then moves you into small groups to discuss how the prompt connects to the course material. Each group contributes key ideas from their discussion to those of other groups, which are projected at the front of the room.

> **Reflect to Learn:** As a student in the class described earlier, how might this feel different from the lecture you were expecting? Looking toward the rest of the semester, how might you feel about future sessions in this course?

Now imagine you're the instructor using those prompts. During those first vital minutes when the tone is being set for the entire term, instead of the usual furious note-taking, you notice that the students are connecting course content to relevant events. As an assignment after class, they're asked to post to an online discussion about how this topic is connected to their lives, and on that discussion board, you read a wide range of responses. Some have shared detailed life experiences. Others have posted links to additional sources. Nearly everyone is contributing and connecting. Visualize how you might feel as the instructor in this course and envision how much learning could occur with those students who were this engaged from the start.

The preceding ideas are examples of dilemmas, issues, or questions (DIQs) that could be used to frame a course or a module within a course. As a frame, DIQs don't replace discipline-specific content; they enhance it and provide students with a compelling reason to learn the facts, models, concepts, and practices associated with the discipline. Additionally, they provide a means for students to think deeply about important, complex issues and problems they will face.

Caralyn's Experience

As a biology major many (many) years ago, I completed a full year of calculus. At the time, I didn't know what I could do with a derivative, but I dutifully learned how to solve all the appropriate problems. I still remember being half-ecstatic and half-dismayed when, as a graduate student, I discovered the many applications of calculus in population and community ecology. I was ecstatic because it was so exciting to see these clear, relatively simple equations applied to messy, noisy ecosystems filled with interacting plants and animals. I was dismayed because I didn't remember any calculus. I still wonder what that initial experience with calculus would have been like if I had been in a calculus class like the one taught by Dale Winter (2007), who revised their calculus course so the mathematics were applied to social and ethical issues – finally providing a reason to know something about derivatives! Students tackled multiple issues, including water security and Native peoples' rights in Botswana, as they learned about the domain and range of a function and interpreting intersection points. In another unit, the students answered the question, "How quickly can polio be eradicated?" by applying and interpreting polynomial functions.

Reflect to Learn: Think back to your undergraduate courses. Which ones had the greatest impact on your learning? What was it about how the course was taught that enabled you to learn so much or that applied to many facets of your life?

At this time when so many are examining the cost/benefit ratio of face-to-face meetings in brick-and-mortar buildings, as well as higher education in general, it seems especially important to draw learners in with compelling contexts for learning. We cannot expect students, their parents, or really anyone to see the value of our specific disciplines if we teach courses that don't deliberately showcase their significance. If the juicy topics, complex questions, and exciting debates are reserved for senior capstone courses and graduate seminars and nothing but dry surveys of concepts, equations, and people comprise the introductory and general education courses, we stand to lose the very people who are in the best position to respond to captivating course work. Not only is this unfair to students, depriving them of important and valuable learning experiences, but it also cements the inaccurate and undemocratic notion that thinking is an elitist activity for addressing a dusty canon of irrelevance. Thus, the tradition of requiring students to "prove themselves" by learning inapplicable material first is especially unfair to students who are already underserved because they are the ones who benefit the most from connecting course content to real-life issues (M. Brown et al., 2009; Winter, 2007). For many reasons, it makes good sense to use an evocative learning context of DIQs because at their core, DIQs are real problems in need of consideration by the very population, students, to whom the responsibility for solving will fall. Practice with relevant issues that foster creative, critical, higher order thinking and call for robust disciplinary knowledge should be front and center in curricula (Hanstedt, 2018).

Activity: Think–Pair–Share

Consider the empathy maps you created in the previous chapter for Juawn, Ameena, Isabella, and Jocelyn. What DIQs might best engage these students?

- Think: Come up with your own answer to the preceding questions.
- Pair: Discuss your answer with a partner.
- Share: Communicate your answers with the group or share them at #learningthatmatters.

DIQs Enhance Learning

Using big, complex questions to frame your course or module within a course can help you generate and hold student interest by enhancing student motivation (Chapter 2). You know that your discipline is fascinating and relevant, but you've had the advantage of years of study in addition to focused, intrinsic motivation. People not as closely connected to the subject matter, which is almost everyone else, need to connect the content to their reality for it to have meaning. Because we ascribe to a constructivist model of learning (Chapter 2), we use DIQs to connect course content to what students already know from their lived experiences.

Imagine an instructor teaching about mutualisms in a non-biology major course. This instructor describes how mutualisms are positive interactions between two different species. Most students can memorize this definition and probably then identify a mutualism from a list of interactions. Now imagine that instead of just giving the scientific definition, the instructor asks students to list what they've eaten in the past 24 hours, indicate which of these foods are insect-pollinated, and describe the type of interaction that pollination is. Next, students explore current concerns in bee die-offs and colony collapse disorder. Then imagine that this instructor doesn't stop there but instead asks students to propose ideas to improve bee survival in the local community, which creates relevance because then there is a reason for the students to know about mutualisms. This then leads to greater retention of material as well as the understanding of key concepts in the discipline (Boyaci Belet & Güner, 2018; Bransford et al., 2000; Chamany, 2006; Chamany et al., 2008). In this scenario, the students not only learned about ecological interactions but also developed problem-solving skills by grappling with a problem that has scientific, economic, and social aspects that make it a worthwhile foundational curriculum for a wide range of citizen-learners. Most of our students will not go on to academic careers in our field of study, but many will go into careers in which they can apply what they learn in our classes creatively. Consequently, we do students a great service by training them to apply disciplinary skill sets to socially relevant contexts and situations.

We assume that anyone reading this book doesn't want students to begin and end their learning by memorizing facts. We know from experience (as well as research) that when students cram the night before the final exam, they forget most of the information by the time winter or summer break is over (P. Brown et al., 2014; Karpicke & Roediger, 2007). On the other hand, teaching content through relevant and compelling topics like DIQs can lead to increased student engagement, higher pass rates, higher course completion rates, and increased knowledge retention (Boyaci Belet & Güner, 2018; Bransford et al., 2000; Chamany, 2006; Chamany et al., 2008). If we value the development of higher order thinking skills that require application, analysis, evaluation, and synthesis, as well as seek outcomes that increase our institutions' sustainability, then we need to design our classes in ways that engage students with material at those elevated levels.

DIQs are those "hooks" that draw in learners and serve as vehicles to engage students in the larger task of sensemaking and connecting disciplinary knowledge. They can motivate and engage students because there isn't an obvious, straightforward answer (Hanstedt, 2018). Because of the multifaceted, arguable nature of these connecting concepts, learners often find them more appealing catalysts that then can frame a unit of study as ongoing inquiry rather than as a neatly wrapped package of knowledge passively acquired. To be fair, in our experience, this type of question could also frustrate those students who are accustomed to memorizing content to ace an exam—which requires instructors to explain the purpose and benefits of this teaching approach and support some as they "unlearn" assumptions.

Now that you've seen the evidence explaining why teaching through DIQs is an effective practice, the question remains, *How?*

> **Reflect to Learn:** How would you describe the DIQ approach to colleagues? Would you be able to tell them how this approach deepens learning?

One or Many?

There are basically two pathways to follow for using DIQs to frame a course. You can select one big DIQ that frames an entire course, or you can incorporate multiple DIQs that may or may not be related to each other. We have found it less intimidating to consider the use of a single DIQ the first time out, whether it is to be the focal point of the whole course or of a single module.

An example of a course-wide DIQ approach was undertaken by four chemistry faculty who decided to rework the first-semester chemistry overview course to meet a new general education critical thinking requirement. Before the revision, the course was a traditional introductory chemistry course for science majors. Students marched through the textbook, learning about the periodic table, atomic and molecular structure, acids and bases, and other topics. In the revised course, students engaged with these same foundational concepts but in the context of issues that impact the climate. Students learned the basic principles of chemistry as applied to ozone depletion, the greenhouse effect, acid rain, and other climate concerns. This gave students a motivating reason to learn the chemistry material and provided a meaningful context. Instead of a multiple-choice exam with questions about the periodic table, students collaboratively created museum exhibits, designed posters, and wrote white papers. Many students who completed the revised course, who were first-year students at the time of their enrollment, upon graduation identified this course as one of the most important learning experiences in their entire undergraduate curriculum.

While that DIQ-centric course tapped chemistry concepts, imagine a common general education course focused on American History, 1865 to the present. Some or all of this course could be framed by the question, "How do events from the past still affect us today?" Students in this course could analyze current events as historians and compare current circumstances to past events, thereby gaining important disciplinary skills and learning historical content.

If you can't see using just one DIQ to frame your course, then instead you might select multiple, smaller DIQs, like the calculus course described previously. In this case, you'll want to focus on the module-level outcomes and select a DIQ well-aligned with them.

Make It Happen: DIQ Creation

Step 1: Brainstorming

Use current events, textbook case studies, colleagues, social media, student focus groups, the resources and websites listed at the end of the chapter, and other sources to create a list of DIQs that could work for your course. At this point, the sky's the limit. We've included a variety of activities and strategies to support you in this first step because we've found that it can be challenging but also exhilarating as you let go of any preconceived notions that you may have about what a course or module "has to" look like.

You Don't Need to Reinvent the Wheel

There are abundant resources that you can mine for DIQ ideas and strategies. Some are outlined in the following.

For anyone teaching science, Science Education for New Civic Engagement & Responsibilities (SENCER; http://sencer.net/) is a wonderful resource whose goal is to help educators make connections between their course content and issues of civic importance. Additionally, the National Center for Case Study Teaching in Science (https://sciencecases.lib.buffalo.edu/) is a great resource for finding case studies that can be applied over one or two classes. The Grand Challenges for Engineering (National Academy of Engineering, 2020) provides complex questions that can be used to engage students.

DIQs are not just for science, technology, engineering, and mathematics (STEM) disciplines. The Evergreen State College's Enduring Legacies Native Cases Initiative (2020) has developed culturally relevant teaching resources in the form of case studies on key issues in Indian country (2020). In *Reacting to the Past* courses, students role-play in complex historical scenarios informed by readings and text and in doing so apply speaking, writing, critical thinking, leadership, and teamwork skills (Barnard College, 2020). TED-Ed (2020) has curated sets of videos focused on themes. Check on these related to your discipline and look for interesting connections and perspectives.

Rittel and Webber first introduced the concept of "wicked problems" in 1973, and the concept is still relevant today. They define wicked problems as "problems that are difficult or impossible to solve because of incomplete, contradictory, and changing requirements that are often difficult to recognize" (Rittel & Webber, 1973, p. 160). These types of problems make excellent issues for guiding a course or unit. Income inequality, climate change, and safe reopening of schools during a pandemic are all examples of "wicked problems." In his book *Creating Wicked Students*, Hanstedt (2018) explains how, and why, courses should be built around these wicked problems.

Another way to generate ideas is to get together with a group of colleagues and complete this DIQ speed-dating activity that may provide some inspiration.

Activity: DIQ Speed Dating

This is for a faculty learning community of four or more members. It can be a bit chaotic, but it's fun and a way to get everyone to think about how to connect their course content to current events and see how different disciplines approach the same topic.

1. Brainstorm a list of five to seven current events or societal issues. For example, COVID-19, Black Lives Matter, U.S.–Russia relations, climate change, and U.S. elections. Write each topic on a separate piece of paper.

2. Divide the group in half. Give each person in Group A one of the pieces of paper with one topic written on it. Ask each person in Group B to sit across from a member of Group A.

3. Set a timer for 2 minutes. In those 2 minutes, have each pair discuss how A's DIQ could be taught in B's class.

4. Then have the B's rotate places and sit across from a new A. Repeat Step 3.
5. Repeat Steps 3 and 4 three times.
6. Then switch groups (people in Group A switch to Group B) and repeat.
7. Wrap up with a group discussion about the ideas you generated.

Still feeling stuck? Here are a few more strategies:

- Open up a newspaper or news site. Pick three headlines and describe how your course could help students address the issues described in the articles.
- Imagine what a course would look like if you co-taught with someone from a completely different discipline.
- Consider the major debates and deep philosophical questions in your field.
- Contemplate community, state, national, or international issues your discipline could address.
- Consider the ideas or questions that first motivated you to pursue your discipline.
- Reflect on ethical dilemmas professionals in your field sometimes face.
- Imagine that there is a new cabinet-level position in the U.S. government called the Secretary of the Future. NPR's Marketplace did a series on this based on a Kurt Vonnegut interview (Brancaccio & Long, 2016). How could your discipline help inform and support this position? What is a student in your class learning that would help them prepare to be the next secretary?
- Ask students (current, former, or potential) what topics they are most interested in.
- Ask students why they think your discipline is exciting and relevant.

Want to enlarge your list of ideas? Complete the DIQ Brainstorming activity on our website.

Step 2: Evaluate Your DIQs

After you have some potential DIQs, you then need to evaluate each for your course. A good DIQ is broad, engaging, complex, aligned, and culturally affirming. Assess each potential DIQ using the following questions:

1. Is the DIQ broad enough to encompass the disciplinary content and skills you intend for students to gain?

2. Is it engaging and relatable to all (or most) students?

3. Is it appropriately complex?

4. Is it sufficiently aligned to your course learning outcomes?

5. Does it include authors, examples, stories, voices, and role models that represent the full range of human diversity (gender, race and ethnicity, ability, socioeconomic levels, etc.)?

Activity: DIQ Evaluation

Evaluate the following DIQs using the earlier discussed criteria. Discuss your decisions with a partner or small group before reading our evaluation.

Here are three DIQs. Evaluate them using the questions from the text:

1. **Flint, Michigan, Water Crisis.** In 2014, the Flint River became the drinking water source for the city of Flint, Michigan. This water was improperly treated, which caused lead from aging pipes to leach into the water supply. Residents were exposed to extremely elevated levels of lead, a neurotoxin.

2. **Who is the more influential of these two feuding American authors: Tom Wolfe or Norman Mailer?** Wolfe is best known for his association with and influence over the New Journalism literary movement. Mailer is considered an innovator of creative nonfiction, which uses literary fiction style and devices in fact-based journalism.

3. **Sales of diamond engagement rings are falling. As a marketer, what strategies could you use to bring back sales?** The Bain Global Diamond Industry Report (https://www.bain.com/contentassets/e225b ceffd7a48b5b450837adbbfee88/bain_report_global_diamond_re port_2019.pdf) suggests that sales of rough diamonds may drop as much as 25% this year, and many jewelry chains closed stores during the COVID-19 pandemic. The diamond industry is facing an uphill climb and will need an extraordinary marketing plan to get it back on its feet.

Our Evaluation

There are many courses that could potentially use the Flint River DIQ. A biology course could focus on the effects of lead on human development. A public policy course could analyze the regulations and decisions that lead to this crisis. A sociology course could examine who had the power to make decisions regarding the water supply and who were the people most impacted by this decision. Ideally, no matter the subject, a course using this DIQ would examine other disciplines and perspectives because this is not a problem that was caused by a single discipline and it will not be solved by one discipline in isolation either.

The authors' feud doesn't meet the earlier stated criteria. It is unlikely that most students would find this engaging or that it is broad enough to incorporate much course content.

Creating a marketing plan for a real industry is complex, authentic, and interesting. However, a focus on the diamond industry may be less relatable than many other businesses you could choose, and it is certainly a questionable choice considering the moral issues surrounding the diamond industry and the difficulty you would have incorporating a diversity of voices. Creating marketing plans for small businesses struggling to stay afloat in difficult financial times would maintain the complexity, allow you to expand on the authenticity by bringing in a diversity of actual business owners, and be more relatable to students.

Step 3: Aligning Course Content With Your DIQ

Once you have DIQs that you are interested in integrating into your course, then you need to align your course content with your selected DIQs. There is no cookbook recipe for this step because there is not a one-size-fits-all approach that will work for all courses. This is an iterative, rather than a linear, process. But no matter how you want to approach this step, you'll need clear, course-level student learning objectives (SLOs; Chapter 4), as well as descriptions of the content, topics, or modules that you want or need to include in your course.

Then you need to evaluate the alignment between your DIQs and the content. It may be that all or most of your content is aligned with the DIQs, or it may be that there are certain modules that don't "fit" into the DIQ model and you teach these separately.

Examine your module-level outcomes (Chapter 4). Be willing to change the order; consider when the skills or content of each module are needed rather than where they appear in the textbook. Give yourself permission to drop certain topics to delve more deeply into others. You don't need to "cover" every chapter in the book (especially since most textbooks keep getting longer and longer); instead focus on the ideas, skills, and attitudes that are most important. In the words of the BlackSpace Manifesto "Choose critical connections over critical mass. Value quality over quantity" (BlackSpace Urbanist Collective, 2020, p.1).

To get your course design juices flowing, write your course SLOs and topics individually on sticky notes. Write the DIQs on whiteboards or larger pieces of paper. Play around with how each SLO and unit could be connected to the DIQ.

Following are two examples of courses that have been redesigned around a DIQ with notes about how it happened:

Example 1: First-year seminar

DIQ: These days every one of us is bombarded on a daily basis with quality news, fake news, facts, and alternative facts. How do we know what to believe? How do we ensure that our own ideas are founded on quality information?

Explanation: In this course, these questions are addressed in an explicit and detailed way in a module that extends for about a quarter of the course, and students have a final project that assesses information literacy. Information literacy is woven into most class periods, and often as students are coming in, there is a current news story projected that relates to the issue of the quality of information we receive and how to best evaluate that information.

Design process: This course existed for many years as a kind of "catchall" for onboarding first-year students. A team tasked with tweaking the course thought that information literacy seemed like a good fit for a course designed to kick off the higher education experience. To engage students, the team began with a focus that was "closer to home": the information students encounter through social media. From there, students were led through considering information of a more academic nature.

Example 2: Sophomore-Level Ecology Course for Majors

DIQ: Agriculture. The application of ecological principles, at the organismal, population, community, and ecosystem levels through the lens of agriculture.

Explanation: In this course, students examine and apply ecological concepts in agricultural settings. Agriculture is not explicitly mentioned in every class. However, a variety of agricultural case studies and scenarios are used throughout. For example, students examine honeybee pollination of crops in the section on community interactions. In the section on ecosystem ecology, students apply knowledge of nitrogen cycling to the impacts of fertilizer runoff.

Design process: This course was taught for multiple terms as a typical ecology course, which started with physiological ecology and ended with ecosystem ecology—basically moving up the steps of ecological organization. In the redesign, the class started with this question, "How do we feed our growing population?" This is an unexpected, "wicked problem" that many students are interested in. A variety of different agricultural systems, such as genetically modified corn and shade-grown coffee, were used to examine and learn ecological principles and concepts. The order of topics changed, but no topics were dropped. One exam was replaced with a group project in which students had to imagine they were working for the Food and Agriculture Organization of the United Nations and needed to design a set of experiments that addressed one of its strategic objectives.

Step 4: Get Feedback

The final step is to get feedback, and then revise based on that feedback. You could ask colleagues, former students, or graduate students you work with to evaluate what you've created so far. If your institution has a Center for Teaching & Learning, then the people who work there would likely be able to provide excellent feedback and advice. If possible, try to get feedback from someone outside your discipline—this way you'll see if your DIQ is motivating and interesting to someone with a different perspective. Ask them to evaluate your DIQ using the questions from Step 2.

Activity: DIQ Gallery Walk

Have each group member write a brief description of their DIQ on a poster-sized "sticky note," whiteboard, or online discussion forum. Everyone else provides feedback and suggestions.

Finding, and then refining, a good DIQ is not easy, so give yourself the time and brainspace to do this. Remember the prototyping step of design thinking from Chapter 3; explore ways to prototype your DIQ with former students or colleagues. Don't be disheartened if there are some rough spots the first time you teach your DIQ. Instead, write down your own notes and observations, ask students for feedback, and revise for the next time you teach the class. One of the benefits of teaching is that you'll have the opportunity to learn from your mistakes and improve your course each time you teach it—and it will never be perfect.

Take time to explain to students why you're using this new approach, that your goal is to enhance their learning by building in more direct connections between course content and their everyday lives. For those students who indicate they prefer simpler, more passive learning, entreat them to consider any of the complex problems facing our society, such as racism, data privacy, or emergent diseases. All these problems will require multifaceted, creative solutions, and by bringing these "real-world" problems into courses, students can develop the skill set that 21st-century employers are looking for and become the leaders, creators, and problem-solvers who our world needs.

Wonderful Resources to Extend Learning

In the book ***Creating Wicked Students: Designing Courses for a Complex World***, **Paul Hanstedt** (2018) presents a compelling argument for building courses around complex "wicked" problems. This is such a wonderful resource that we are recommending no others here.

References

Barnard College. (2020). *Reacting to the past.* https://reacting.barnard.edu/

BlackSpace Urbanist Collective. (2020). *Blackspace manifesto.* https://www.blackspace.org/manifesto

Boyaci Belet, S. D., & Güner, M. (2018). The impact of authentic material use on development of the reading comprehension, writing skills and motivation in language course. *International Journal of Instruction, 11*(2), 351–368.

Brancaccio, D., & Long, K. (2016, March 1). *What if we had a secretary of the future?* Marketplace. https://www.marketplace.org/2016/02/29/elections/secretary-future/secretary-future/

Bransford, J. D., Brown, A. L., & Cocking, R. R. (2000). *How people learn.* National Academies Press.

Brown, M. K., Hershock, C., Finelli, C., & O'Neal, C. (2009). *Teaching for retention in science, engineering, and math disciplines: A guide for faculty* (CRLT Occasional Papers, 25). Center for Research on Learning & Teaching.

Brown, P. C., Roediger, H. L., & McDaniel, M. A. (2014). *Make it stick: The science of successful learning.* Harvard University Press.

Chamany, K. (2006). Science and social justice. *Journal of College Science Teaching, 36*(2), 54–59.

Chamany, K., Allen, D., & Tanner, K. (2008). Making biology learning relevant to students: Integrating people, history, and context into college biology teaching. *CBE—Life Sciences Education, 7*(3), 267–278.

Graffiti (n.d.). Merriam-Webster. https://www.merriam-webster.com/dictionary/graffiti

Hanstedt, P. (2018). *Creating wicked students: Designing courses for a complex world.* Stylus Publishing.

Karpicke, J. D., & Roediger III, H. L. (2007). Repeated retrieval during learning is the key to long-term retention. *Journal of Memory and Language, 57*(2), 151–162.

National Academy of Engineering. (2020). *Grand challenges for engineering.* http://engineeringchallenges.org/

National Center for Case Study Teaching in Science. (2020). University at Buffalo. https://sciencecases.lib.buffalo.edu/

Rittel, H. W. J., & Webber, M. M. (1973). Dilemmas in a general theory of planning. *Policy Sciences, 4*(2), 155–169.

SENCER. (2017). *SENCER.* The National Institute for Science and Civic Engagement. http://sencer.net/

TED-Ed. (2020). *TED-Ed lessons series.* https://ed.ted.com/series

The Evergreen State College. (2020). *Enduring legacies Native cases.* http://nativecases.evergreen.edu/

Winter, D. (2007). Infusing mathematics with culture: Teaching technical subjects for social justice. *New Directions for Teaching and Learning, 2007*(111), 97–106.

CHAPTER SIX

Connected Assessment

> *Preflection*
> If you were observing students in their courses, what would be the "field marks" of learning that you could use to identify when it is occurring? (A field mark is a characteristic useful for species identification; it is often used in birding. For example, one field mark for snowy egrets is their yellow feet).

AS YOU READ THIS chapter, reflect on it, and engage with the activities both independently and with fellow readers, note that it has been designed to support you in the following ways:

- Examining the continuum of formative to summative assessments and connected and unconnected assessments
- Applying a critical lens to assessment purposes and questioning assumptions embedded in common assessment practices
- Developing a mindful, equitable assessment practice that stems from an asset orientation by building more formative, connected assessment into your course

In the writing process, this chapter provoked a great deal of ongoing discussion among us as it was being written. The exchange centered on our desire to pack the chapter with practical ways that readers could begin to design and implement assessment tools as a part of an inclusive teaching practice. This pragmatic bent contrasted with our desire to catalyze change by fostering interrogation of the systemic oppression that occurs when courses are based on competition and learning is reduced to grades. This proportionately important commitment to equitable education for all learners stems from our philosophical positions to work to improve society as best we are able. While we don't pretend to understand what this oppression feels like, we recognize that the outcomes from these oppressive practices for students who are members of groups that have been marginalized are indefensible. Sometimes these unwarranted outcomes occur because multiple levels of decision-makers have justified excluding learners based on unfounded assumptions that many are "unable to handle that level of rigor" when the learners have never had the opportunity to operate in those domains. At other times, unnecessary barriers to participation, such as access to technology or transportation, have been placed at potential students' every turn. We believe that developing the right skills and knowledge will allow us collectively—as educators in higher education—to exercise our will to interrupt these patterns and call out injustices we have observed. That is what we aspire to prepare you to do through this chapter and book.

In the end, we decided to make this tension transparent to you by including a brief introduction to why current assessment practices are troubling to us. Our hope is that this evidence will convince you to implement the alternatives we offer as soon as possible. The countless students for whom the current system doesn't work have been dismissed for far too long. Rectifying injustice demands our actions now. In the longer run, we hope that you will begin to have open dialogue at your institution about the purpose and outcomes of assessment and evaluation, particularly the use of grades as gatekeeping to learning and success. We frame this chapter around assessment as the opportune platform for developing asset orientations—in students and in those who divvy out grades. Those with asset orientations notice what they, and others, *can* do and where they *can* go next to improve, while those with deficit orientations focus on what *can't* be done, relegating learners to be satisfied with their lot. Asset orientations are aligned with world views that frame the future in terms of possibility. Therefore, as folks with asset orientations ourselves, we further appeal to your moral obligation to assimilate the practical strategies presented in this chapter to redress the one-sidedness entrenched in our education system that leads to many of these unjust, inhumane outcomes.

Who Benefits From Education?

As an educator, you might think this heading an odd question. "Why, everyone benefits from education," you say. We agree that all *might* benefit from education, but we also know that for some, the price of education is so high they do not reap the benefits of education commensurate with the cost. Of course, those costs may be financial, but often they are deeper, more damaging, and less obvious, having negative consequences for generations.

For example, we are well aware that almost nowhere other than in the disciplinary practices commonly used in PK–12 schools is it as apparent that Black, Indigenous, people of color (BIPOC) have a far different experience in the United States than do their White counterparts. Ameliorating costs with regard to degree completion, debt, and experiences that build students' confidence and send them into the world ready to contribute are some inequities we will address.

To begin with, college completion rates examined along racial and ethnic lines show great variation, with Latinx and Black students earning credentials within 6 years at much lower rates than White and Asian students do. According to the 2017 report by Shapiro et al., released by the National Student Clearinghouse Research Center, among students who started in four-year public institutions in 2010, Black men had the lowest completion rate (40%) and the highest stop-out rate (41%) while in that same period, 62% of White and 63% of Asian students graduated. Fully 76% of Asian women completed their degrees in six years. Completion rates were more dismal for students who began college at two-year schools and transferred to four-year public institutions. The National Student Clearinghouse Research Center (Shapiro et al., 2017) reported that after six years, about a quarter of Asian students, a fifth of White students, and about a tenth of Latinx students had finished their degrees while only about one in 12 Black students had done the same. As unsatisfactory as those numbers are for all groups, the college completion rates experienced by students of color are truly unacceptable.

Second, student debt is hurting learners across all spectrums, and Black students typically have higher rates of debt than their White complements. Not only are there Black–White disparities in student debt, but these disparities also increase throughout early adulthood, meaning that it is unlikely that Black students will catch up economically to their White peers in their lifetimes. This leads to generations of inequality (Houle & Addo, 2019). In explaining the severity of their findings, Houle and Addo (2019) stated that "student debt may be a new mechanism of wealth inequality that creates fragility in the next generation of the black middle class" (p. 562).

Finally, even students from BIPOC communities who complete college don't always find the environment an academically challenging, responsive one that then enables them to operate successfully in a fast-paced globalized world (Brooms, 2016). Granted, this is true for many students who don't feel they are taken seriously as intellectually capable learners. Yet, for those students who, in their educational careers, may have interacted with few teachers who looked like them and with many fellow students who did not, being able to establish meaningful relationships with faculty and peers is a particularly difficult hurdle to overcome. Here, the costs may be measured in dollars but more than likely are manifested in students being denied the development of soft skills, efficacy beliefs, or social-emotional competencies that go a long way to ensuring success in the 21st century. As pointed out in Chapter 2, self-motivational assets are called upon throughout the lifespan in settings far beyond the classroom.

The list could go on, but we believe you can see how our perspectives led us to the decision toward building your capacity for implementing inclusive and equitable teaching practices. With that explanation, we move on to helping you learn about and develop equitable assessment practices connected to learning. As you revise and implement new assessment practices in your course, please keep in mind that creating a more equitable learning environment will make a difference for learners—both for those who have faced oppression in higher education and society, as well as those who, up to now, have been traditionally advantaged. You are also providing all students a learning template to compare other experiences to and to build on in their futures.

Reflect to Learn: Besides financial, what costs do students pay because of current course structures and practices entailed by educational systems?

Now might be a good time to put the book down and reflect on what you just learned. Here are some resources you can review for additional information and support:

- Carnevale, A. P., & Strohl, J. (2013). *Separate and unequal: How higher education reinforces the intergenerational reproduction of White racial privilege.* https://cew.georgetown.edu/cew-reports/separate-unequal/

- Center for Organizational Responsibility and Advancement (CORA). https://coralearning.org

- The representation of African-American women: An interview with Patricia Hill Collins. *Global Dialogue.* https://globaldialogue.isa-sociology.org/the-representation-of-african-american-women-an-inter view-with-patricia-hill-collins/

- Wheaton College. *Becoming an anti-racist educator.* https://wheatoncollege.edu/academics/special-projects-initiatives/center-for-collaborative-teaching-and-learning/anti-racist-educator/

Now, we're going to move into more practical assessment concepts and ideas. After encouraging you to reexamine some of your currently held ideas about assessment, we introduce you to the idea of connected assessment. Then, we compare formative and summative assessment practices, with an aim for you to begin including more feedback for learners. The chapter concludes with a discussion of rubrics and rethinking grading. Reflective exercises are placed throughout the chapter that invite you to examine feedback, grades, and equity in your course.

Activity: Assessment Anticipation Guide

The anticipation guide is a teaching tool and assessment strategy that we use frequently to activate learners' prior knowledge and promote discussion, so you might use one at the beginning of a new lesson. Pay attention to how well you think the following anticipation guide taps into your prior knowledge about assessment.

Following are statements about assessment practices. You may or may not feel that you know the correct response. However, use your best judgment to complete this anticipation guide by writing A for those statements that you agree with and D for those with which you disagree.

_____ 1. The terms *assessment*, *grading*, *test*, and *evaluation* basically mean the same thing.

_____ 2. A test grade is an effective means for students to receive feedback and improve performance.

_____ 3. Multiple-choice questions are effective at measuring content knowledge while open-ended essay questions are better suited to assess higher order skills.

_____ 4. Information from student performance on assignments can assist the professor in teaching better.

_____ 5. It is beneficial to test students on material that you expect them to know but that you don't explicitly teach.

_____ 6. Grades are an objective measure of learning.

_____ 7. It is good practice to review your assigned final grades over several terms to identify trends across different demographic groups.

_____ 8. A bell-curve distribution of final grades is indicative of a well-taught course.

_____ 9. Independent work should be weighted more heavily than collaborative work in final grades.

_____ 10. An anticipation guide can be a useful assessment tool for the instructor and students.

We encourage you to discuss your answers with a partner or group before moving on in this chapter. If you'd like our thoughts on these questions, please visit our website.

Why Assessment Matters

First of all, what is assessment? The term is often used as a noun to mean a data collection instrument as well as to refer to processes for informing decision-making. For instance, you could say, "The assessment for this course is a research paper." In that sense, assessment refers to the instrument. However, a broader meaning of assessment is a continuous process for gauging student learning. For example, "Last time I taught this course, most students gained the expected knowledge and skills. However, many didn't demonstrate the dispositions I expected." How can the instructor make that claim? Because they used an assessment *process* to gather data to inform their decision-making. Notice, assessment is done both to measure student learning and to improve teaching.

Many people think of evaluation and assessment as the same behavior. However, we consider evaluation, or the step of judging, to be just one part of the assessment process. Therefore, gathering information to inform judgments, or assessment, is a crucial undertaking. Assessment matters because at most institutions, course assessments are connected to grades, and grades are the means by which students are evaluated and "sorted." The somber statistics stated previously exist, in part, because of how well students do, or don't do, in specific courses. When students fail a class, it does more than just factor into their grade point average. Depending on the student, it means she falls behind in the curriculum or her time to graduation is lengthened—or she doesn't persist to graduation. All of these outcomes have negative financial implications. Even more important, these "failures" can reinforce the perception they simply are not college material (Domina et al., 2017).

Reflect to Learn: Have you ever taught or been a student in a "weed-out" course? Naturally, this terminology is not found in the course description, yet the idea that the course is there to remove "unwanted" students, usually early on in a degree program, from pursuing that area of study persists in higher education. Whose purposes do "weed-out" courses serve? How do these courses prevent equity in higher education?

Putting Assessment on the Grid

The message we want you to absorb here is that assessment is a tool with a specific function, namely, to make learning visible so as to inform your decision-making and that of students. We don't believe spending hours learning assessment jargon so you can correctly distinguish projects from performance assessments or a standardized test from an informal assessment is the best use of the time you've devoted to transformative course design. By examining assessment along two continuums (Figure

6.1), we hope to simplify the processes and demonstrate that assessment practices are valuable tools for fostering learning. The vertical axis on the continuum is from unconnected to connected assessment. The horizontal axis runs along a continuum from summative to formative assessment. Each of these continuums is described in detail in the following sections. Our goal is to convince you that for learning to be equitable and transformative, educators with expertise in assessment need to spend a significant amount of time in the connected and formative quadrant of this grid. Your goal is to focus your efforts on assessments in the formative and connected quadrant.

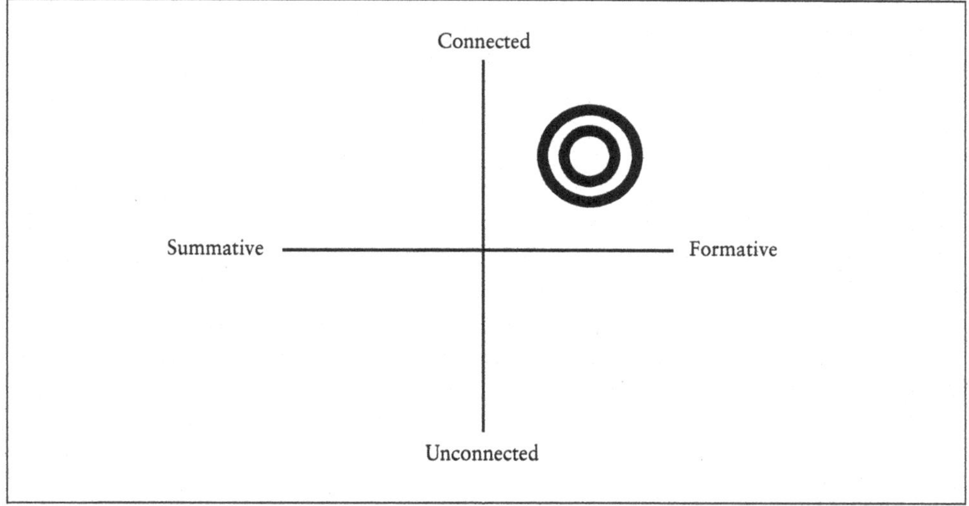

Figure 6.1: *Assessment Grid for Two Continuums: Summative to Formative and Unconnected to Connected*

Connect to Learning

In Figure 6.1, the vertical axis on the grid represents the continuum from unconnected to connected. Connected assessments are transparent, holistic, and affirming. They should also be *aligned* with student learning outcomes (SLOs), which you wrote in Chapter 4. Standardized proficiency exams such as the SAT and GRE are good examples of unconnected assessments because they are far removed from the learning experiences of the test taker. High-stakes standardized tests, by definition, privilege specific academic knowledge, and are delivered in a one-size-fits-all fashion requiring one-size-fits-all responses. As their purpose is for ranking, there must be winners and losers. As unconnected assessments, these tests have limited the options of many learners.

Alignment is a hallmark of connected assessment. If you are not consistently teaching toward your SLOs and providing students with opportunities to demonstrate learning through an aligned assessment, then it is unlikely that students will hit the target you've put in front of them. Imagine a course with this SLO: *Students will be able to compare and contrast community responses to contemporary water issues*. A multiple-choice exam would be a poorly aligned assessment because it would not measure how well students can compare and contrast community responses. This misalignment commonly happens when instructors don't use their SLOs as course guides. It also occurs when professors are rushed or feel they don't have the time to create or grade anything beyond multiple-choice questions, or the class is so large they think there are no other options outside of Scantron-gradable, multiple-choice questions. We call this haphazard approach to assessing learning "unconnected assessment." Our hope is that you become skilled in deploying holistic and connected means for determining student learning and move away from this unconnected process.

Now if we return to that SLO (*Students will be able to compare and contrast community responses to contemporary water issues*), a take-home essay question in which students are asked to select two regions (from an instructor-generated list) and compare those regional responses to the problem of water scarcity would be much better aligned with this outcome. Even better would be if this exam were preceded by in-class discussions analyzing water scarcity in different regions, including the local watershed. The professor could then provide guidelines for how she expected the students to formulate their comparisons along with examples of high- and low-quality comparisons. Next in the sequence, the students would practice writing their own comparisons in groups and then receive peer feedback. While the specific regions listed in the exam question were new to the students, both professor and students would be confident in the students' ability to successfully answer this type of question.

Depending on the course-level SLOs you wrote in Chapter 4 and the overall structure of your course, you may assess an SLO multiple times throughout the course, or an SLO may be assessed only once or twice. Table 6.1 shows what these two patterns might look like.

Connected assessment is transparent to students. Students are often skeptical of the benefits of assessment and judge the process to be lacking transparency (Fletcher et al., 2012). The feeling that projects, papers, and exams are just there to highlight what they don't know prevents deep learning and contributes to an adversarial relationship between students and faculty. For an assessment to be connected, both faculty and students need to understand what it is, how it can facilitate learning, and how information gained from assessment moves learners closer to their learning goals. We believe that students should know what they're aiming toward and that

Table 6.1: *Assessment Schedules in Two Courses*

Course and Student Learning Outcomes (SLOs)	Assessment
Public speaking course Upon successful completion of the course, you will be able to: SLO 1: Create and give clear, well-organized, educational oral presentations. SLO 2: Demonstrate critical thinking skills by writing and delivering speeches that utilize reliable evidence and argumentation. SLO 3: Collaborate with classmates by providing constructive feedback. SLO 4: Effectively overcome public speaking anxiety and become more comfortable speaking in public.	The course repeatedly assesses all four SLOs through multiple in-class presentations and a final public presentation styled after a TEDx event. Initially, the presentations are short, but they develop in length and complexity. Students present "rough drafts" of all presentations in pairs and small groups and provide feedback. Prior to the final event, each student gives their TEDx presentation to the class for feedback and review (including review from the professor).
Introduction to Psychology Throughout this class, engaged students will: SLO 1: Describe the major movements in the history of psychology and make historical comparisons. SLO 2: Identify structures in the brain and connect these structures to mental function. SLO 3: Explain theories of social, moral, and personality development. SLO 4: Explore the relationships between motivation, emotion, and behavior in the context of learning. SLO 5: Use psychological knowledge to interpret images, themes, and scenarios from popular culture.	Throughout the semester, students engage in small group discussions, in person and online, connecting course material to images, themes, and scenarios from popular culture (SLO 5). For SLO 1 (weeks 1–4), students role-play interactions among historical figures, including the perspectives of individuals who may have been harmed or ignored by psychological practices. Groups conduct research, write scripts, and make short videos depicting these interactions. Multiple choice questions (two quizzes and a test) assess SLO 2 (Weeks 5 & 6). SLO 3 (Weeks 7–11) is assessed through a mix of quizzes, essay questions, and by developing short videos explaining these theories for a high school Intro Psych class. SLO 4 (Weeks 12–14) is assessed through quizzes, reflective journal entries where students analyze their studying behavior, and by a class-created Wiki.

Note: The SLOs are assessed repeatedly throughout the public speaking course, while the psychology course SLOs are assessed sequentially.

you should know if the trajectory you've planned for them to follow is likely to end with them meeting the target. This doesn't mean that your tests have to be "dumbed down" so that all students can pass. Rather, connected assessment requires that you be purposeful in selecting outcomes and using assessment information to determine the degree to which course activities are supporting learning. We advocate connected assessment that is informed by the learning outcomes and planned in advance of content delivery, occurs frequently (even daily) throughout the course, allows for course correction, and is conducted by the instructor, students, and peers to emphasize growth and gains rather than deficits.

Connected assessment is holistic. Students are more than just the sum of their exam grades, but too often, that is what students feel they are reduced to. A physician who employs holistic medicine is going to ask her patients about their mental and emotional health in addition to reviewing their vitals. Likewise, educators who employ connected assessment are going to look at multiple lines of evidence when making recommendations that lead to learning. Think back to what you learned about Universal Design for Learning (UDL) in Chapter 3. One of the three principles of UDL, is *Provide multiple means of action and expression*: "Learners differ in the ways they can navigate a learning environment and express what they know" (CAST, 2018, "Action and Expression" section). Providing students with opportunities to express their learning in multiple ways helps reinforce learning for all students. For example, if students are assigned to write essays and they discuss the topic in a small group either before or after writing, then they are much more likely to process this idea deeply. Because this sequence of activities draws on students' intellectual, social, and emotional domains, the learning they experience becomes embedded in multiple neuronal networks, thereby increasing the possibility that that information can be easily retrieved later (Jaipal, 2009). Holistic, connected assessment focuses on more than just cognitive domains; it also includes skills and dispositions. Remember the head, heart, and hands activity of Chapter 4? And by looking holistically at the learners, connected assessment not only measures students' academic accomplishment but also provides insight as to the type of people they are becoming.

Connected assessment is affirming; it is not reductive or punitive. Too often, we create relevant and authentic activities that conclude with students taking a test or writing papers. It becomes apparent that creative energy and effort were incorporated for nothing when instructors begin reviewing students' work and find themselves taking points off for errors, miscalculations, or mental slipups, focusing on these mistakes rather than on the learning that has occurred. It is our position that this tradition of finding fault needs to be challenged—instead, teachers should be taking into account how they have ensured that students can show their learning. Assessment is connected in this sense because it is one of the first considerations professors make and their intentions can be traced all the way through to student performance. In other words, instructors ask themselves, "In what ways have I foreseen a pathway where students can demonstrate meeting the learning outcomes in multiple ways and with plenty of room for improvement, feedback, and support?"

Activity: Connected or Not?

Categorize these statements as to whether they suggest connection and alignment (C) or assessment practices that are fragmented and lead to unconnected assessment (U). Once you have decided how to categorize, discuss with a colleague to see what from the reading would support that judgment. The answers are provided at the end of the chapter.

1. When writing exam questions, the instructor checks to see if the course outcomes and lesson objectives are being measured by the questions.
2. The professor decides to give pop quizzes to ensure students "do the reading."
3. Extra-credit projects unrelated to SLOs are assigned so that students can raise their grades.
4. The teacher checks to see if the assessment instrument for the upcoming term needs to change because her delivery mode will change.
5. Problem-solving and collaborative tasks are woven through the curriculum so the instructor is able to assess for higher order and affective gains.
6. The professor sticks to a preset exam schedule when a majority of students scored poorly on all the preceding quizzes.

From Summative to Formative

Assessment can also be considered along a continuum of formative to summative assessment. Formative assessment provides immediate (or as close to immediate as possible) feedback to improve student learning and instructional methods. These assessments aren't necessarily graded. Formative assessment helps learners and instructors change their approaches while the learning is still forming and before students will be evaluated, thereby increasing student achievement (Black, 2003).

At the other end of the continuum are summative assessments. Projects, lab reports, essays, presentations, exams, and portfolios—these are all summative assessments. As noted earlier when explaining how judging the quality or degree to which a learner performed is part of the assessment undertaking, the key characteristic of summative assessment is *evaluation*. Summative assessments carry high stakes for students and are typically given at the end of a course, module, section, or chapter. Summative assessment comes at a juncture at which a judgment that the learning has indeed occurred (or not) and at what levels of mastery various students have met the outcomes is to be made. Keep in mind that some evaluations of student mastery will be "not yet" and imply continued learning should occur.

Not surprisingly, there is significantly more student stress associated with summative assessment than formative assessment. The "high-stakes," all-or-nothing perception of summative assessments can lead to inequitable outcomes for students. A student who has to make a choice between studying for an exam and tending to a family emergency may have been put in an untenable situation of weighing immediate needs with their future success.

We fear that summative assessment practices traditionally used throughout colleges and universities in the United States are inequitable and come from a culture of White supremacy. Too often, professors use grades to "weed out," or sort, students. These professors use summative assessments to highlight the inadequacies or deficiencies they perceive in their students and to justify the sorting of students into different categories.

Reflect to Learn: Robert Marzano and associates (2006) have collected data showing how arbitrarily grades are often assigned and how poorly they serve to communicate student achievement: "Research indicates that the score a student receives on a test is more dependent on who creates the test, who scores the test, and how they score it than it is on what the student learns and understands" (p. 30). Are you surprised by this statement, or does it reflect your own experience? What implications does this have for your own practice?

Activity: Teaching Observation

As you read the following scenario, list what this instructor is doing well. Describe improvements they can make to boost student learning.

Sami MacMenz has been teaching at City Community College for the past four years in the Criminal Justice & Sociology Department. They teach three sections of Introduction to Criminal Justice. It is mid-semester. Professor MacMenz walks into their Monday morning class a few minutes before class begins, powers up their computer, opens their PowerPoint file, and greets students by name as students walk in. As they set up, they talk with a few students about what the students did over the weekend.

Sami always begins class the same way. First, they announce any deadlines for readings or assignments due within the next two weeks. Next, they list the lesson objectives for the day's lecture so that students know what to expect. They also post this information on Blackboard after class.

After answering a few questions about upcoming assignments, Professor MacMenz launches into the lecture. The other day, they heard a Criminal Justice story on NPR, so they begin the lecture by having students listen to this broadcast. They explain how this news story is connected to the course content. As they lecture, they regularly check in to see if students are paying attention. They regularly ask, "Any questions?" but they rarely get any replies. The slides are easy to read and include at least one relevant picture or diagram.

Sami finishes their lecture with two minutes to spare. Once again, they ask, "Any questions?" And once again there is silence. They announce the upcoming deadlines once more and then tell everyone they are looking forward to the next class.

A few of us, and we're betting a few of our readers, may have once taught much like Professor MacMenz. They are doing some things very well—they connect with students, add relevance to course material, and are organized. At the end of class, Sami doesn't know how well the students understood the material, and it is unlikely that the students know how well they understand things either. This is where formative assessment comes in, by gathering and using information to make changes *during* the learning process.

Another issue in this scenario is that Sami's class lacks active learning. For example, you may have multiple-choice "clicker" questions dispersed throughout a lecture. Both you and the students can see the results from this assessment and—this is the important part—change behavior based on the results. If your class is acing all the questions, then you know you can move quickly through the material and in the future move this information to a preclass reading. However, if most students don't yet know the correct answers, you know you need to stop and explain the concept again and include more practice questions. Another common formative assessment is the "minute" paper in which students write for one to two minutes in response to a question such as, "What was the most important point from today's class?" (Angelo & Cross, 2012). If half the class identifies an extraneous detail as the most important concept, then you can choose to spend a few minutes during the next class clarifying the idea or posting a video or additional reading online that explains the concept and in the future, you know to more clearly highlight the main idea in class.

We highly recommend the book *Classroom Assessment Techniques* by Angelo and Cross (2012); it contains a wide variety of formative assessment ideas. Some of our favorites include think–pair–share, minute papers, the muddiest point, and one-sentence summaries.

Reflect to Learn: Reflect back to Chapter 2, where we introduced the anchor concept "Motivation Matters." Where can you draw connections between student motivation (intrinsic/extrinsic, mastery/performance) and connected assessments? As we move to consider connected and formative assessment strategies in the next few sections, consider how each might impact (or be impacted by) student motivation.

Feedback—Connected and Formative

Feedback is common in courses designed around connected assessment. Feedback fosters learning because it alerts the students in time for them to modify their behaviors or actions. Instructors who intend to be transparent about what the learning entails and how it can be demonstrated provide feedback. This kind of formative assessment also reinforces students' consideration of the criteria that will be used to gauge their progress and helps close the gap between the learners' current states and where you mean for them to end. Yet, as Hattie and Timperley (2007) have shown, all feedback is not equal. To improve learning, effective feedback must provide learners with information about those areas in which they are on track and suggest to learners what they need to do to increase the quality or depth of their learning.

All the feedback gurus we have learned from indicate that good feedback focuses on one or more of the following "3Ps": (1) process—how the learner is going about the task, (2) product—how well the product meets expectations, or (3) progress—how the learner is moving toward the goal (Hattie, 2012; Juwah et al., 2004; McKeachie & Svinicki, 2013; Nicol & MacFarlane-Dick, 2006).

Descriptive feedback, information that is nonevaluative and indicates what the student has demonstrated and what the next target should be, is generally well received and easily applied by learners. Simply communicating to a student, "This is a good essay—I really liked the introduction," or highlighting an item and writing, "Don't jump to conclusions," are not especially helpful statements for improving learning. This information *evaluates* rather than educates. Suggesting that the product is good or bad but communicating nothing about how to get better or what to do to avoid jumping to conclusions does little to move students to the next point in the learning progression. Correcting work by providing the correct answer to a problem or rewriting a sentence is similarly unhelpful because the student didn't take the action themselves. Remember the adage, "She who does the work does the learning." Descriptive feedback is effective because the learners understand what to continue and what to change. It motivates them to incorporate the feedback on their next attempt.

How do you think learners would proceed if they received this information instead of the information described earlier?

> This feedback is critical but hopefully helpful. I wouldn't give you this feedback if I didn't think that you could write an excellent essay. Your essay has a witty introduction that kept me reading. It was easy for me to trace your thesis throughout the piece (see sentences I underlined in blue). I didn't see many details that supported your argument that offering college football detracts from academics. Did you find any sources you could include in paragraphs 2 or 3 to make that point?

> This lesson is challenging, but you've already demonstrated your ability to master challenging concepts. Remember that $1/\infty = 0$ differs from $1/\infty \to 0$. It seems like you jumped to a conclusion that the analysis would be the same for items (c) and (d). Graph the functions and x on one display screen on your calculator to see the difference. Put the difference in the meaning of those formulas in your own words and keep your wording in your notebook to help you recognize this overgeneralization.

You probably noticed that this second set of examples, which are descriptive, are longer and include information that offers learners clarity with regard to these questions: Where am I going? How am I going? Where do I go next? These comments also contain specific observations about the student's work. They are motivating in the sense that they are constructive without being so crushing that the students can't "hear" them. When comments are predominantly negative, students may protect themselves by ignoring the feedback or judging you as incompetent. Moreover, feedback alone, rather than feedback accompanied by a grade or a grade with no feedback, is the least threatening to students and strengthens intrinsic motivation (Butler, 1988).

Different learners will require more or less directedness in the feedback for them to find it helpful. However, our advice to you if you are just beginning to develop this skill is to choose only one of the 3Ps—the product, the process, or the progress of the student—to emphasize. Provide all learners with one or two comments about the quality of the product and one or two comments about what to do to improve it. Pay attention to how this goes—who uses the feedback and what specific feedback leads to changes. As you become more adept at providing feedback that fosters learning, then you can begin to differentiate for diverse learners by varying the amount, type, and specificity of the feedback for different individuals as you recognize who is self-directed, who is more reluctant, who needs focused comments for achieving particular outcomes of the assignments, and who can generalize the strategies to various situations. To illustrate, the feedback for the student writing the essay is more direct and acknowledges that student's need for encouragement while the openness of the second set of remarks suggests the math student is a self-directed learner who is close to meeting the mark. The feedback provided about math includes a strategy (put meanings in your own words) that learners can use across contexts, not apply merely in the immediate one.

Notice also that the feedback above conveyed high expectations and the instructor's belief that the student can meet those expectations. These are the characteristics of "wise feedback." Wise feedback is especially important for students who are vulnerable to stereotypes, so don't expect to be treated fairly (Cohen et al., 1999; Yeager et al., 2013). Many students from BIPOC communities have good reasons not to expect fair or equitable treatment from instructors from past experiences, so giving wise feedback is critical.

Providing feedback is crucial for learning. Hearing this may make you feel overwhelmed. After all, we tend to associate quality feedback with requiring much time; picture a towering stack of papers and a red pen. Ugh! But feedback does not need to only come from you. A great deal of it can come from other sources:

- Peers—You will need to teach students how to give their peers quality feedback, but it is well worth it (Gielen et al., 2010; Nilson, 2003). Ask peers to complete checklists, sentence stems, or other feedback forms.
- Self/Self-Evident—Sometimes, results speak for themselves. When you taste soup and discover it needs more salt, that is feedback. When the experiment doesn't work, that is feedback. See if you can create situations where the results speak for themselves.
- Expert—Consider bringing in experts to give feedback. This could be experts from your field, but it could also be other professors. The most underutilized experts are more advanced students such as seniors or graduate students. Many of them would actually enjoy being of help.
- Tech—Technology can also provide feedback. Consider, for example, online quizzes or applications such as "ProWritingAid," which allows students to submit papers and get feedback on grammar, punctuation, and so on.
- Low-Tech Tech—When students use flashcards, those cards give them feedback. When students take three-column notes (discussed in Chapter 8) and then use the questions in the first column to quiz themselves, they get feedback on what they know and don't know.

> **Reflect to Learn:** Consider times when you've received feedback, it could be student course evaluations, a critic's comments on your performance, or peer reviewer comments on a submitted manuscript. When were you able to "hear" the comments, and when did you react defensively and shut down? When have you received feedback that motivated you to improve? What can you do to create a culture of feedback in your courses that enables you and students to hear feedback and motivates learning?

Feedback falls squarely in the formative and connected quadrant (we don't imagine that you're going to spend precious time and effort on feedback not relevant to your learning outcomes). What if you want to nudge your summative assessments toward the formative assessment end of the continuum? To help you do this, we present two ways for you to build more formative assessment into exams.

Formative Exams

Before we offer some strategies that move exams toward formative on the summative–formative continuum, let's try a little thought experiment. Remember TRIZ—the counterintuitive idea generation technique we introduced in Chapter 3? Take a moment to imagine what the worst-possible exam might entail. What would guarantee that students couldn't demonstrate their learning? How could you guarantee students wouldn't do well? After you imagine this nightmare scenario, take a second look. Is there anything in the scenario that at all resembles your current exams?

Two-Stage Cooperative Exams

Also called pyramid exams, tiered exams, group exams, or team-based tests, in these assessments, students take the exam twice. The first time, students complete the exam closed-book and independently (and turn in their answers for grading). They repeat the exam again in groups with access to resources, that is, open note. Cooperative exams are a way to build collaborative learning into summative assessment, and they lead to better short-term and long-term learning (Bloom, 2009; Knierim et al., 2015; Vogler & Robinson, 2016). Implementing cooperative exams in your class also sends the message that you value collaboration and want to use exams for learning, not just as evaluative tools.

Caralyn's Experience

I call them "exam redos" in my large lecture (over 200 students) Introductory Biology I and II courses. Part 1 is administered in the evenings (outside of class time). Part 2 is in-class the following Friday, and it takes the entire period. Part 1 counts for their normal exam grade, and Part 2 is a separate "exam redo" grade worth 25% of the exam grade. While my exams contain multiple-choice and open-response questions, the exam redo is only the selected response items. Many students show up early for class for the exam redo, ready to review their notes and discuss answers with friends. During the exam redo, the teaching assistants and I run around the room answering questions and guiding students to the right diagram or section of notes. The sound in the room is amazing, punctuated by groaning "Ohs" when students realize why they got an answer wrong or loud slaps when giving each other high-fives. While colleagues have commented they don't want to "give up" an entire lecture period for this type of activity; I think the learning benefits outweigh any loss of lecture time. When I have lectured after an exam, I notice that most students are exhausted from studying and not ready to learn new material, so an "exam redo" seems like a much better use of class time.

Exam Wrappers

What is the first thing students do when exams, papers, or reports are passed back in class? They flip open to whatever page their grade is written on and stare at that number or letter. Maybe if they have a performance-approach orientation (Chapter 2), they compare their grade to their neighbors. Notice the laser focus on grades, which means extrinsic motivation rather than intrinsic. The focus is on what the grade means to their final grade in the class, not how it represents learning or what changes need to be made. Maybe a few students come to your office hours to discuss how to improve their studying strategies, but many students will be too embarrassed, mad, or overwhelmed to take that step.

Exam wrappers, also called cognitive wrappers, are short, reflective exercises that encourage students to think about their study habits and the learning process. Exam wrappers help students develop their metacognitive abilities (Achacoso, 2004; Gezer-Templeton et al., 2017; Lovett, 2013). Metacognition is an awareness and understanding of one's own thinking.

Metacognition "encompasses the awareness individuals have of their own mental processes (cognitive and affective) and their consequent ability to monitor, regulate, and direct their thinking to achieve a desired objective" (National Academies of Sciences, Engineering, and Medicine, 2018, p. 70). Metacognitive practices develop students' awareness of their strengths and weaknesses as learners, and then once they know about these, they are more likely to actively monitor their learning strategies and be better able to know what they do and don't know.

The exam wrapper, which isn't graded but can be worth points, contains guiding questions that ask students to consider how they prepared for the exam (or project), what worked, and how they can improve. After you've reviewed students' answers, you can share the successful studying strategies. Additionally, a student's responses can be a great basis for an office-hours discussion. Because different disciplines use and emphasize different ways of thinking and learning, there is no one-size-fits-all exam wrapper, and you can customize yours. In the following, we've listed some questions that you'll commonly find on exam wrappers. A quick Google search will help you find more.

1. Approximately how much time did you spend preparing for this exam?
2. What percentage of your exam studying was spent in each of the following activities?
    a. Rereading the textbook
    b. Reviewing posted class notes
    c. Reorganizing or rewriting class notes in your own words

   d. Redoing quizzes

   e. Group studying

3. As you look over your graded exam, analyze where/how you lost points. Indicate the number of points you lost due to each of the following:

   a. Trouble remembering processes:

   b. Lack of understanding of a concept:

   c. Trouble applying concepts or ideas:

   d. Careless mistakes:

   e. Misunderstood the question:

4. Based on your responses to the earlier questions, name three things you plan to do differently in preparing for the next exam. For instance, will you just spend more time preparing, change a specific study habit (which?), try to sharpen some other skill (which?), and/or use other resources more, or something else?

Well-Timed and Informative

Think about when you took your driver's license exam. You didn't take it your second day behind the wheel, did you? Instead, you went out on many practice trials; you studied the rules of the road and formed good habits; you probably even spent time observing how other experts drove (thanks, Mom!). Your driving instructor was pretty sure that you would pass before she allowed you to take that trip to the Department of Motor Vehicles. Yet, instructors often evaluate early on when the learning is still in process, which is like taking your driving test right after you've been given your learner's permit. This doesn't mean that students should be unaware of their progress or that there should be a single winner-take-all test at the end of the term. Rather, we're advocating that students have multiple opportunities to practice, receive feedback, and improve before being expected to show overall competency. Evaluating student work early in the term and assigning it equal weight to that which students demonstrate at the end of the term sends the message that learning does not take time, effort, or practice. It also can be seen by students as a "gotcha" move because they know they aren't prepared to perform optimally. Evaluating (not assessing) too early in the process is likely the practice of an instructor with a deficit orientation. It's much better to build student confidence and learn what students have accomplished rather than administering assessments that you know will reveal little learning.

Reflect to Learn: Consider a concept from one of your courses that many students find challenging. Should a student who already knew the concept or learns it early in the term be rewarded for learning it quickly compared to someone who learns it later in the term? If a student earns an "A" on a comprehensive final project or exam after struggling through the semester, is it unfair for him to be assigned the final grade of "A"? If so, to whom is it unfair—to that student who sailed through the term with high marks from the beginning?

It can be hard to break away from traditional assessment approaches such as taking grades from three midterm exams and a final, averaging scores from four short papers followed by a lengthier term paper, or simply one high-stakes cumulative final. Of course, we recommend multiple assessments throughout the course rather than one or two major ones. This wider sampling scheme provides more validity to the inferences you'll make about student learning. Having multiple assessment opportunities provides students a means for learning from past mistakes, which are often the best teacher. Additionally, limiting the occasions for students to show what they have learned is stressful, de-motivating, and turns routine events into unnecessarily high-stakes occasions. The anxiety can impede learning and make it less likely that students who experience test anxiety will succeed (Fulkerson & Martin, 1981). Furthermore, having one, or only a few, summative assessments in a course encourages cramming and surface, rather than deep learning (Bangert-Drowns et al., 1991).

But for course assessment to be truly transformative, for it to support all learners rather than punish and demoralize them, we need to challenge ourselves to think deeply about how students demonstrate learning and interrogate the structures that many of us assume are "just the way" courses are. We encourage you to continuously assess and use those assessments to evaluate student achievement with greater validity. We believe the emphasis on evaluation has led to the deficit perspective held by many higher educators that we hope to address with this guide—to focus on what a few students cannot do or are not demonstrating rather than thinking about how to support all students' progress and recognizing the strengths everyone brings.

Activity: Pin the Assessment on the Grid

Examine each of the statements below and decide where on the assessment grid (Figure 6.1) they belong. For any of the statements that you judge to be unconnected, how could you revise them to make them more connected? How could you build more feedback into any of the scenarios that emphasize evaluation? Then discuss your answers with a partner or group.

1. The instructor marks essays with grades but no other information. Students see these grades a few days before the next set of essays is due.

2. Each new chapter is introduced with the learning objectives for that chapter. Students have access to resources where they are able to repeatedly quiz themselves online.

3. Every week, there is a short, graded quiz in addition to a single, open-response homework question that provokes connections amongst topics. Exams contain multiple-choice and open-response questions that align with the objectives and the previous work.

4. The professor has students complete an ungraded essay on the first day of class to assess students' incoming knowledge of the topic. He then uses this information to create discussion groups for students, highlighting the previous knowledge and experience that each group member brings to the group.

5. Exams completed early in the term are weighted equally to those completed at the end of the term to form a mean average final course grade.

6. In a two-year professional program, students in a seminar course meet with the instructor at the beginning of each term to set goals. Half of the final grade is based on evidence students have collected and presented regarding their progress toward the goal.

7. After they submit their lab reports and receive a grade and comments, students are expected to revise and resubmit in order to earn an A.

8. A course called Introductory Discipline I covers the first half of the textbook, and Introductory Discipline II covers the second half. The faculty teaching Intro I continues on with the required content even though the majority of class failed the assessment from the previous chapter.

9. Before students submit their final product, they work in pairs to apply the class-constructed rubric to their partner's product.

10. Students spend many class periods discussing biomedical ethics, writing op-ed newspaper articles, providing feedback to each other, and receiving descriptive feedback from the professor. The unit ends with a multiple-choice exam on the textbook material.

Rubrics

As you shift your assessment practice from exam-based toward a more connected proceeding, you need to be aware that performance assessments are generally accompanied by a rubric. Just as the entire process of assessment offers a spectrum of tools to guide teaching and learning, using rubrics is part of a kit that makes expectations transparent and success more likely. Rubrics are often used for summative assessment purposes as scoring tools that list what "counts" for points; however, rubrics can function in both formative and summative assessment roles. Because rubrics provide feedback to learners, they are a particularly helpful component of the assessment toolkit. Rubrics can be used to assign scores, but more important, they are practical self- and peer-assessment tools. Although well-aligned rubrics are time-consuming to create, once implemented they become an effective way to provide feedback and support student ownership of learning. Although our intent isn't to teach you how to construct rubrics here, there are literally hundreds of resources that will support you in mastering this skill at a later date. Once you understand the value of rubrics for making expectations clear, we think you'll find improved student learning to be worth the effort. Of course, with practice and feedback, you will become more efficient in designing rubrics.

No matter the type of rubric—holistic, which includes all criteria allowing for an overall judgment of a product; analytic, which, due to its graduated descriptors of quality and specificity of expectations, offers detailed feedback to a learner; or single point, which is less wordy yet offers room to provide open-ended feedback on areas of excellence and growth—they all share some features. One common feature of all rubrics is the stipulation of criteria on which the product will be judged, although how concretely criteria are described can depend on the purpose of the assessment. An analytic rubric is the most detailed in this regard, while the holistic is the most general. The second common feature of rubrics is the capacity to provide feedback, usually in terms of identifying high points of the product and/or areas for improvement. Because rubrics clarify what the expectations are, they help learners get a fix on the objective before undertaking the task. Feedback related to criteria also helps learners understand their strengths and points to targets to develop in later steps.

Rubrics can also help you focus on your specified evaluation criteria and prevent biases or impressions from creeping in. For example, imagine students are creating documentary videos that you are evaluating based on the following criteria: accuracy, organization, camera use, and editing. It could be easy to be biased in favor of a male student with a Morgan Freeman-like authoritative voice simply because this fits your presupposed image of what a documentary narrator sounds like. Voice tone, which is not something students were expected to address in the course, wasn't included as a criterium on the rubric and therefore shouldn't influence grades. When you create rubrics based on the core competencies to be demonstrated, you are able to reduce the impact of this type of bias. Similarly, consider a rubric that will be used to evaluate open-response items for accuracy and use of correct terminology. A student who is emergent bilingual accurately uses the discipline-specific terminology correctly in her response but uses articles *a* and *an* incorrectly. It would be unjust and invalid to deduct points for those mistakes because appropriate grammar is not a stated criterion. It's also unlikely that grammar was an area of instruction in the course, or it would have been included on the rubric. Of course, for the student learning the language you might well add information as feedback about article use in English that might be educative but not punitive. Indeed, this would be an example of differentiating feedback. We warn you of this pitfall because it is one that we've all made. Karynne remembers well that as a young middle school science teacher, she had to learn this lesson the hard way and then had to repair damaged relationships with trusting young adolescents newly emigrated from Korea.

While creating rubrics is beyond the scope of this book, we encourage you to explore rubrics online (no need to reinvent the wheel), and to ask colleagues to share their rubrics with you. As you explore rubrics and decide which ones you may use, you'll also need to conduct a cost-benefit analysis. Typically, the more details you have in a rubric, the more time you'll spend when you have to apply it—meaning that more complicated rubrics lead to more time providing feedback. Whatever rubric you decide to use, be sure to share your rubric with students well before any final deadlines. Don't assume that students (or even colleagues) will interpret your rubric in the same way that you do. To help students acclimate to how you use your rubric, provide work samples (from previous semesters or that you create yourself) and ask students to evaluate them using the rubric. Working in small groups, have students discuss each criterion. Have groups share their answers, then you can add additional information and lead a class discussion to ensure similar understanding for all.

Grading

Finally, a topic that is perennially addressed under the banner of assessment is grading. A common misconception is that all student work must be graded and, of course, that the grade will be reported on a 100-point scale. Hours of time are spent marking products that offer little information about performance and could be better used in designing engaging activities or building relationships. Thus, we know that although a significant amount of any teacher's effort is spent grading, very little is directed toward questioning *why* we grade the way we do. Please note that there are more equitable alternatives to traditional practices such as mastery-, contract-, or standards-based grading. If these ideas intrigue you, "ungrading" is a movement of educators exploring grading alternatives you might want to investigate. If you return to Chapter 2 on motivation and learning theories, you'll recall why current practices tend to inhibit learners' development of lifelong, self-directed learning habits, which, in turn, begets inequity. We know this area needs to be aired more critically at many institutions.

Reflect to Learn: Consider one or more of the following questions and then discuss these questions with a partner or in small groups:

- How did you decide how students will be graded? Is your grading scheme aligned with your course SLOs and your values? What messages are sent/received by your grading scheme?
- What do grades communicate? How are grades interpreted? Is that what you intend for them to communicate?
- How does grading affect inclusivity and access? Is rigor defined by failing a percentage of students at the end of the course? Is having a low course average a badge of honor at your institution?
- Why are grades based on a 100-point scale when at least 50 of those points constitute failure rather than a 5-point scale where the intervals for each letter grade are equal?
- Does your department or institution value "hard" courses more than ones in which most students succeed?

Broadening Your Assessment Horizons

We close this chapter by highlighting some potential areas of assessment exploration. After you have reflected on the questions in the Reflect on Learning activity, consider some of the ideas that follow. While we don't consider these approaches radical, they are significant departures from norms. You may immediately think that there is no way you could do that in your class. We encourage you to sit with them a bit and consider how the grading and evaluation section of your syllabus compares to these ideas. What message does each send compared to your current methods?

- A truly connected approach to assessment is to co-design the assessment and evaluation with students. Consider inviting students into a conversation about how they would like to demonstrate they've achieved the learning outcomes—and what excellent work looks like. They might surprise you.
- Rather than providing students with grades throughout the semester, provide them with process, product, and progress feedback. At the end of the semester, meet individually with each student to discuss the learning and how they accom-

plished this learning. At the end of this conversation, ask the student what grade would reflect this learning and, unless you see a huge discrepancy between the grade you had in mind and the grade they propose, the student earns that grade (Kohn, 2013).

- Develop an assessment plan for the course in which students have unlimited choice in demonstrating how they've met the learning outcomes. You provide options for projects, activities, and other learning—or they contribute their own. Periodically through the term, students submit a portfolio that collects the artifacts that best demonstrate their achievements. You provide feedback and guidance as to where they should focus their attention.
- Ask students to create the rubric that will be used for their major assignments or tests.
- Kick grades and points to the curb! Instead, replace all your evaluations of students with evaluative language (e.g., novice, emergent, developing, proficient, mastery). Kohn (2013) suggests that even these mastery levels are counterproductive.
- Consider specifications grading:

> Imagine another (kind of) grading system, one where you grade all assignments and tests satisfactory/unsatisfactory, pass/fail. Students earn all of the points associated with the work, or none of them, depending on whether their work meets the particular specifications you laid out for it. This is why I call this grading system specifications, or specs, grading. Think of the specs as a one-level, uni-dimensional rubric. Don't think of them as defining D or even C minus work. Rather, imagine they define truly "satisfactory" as at least B work—maybe even A minus work. (Nilson, 2016, para. 4)

Make It Happen: Beginning Your Assessment Plan

Now that you have a better idea of what connected assessment is and its importance to improving learning, we'd like you to *begin* crafting your assessment plan for a specific SLO in your course. The emphasis is on "begins" because you'll be continuing this work through the next chapter.

Step 1—For the purpose of this activity select one or two of your SLOs to assess. (You'll eventually do this for all your outcomes.)

Step 2—Decide on one or more summative assessments for this SLO. In Chapter 7, you'll flesh out the details. For now, focus on sketching the assessment, knowing you'll add more depth later:

- What could students do or create to demonstrate they meet this SLO?
- How can you build on your DIQ and connect your assessment to it?
- Is this a project that students will complete individually or in groups?

Step 3—What type of feedback would students need from you, themselves, their peers, or outside experts to know they are making progress? How often will students receive actionable feedback they can use to improve?

Reflect to Learn: Anticipation guides can also function as self-assessment tools when learners repeat the guide after the lesson, and are encouraged to change any response. Revisit the anticipation guide from the beginning of this chapter. Have any of your responses changed? If so, what precipitated these changes in perspective?

Wonderful Resources to Extend Learning

Classroom Assessment Techniques, a classic by **Angelo and Cross** (2012), will help you expand your ideas about what assessment could look like.

In a short blog post, **Jesse Stommel** (2018) discusses ***How to Ungrade*** and explains why grades can hinder learning. Read it at https://www.jessestom mel.com/how-to-ungrade/.

Faculty across the world are sharing their experiences with ungrading using the **#ungrading**. Learn new techniques or join in the fun and share your experience.

Grading for Equity. What It Is, Why It Matters, and How It Can Transform Schools and Classrooms by **Joe Feldman** (2018) helps you challenge unquestioned conventions that perpetuate inequality and commit to constructive change.

Although written for K–12 teachers, ***Hacking Assessment: How to Go Gradeless in a Traditional Grades School*** by **Starr Sackstein** (2015) can be used to help any instructor consider what either going gradeless or minimizing grades could look like.

W. James Popham's (2011) ***Transformative Assessment in Action*** dives into applying formative assessment and feedback and will help you take action. Popham's quirky style makes this an easy read about a consequential subject.

Answers to the connected assessment activity: 1. C; 2. U; 3. U; 4. C; 5. C; 6. U

References

Achacoso, M. V. (2004). Post-test analysis: A tool for developing students' metacognitive awareness and self-regulation. *New Directions for Teaching and Learning, 2004*(100), 115–119. https://doi.org/10.1002/tl.179

Angelo, T. A., & Cross, K. P. (2012). *Classroom assessment techniques.* Jossey-Bass.

Bangert-Drowns, R. L., Kulik, J. A., & Kulik, C. (1991). Effects of frequent classroom testing. *Journal of Educational Research, 85*(2), 89–99. https://doi.org/10.1080/00220671.1991.10702818

Black, P. (2003). The nature and value of formative assessment for learning. *Improving Schools, 6*(3), 7–22. https://doi.org/10.1177/136548020300600304

Bloom, D. (2009). Collaborative test taking: Benefits for learning and retention. *College Teaching, 57*(4), 216–220. https://doi.org/10.1080/87567550903218646

Brooms, D. R. (2016). *Being Black, being male on campus: Understanding and confronting Black male collegiate experiences.* SUNY Press.

Butler, R. (1988). Enhancing and undermining intrinsic motivation: The effects of task-involving and ego-involving evaluation on interest and performance. *British Journal of Educational Psychology, 58*(1), 1–14. https://doi.org/10.1111/j.2044-8279.1988.tb00874.x

CAST. (2018). *Universal Design for Learning guidelines version 2.2.* http://udlguidelines.cast.org

Cohen, G. L., Steele, C. M., & Ross, L. D. (1999). The mentor's dilemma: Providing critical feedback across the racial divide. *Personality and Social Psychology Bulletin, 25*(10), 1302–1318. https://doi.org/10.1177/0146167299258011

Domina, T., Penner, A., & Penner, E. (2017). Categorical inequality: Schools as sorting machines. *Annual Review of Sociology,* 43(1), 311–330. https://doi.org/10.1146/annurev-soc-060116-053354

Feldman, J. (2018). *Grading for equity: What it is, why it matters, and how it can transform schools and classrooms.* Corwin.

Fletcher, R. B., Meyer, L. H., Anderson, H., Johnston, P., & Rees, M. (2012). Faculty and student conceptions of assessment in higher education. *Higher Education, 64*(1), 119–133. https://doi.org/10.1007/s10734-011-9484-1

Fulkerson, F. E., & Martin, G. (1981). Effects of exam frequency on student performance, evaluations of instructor, and text anxiety. *Teaching of Psychology, 8*(2), 90–93. https://doi.org/10.1207/s15328023top0802_7

Gezer-Templeton, P. G., Mayhew, E. J., Korte, D. S., & Schmidt, S. J. (2017). Use of exam wrappers to enhance students' metacognitive skills in a large introductory food science and human nutrition course. *Journal of Food Science Education, 16*(1), 28–36. https://doi.org/10.1111/1541-4329.12103

Gielen, S., Peeters, E., Dochy, F., Onghena, P., & Struyven, K. (2010). Improving the effectiveness of peer feedback for learning. *Learning and Instruction, 20*(4), 304–315. https://doi.org/10.1016/j.learninstruc.2009.08.007

Hattie, J. (2012). *Visible learning for teachers: Maximizing impact on learning.* Routledge.

Hattie, J., & Timperley, H. (2007). The power of feedback. *Review of Educational Research, 77*(1), 81–112. https://doi.org/10.3102/003465430298487

Houle, J. N., & Addo, F. R. (2019). Racial disparities in student debt and the reproduction of the fragile black middle class. *Sociology of Race and Ethnicity, 5*(4), 562–577. https://doi.org/10.1177/2332649218790989

Jaipal, K. (2009). Meaning making through multiple modalities in a biology classroom: A multimodal semiotics discourse analysis. *Science Education, 94*(1), 48–72. https://doi.org/10.1002/sce.20359

Juwah, C., Macfarlane-Dick, D., Matthew, B., Nicol, D., Ross, D., & Smith, B. (2004). Enhancing student learning through effective formative feedback. *The Higher Education Academy, 140,* 1–40.

Knierim, K., Turner, H., & Davis, R. K. (2015). Two-stage exams improve student learning in an introductory geology course: Logistics, attendance, and grades. *Journal of Geoscience Education, 63*(2), 157–164. https://doi.org/10.5408/14-051.1

Kohn, A. (2013). The case against grades. *Counterpoints, 451,* 143–153.

Lovett, M. C. (2013). Make exams worth more than the grade. In D. D. LaVaque-Manty, D. Meizlish, N. Silver, & M. L. Kaplan (Eds.), *Using reflection and metacognition to improve student learning: Across the disciplines, across the academy* (pp. 18–52). Stylus Publishing.

Marzano, R. J. (2006). *Classroom assessment and grading that work*. ASCD.

McKeachie, W., & Svinicki, M. (2013). *McKeachie's teaching tips*. Cengage Learning.

National Academies of Sciences, Engineering, and Medicine. (2018). *How people learn II: Learners, contexts, and cultures*. National Academies Press.

Nicol, D., & MacFarlane-Dick, D. (2006). Formative assessment and self-regulated learning: A model and seven principles of good feedback practice. *Studies in Higher Education, 31*(2), 199–218. https://doi.org/10.1080/03075070600572090

Nilson, L. B. (2003). Improving student peer feedback. *College Teaching, 51*(1), 34–38. https://doi.org/10.1080/87567550309596408

Nilson, L. B. (2016). Yes, Virginia, there's a better way to grade. *Inside Higher Ed*. https://www.insidehighered.com/views/2016/01/19/new-ways-grade-more-effectively-essay

Popham, W. (2011). *Transformative assessment in action: An inside look at applying the process*. ASCD.

Sackstein, S. (2015). *Hacking assessment: 10 ways to go gradeless in a traditional grades school*. Times 10 Publications.

Shapiro, D., Dundar, A., Huie, F., Wakhungu, P. K., Yuan, X., Nathan, A., & Bhimdiwali, A. (2017). *Completing college: A national view of student completion rates – fall 2011 cohort* (Signature Report No. 14). National Student Clearinghouse Research Center. https://nscresearchcenter.org/signaturereport14/

Vogler, J. S., & Robinson, D. H. (2016). Team-based testing improves individual learning. *Journal of Experimental Education, 84*(4), 787–803. https://doi.org/10.1080/00220973.2015.1134420

Yeager, D. S., Purdie-Vaughns, V., Garcia, J., Apfel, N., Brzustoski, P., Master, A., Hessert, W. T., Williams, M. E., & Cohen, G. L. (2013). Breaking the cycle of mistrust: Wise interventions to provide critical feedback across the racial divide. *Journal of Experimental Psychology: General, 143*(2), 804–824. https://doi.org/10.1037/a0033906

CHAPTER SEVEN

The Power of Projects

> *Preflection*
>
> Think about a recent project that you completed in your personal or professional life that makes you especially proud. What about this accomplishment satisfies you the most? When you observe the finished product, can you still picture the time that went into it?

As you read this chapter, reflect on it, and engage with the activities both independently and with fellow readers, note that it has been designed to support you in the following:

- Incorporating projects into your course design in order to provide students with fruitful means for demonstrating learning
- Designing projects that are relevant, collaborative, and transparent

In the previous chapter, we examined formative and summative assessment. In this chapter, we focus on the practical skills needed to design the *activities* that can simultaneously engage students in learning while also offering you an opportunity to conduct formative checks for understanding and provide feedback. When formative *activities* are effectively enhanced, they become summative *projects*. Activities and projects are quite similar, differing mainly in degree and duration; therefore, the ideas presented in this chapter can be dialed down for quick activities or dialed up for long-term projects. We will use the term *project* throughout this chapter knowing that sometimes you'll be creating activity-type projects that might take students 20 minutes to complete while other times you might design projects that could span weeks or months. We begin this chapter by examining what makes projects advantageous. We introduce you to a template for creating a subtype of projects called "performance tasks." Because many projects can and should involve students working in teams, we discuss ways to avoid common pitfalls of group work. After that, we suggest ways to foster equity by designing projects with transparency in mind. By the end of this chapter, you'll be ready to design your own innovative, creative projects that students will find motivating and affirming.

Why Projects?

As an array of constructivist learning approaches have entered the mainstream, a proliferation of texts on inquiry-based learning, problem-based learning, case-based learning, and other context-based learning have emerged. Many of these methods differ minimally; thus, we classify them under the umbrella of "project-based learning" (Larmer, 2015). We invite you to take a deeper dive into one or more of these pedagogies once you feel comfortable with course design as they are all remarkably interesting. However, now we're going to introduce you to the elements in and reason for the popularity of project-based learning.

Project-based learning links to key concepts we have already addressed. The statement, "The one who does the work does the learning," encapsulates the research findings on projects. That projects thoroughly involve learners is but one of their strengths. Additionally, in part because of their novelty, projects tend to be motivating. If motivation is a combination of autonomy, mastery, and purpose (Pink, 2009), those elements are addressed through projects. They're also strong in providing purpose for learning as projects can simulate the "real work" that professionals do. Instructors are able to design projects that mimic what professionals engage in or require students to solve actual problems. When the project has the potential to benefit others, it becomes imbued with purpose. Projects also tend to be "stickier" than tests or quizzes. We'd even go so far as to bet that academic knowledge you best remember from more than 10 years ago is still with you as the result of project work. Moreover, projects have great potential for maximizing portable thinking skills.

But perhaps most important, a well-designed project can be tailored for different student profiles. It can be a more equitable choice because projects can serve all students well. Small activity-type projects can be easily designed to promote collaboration in ways that support learners who don't readily navigate the hidden curriculum. Larger scale, higher stakes projects can also be cooperative, with benefits for students who traditionally have been left behind or minimally challenged. Larger projects can and should have checkpoints where students receive feedback, potential problems are identified, and direction is reassessed before the final product is due. Often, projects can be completed within flexible timelines, which assists students in balancing coursework with out-of-class obligations. We can offer students a choice of two or three projects that allow them to demonstrate the attainment of outcomes in varied formats. When we build in choice, projects can be differentiated to meet the divergent needs of a host of learning profiles. Furthermore, projects can alleviate the "test anxiety" experienced by some students, such as those who respond negatively to stereotype vulnerability (Spencer et al., 1999; Steele & Aronson, 1995) or neurodiverse students who may struggle to perform when timed or overwhelmed when facing seemingly countless test bank items. The advantages go beyond student benefits. We've noted that project work products are often more enjoyable to evaluate, improving our own engagement in this important task. Is it any wonder that we're so keen on the power of projects? Let's look at some specific emphases in projects.

Strengths-Focused Projects

Research suggests that students solve problems more efficiently when taught to utilize their strengths as they are tackling problems (Rashid et al., 2013). Furthermore, students find projects more meaningful when they are intentionally designed to foster learner reflection and develop their strengths. In turn, students are motivated when educators show interest in their strengths (Meyers et al., 2015; Scheidecker & William, 2015). Applying this finding is simple; when introducing a project, ask students to choose a strength from the "Values in Action" (VIA) on the Institute on Character website (https://www.viacharacter.org/) to develop within the project, and then write for two minutes about what that might look like. At the end of the project, students again reflect for two minutes, noting how they used and developed that strength. With this priming, the project's significance is magnified as the learners build skills that are useful for a lifetime while they improve content knowledge. This under-five-minute intervention increases the likelihood that students will value the project and judge it to have been worthwhile (Rashid et al., 2013).

Connecting to student strengths leads the way to exceptional projects. Exceptional projects are generally authentic, often collaborative, and always transparent. We examine each of those features in the following sections.

Authenticity

Wiggins and McTighe (2005, p. 153), the creators of the backward design process, use "authentic" to describe assessments that ask students to grapple with real-world problems, often in groups, to complete projects. They advocate that meaningful projects occur in real-world settings, closely adhering to what professionals do in the world of work or benefiting others outside the classroom. Projects that guide students' deeper learning in this manner can easily become "performance tasks," providing an authentic assessment context.

A performance task is any learning activity that asks students to create a tangible product or performance to demonstrate their knowledge, understanding, and proficiency. Like projects themselves, performance tasks can be small, taking part of a class period to complete, or large, spanning an entire semester. As we noted earlier, through projects, learning and assessment can occur simultaneously. Performance tasks can provide the context of assessment *for* learning and assessment *of* learning. Rather than following the pattern of the teacher lecturing, the students studying, and then a test, the norm is challenged as students engage with a performance task whereby they are learning the material while you (and they) are determining how well they understand it (Chun, 2010). Repeated engagement in performance tasks can help students develop higher order thinking skills and valuable dispositions (Cargas et al., 2017).

You might imagine that creating an authentic "performance task" would be difficult, but Wiggins and McTighe (2005, pp. 157–158) have a formula that makes designing them a breeze. They recommend the "GRASPS" framework: **G**oal, **R**ole, **A**udience, **S**ituation, **P**roduct/Performance, and **S**tandards/Success criteria. Once you have determined what outcomes you want students to be able to demonstrate through this project, ask yourself what do professionals (or others) in the world outside your classroom use this knowledge and these skills to do? Starting with the role is often the easiest.

Let's say you're teaching an American history course with the DIQ, "How can we ethically and thoughtfully weigh historical evidence to come to stronger conclusions?" In this particular unit, you want students to be able to weigh evidence to draw reasonable conclusions from conflicting historical accounts. You ask yourself, "When would a professional need to draw reasonable conclusions from conflicting historical accounts?" Of course, there are many possible answers, but one that many students would find intriguing is the professionals who write for the History Channel. So, there's your role: "You are a team of writers for the History Channel (R)." Now you need a goal (G), an audience (A), and a product (P). "Your goal is to help your audience, a broad range of individuals ages 15 and up, understand how to make sense of conflicting historical accounts through a part of an episode for a series on the American Civil War focused on the Sand Creek Massacre."

Now what are some of the particulars of the situation (S) that these History Channel creators might need to know? "Some refer to the incident at Sand Creek as a massacre of the Cheyenne people, but others insist it was not. In order to write this episode, you will have three weeks to read Senate transcripts and various conflicting, first-hand accounts leading to your own 10-minute script which will present various points of view." What standards (the second "S") should the script then meet? "The script should (a) explain the evidence for and against the 'massacre' designation, (b) explain how the evidence might be weighed, and then (c) draw some conclusions as to whether the preponderance of evidence does or does not suggest a massacre."

Later in the chapter, we'll determine how to best present this performance task to students, but this example serves to provide an example of each of the basic parts. Let's look at another example:

Course: Chemistry & Climate

Unit: Ozone Depletion

Imagine you are a chemist in the year 2020 working in a stratospheric ozone depletion research group. You travel back in time to 1987, prior to adoption of the Montreal Protocol, with the scientific evidence you have available to you. Your task is to prepare a persuasive yet accurate presentation that will convince politicians and the general public of the importance of adopting the protocol.

You've been asked by your research director to prepare a poster presentation that addresses the following criteria:

- Provide context for the issue that will convince scientists and nonscientists unfamiliar with the controversy and the data.
- Use a minimum of four of the datasets discussed in class.
- Explain the chemical basis for the issue, which includes chemical structures and reactions.
- Provide a timeline for ozone depletion and recovery.
- Use additional, scientifically valid resources to make your case.

In this example, the Goal is to defend a position on the Montreal Protocol with data. The Role is a chemist and the Audience is politicians and the general public. The Situation is the 1987 Montreal Protocol discussion. The Product or Performance is a poster that presents a convincing argument. The Standards for Success are to provide a context appropriate for nonscientists, support your argument with data presented in class and scientifically valid sources, provide scientifically accurate explanations, and prepare a plausible timeline for ozone depletion and recovery.

Activity: Grasping GRASPS

We have found that it helps those new to the GRASPS framework to see examples and label the parts of each. Working in groups, identify the goal, role, audience, situation, product or performance, and standards for success in each of the following examples. Check out our website for the answers and more examples.

Example 1: Ethology

Unit: Canine Communication and Behavior

Student Learning Objectives (SLOs):

- Students will be able to analyze the body language and vocalizations of dogs.
- Students will be able to create an action plan to address common problem behaviors in dogs.

Assignment description: You are a professor of ethology and on the side, you help people who have problem dogs. Currently, you are assisting two individuals. They have each sent you a videotape of their dog displaying the problem behavior. Your task is to write a letter to each dog owner including the following:

- Explain the dog's vocalizations and body language to the owner. What is the dog trying to communicate? (Your letter needs to address vocalizations, eyes, ears, mouth, body, and tail.)
- Make suggestions to the owner concerning the best way to react to their pet when the dog is sending these messages. (Your work will be judged at how close your suggestions come to those of a professional canine ethologist.)

The best letters will be sent to the dog owners.

Example 2: Research Methods

Unit: Multivariable Experimental Design

SLOs:

- Students will be able to develop an experimental design for isolating key variables.
- Students will be able to clearly communicate experimental methods.

Assignment description: You are a researcher with *Consumer Reports* magazine. Your task is to design an experiment to determine which of four brands of detergent will most effectively remove three different types of stain on cotton fabric. You have a two-part challenge: to develop an experimental design for isolating the key variables and to clearly communicate the procedure so the staff of the testing department can conduct the experiment to determine which cleaner is most effective for each type of stain.

You need to develop a written experimental procedure outlining the steps in sequence. You may include visual aids to accompany the written description. Your design needs to follow the criteria for quality design, appropriately isolate the key variables, and include a clear plan for the testing department staff to determine which cleaner is most effective for each type of stain.

Example 3: Architecture

Unit: Final project

SLOs

- Students will be able to design sites that are responsive to relevant regulations and include the principles of life-safety and accessibility standards.
- Students will be able to make technically clear drawings and prepare outline specifications appropriate for a building design.
- Students will be able to productively work in groups.

Assignment description:

A local condominium community has been struck by an EF3 tornado, and several homes in the development were destroyed. Luckily, no one was seriously injured. As an architect, you have been asked to design new homes for the families in this development. The insurance settlement and Federal Emergency Management Agency (FEMA) money allows you to build homes that are between 1,200 and 1,500 square feet of living space, not including attics, basement, or garages. Choose whether you will design a three-, four-, or five-bedroom home. A plot plan will be provided, and you may site your home on any of the available lots. Prepare a first-floor plan, a second-floor plan, and a foundation plan. Choose your client from one of the following displaced families:

- A young family of five with two boys and one girl ages 5 to 12.
- A retired couple who have adult children that live out of state.
- A couple with one infant child; the father is a disabled veteran who requires a wheelchair.
- A single mother with two teen children, a boy and a girl ages 15 and 17.
- A single adult (age 55) who cares for an aging parent (age 80).

> Your house design should be appropriate for your client and the lot that you have chosen and must fall within the square foot budget provided. The design must meet all applicable codes (provided) and should also take into account universal design and sustainability (provided). You will need to present your design to the instructor and several students, who will act as the clients.

Make It Happen: Design Your Own Performance Task

Remember that you don't have to start with the goal. Often it is easier to start with the role.

Create a performance task around a real or imaginary scenario that

- requires the student to use what they've learned in class.
- aligns with one or more of your course's outcomes.
- builds on the DIQ that you are using to frame your course.

SLO: What do you want students to demonstrate they know or are able to do? (Note: You can use a performance task to allow students to demonstrate they meet several learning outcomes, but for the sake of practice, just start with one.)

What is the DIQ you are aligning with?
Now the parts of your performance task:

Goal:

Role:

Audience:

Situation:

Product or performance:

Standard for success:

Design for Cooperation

Most professions require individuals to work productively with others. In the Association of American Colleges and Universities 2018 survey of hiring managers conducted by Hart Research Associates, 87% listed the ability to "work effectively in teams" as a very important skill, second only to the ability to "effectively communicate orally" (p. 12). Yet, many students are not yet skilled at working in teams. Projects can be particularly effective at helping students develop these skills.

Julia's Experience

Early in my teaching career, I didn't understand the importance of building cooperation and interdependence skills in groups. One particularly memorable experience was a time when I was teaching a survey chemistry class to majors. I thought it might be fun to have them do some exploration, so I randomized them into teams and assigned them a biomolecule and a list of things to make sure they included in their reports. This project was worth a significant part of the final grade (15%), so the stakes were high. It wasn't 24 hours before I had my first email from a student. She wanted to know what "part" of the project she was supposed to complete and how she would be graded. She reported that she had tried repeatedly to contact her group mates (who were all members of a different sorority) with no response. I didn't quite get what the sorority membership had to do with anything, but I was sensing that my project might not be as fun as I imagined. Sure enough, when the projects started rolling in, I could see they were either Frankenstein composites built from a "divide and conquer" approach *or* I couldn't tell if the entire project was completed by one enterprising group leader. I didn't have any clue how to effectively grade the projects, and I knew that some justified complaints were likely coming my way. That was such a fail that I avoided group work for a while.

Looking back, I can see how I failed those students. First of all, we hadn't done any group work in the course, so they didn't have any ability to build relationships or negotiate how they might share responsibility with one another. Furthermore, the evaluation scheme for the group work wasn't transparent—and if I am honest, I probably was planning to figure it out as I was grading the projects. So, I set up a high-stakes project with an opaque assessment and no opportunity to practice.

About six years after the failed group experiment, I taught that course again. This time, I designed the course around case studies. Students spent time in class working through the case study analysis in groups. These groups constructed charters where they shared their strengths, described their commitments to one another, and developed a plan for managing conflict. When it came time for the final project, these teams were well positioned for success. They were supported by a much more transparent project description and clarity about evaluation. This approach didn't completely eliminate student complaints about group work, but I had a good rationale for why working in teams was valuable and could point to the ways in which the projects were designed for their success.

Surely, you've experienced some truly terrible group work as students and perhaps also as instructors. In the 1990s, David W. Johnson and Roger T. Johnson, among others, made a conscious effort to redesign group work to save what was working and remedy what wasn't. They noted,

> There is nothing magical about putting students in groups. Students can compete with groupmates, students can work individualistically while ignoring groupmates, or students can work cooperatively with group mates. In order to structure cooperative learning effectively, teachers need to understand how to structure positive interdependence, individual accountability, promotive interaction, appropriate use of social skills, and group processing into learning situations. (Johnson & Johnson, n.d., "Conclusions and Summary")

You will often see references to collaborative learning, which is similar to, but distinct from, cooperative learning (Bruffee, 1995). However, even in the literature, the terms are not always used consistently. We're not going to wade into the specific differences between the two, but we invite you to take a deeper dive when you have the opportunity.

A goal of cooperative learning is to create positive interdependence, which occurs when students accomplish more by working together than working independently. With positive interdependence, members feel they are valued by the group and contributing in equitable ways.

When cooperative learning is done well, it can have enormous benefits for both instructors and students. It can help students develop important professional skills, such as the ability to clearly communicate, work with a diverse team, and complete complex tasks. Positive team experiences have also been shown to contribute to student learning, retention, and overall college success (Barkley et al., 2014). On the instructor side, cooperative learning allows an instructor to assign more complex, authentic problems to groups than they could to individuals. Group activities can be useful when there are a limited number of viable project topics to distribute among students. Group projects can reduce time spent grading. What does it take to transform that dreaded "group work" into a successful cooperative learning project?

Design Cooperative Learning Well

There is a degree of uncertainty and complexity introduced whenever independent learners are expected to work together. Thus, providing an explanation as to how the product will be enhanced through teamwork can decrease students' anxiety and increase student motivation. You may recall references to self-determination theory from Chapter 2. By applying self-determination theory to designing cooperative learning activities, you can also ensure that the cooperative activities you create are purposeful and offer autonomy and relatedness to foster motivation. This will allow you to further boost the value of cooperative learning in the eyes of students.

Many students may have had negative group work experiences, so you may need to convince them of the benefits and explain how you will overcome the issues they have likely experienced in the past. For example, provide professional examples of how they will be expected to work as part of a team in their future career, and explain how they could use this course work to respond to an interview question about how they have successfully worked on a team. Here, we've provided project design criteria that can help alleviate many common student (Table 7.1) and faculty (Table 7.2) group-work pitfalls.

Table 7.1: *Project Design Criteria That Avoid Common Group-Work Pitfalls Experienced by Students*

Cooperative Learning Design Solutions	Group-Work Challenge
Design the project so there are individual grades, as well as group grades, or even consider feedback on teamwork as opposed to group grades. (Individual accountability)	Students perceive group grades as unfair.
Create "positive interdependence." Assign roles or tasks, or have students assign them and you approve them. Discuss strategies for distributing work and handling common issues. Use issues that arise as "teachable moments" to help students develop their teamwork skills.	One person does all the work ("social loafing").
You may not want to ask students to get together outside of class. Too many students have difficult schedules, no transportation, etc. Provide class time for students to do much of the work together while also assigning each person in the group some part of the project to do at home on their own in preparation for the next meeting or provide the means for the group to work together virtually if every student has easy online access.	It is difficult to get together outside of class.
Provide "transparent" instructions in writing at the beginning to provide organization, decrease anxiety, and promote equity.	The project feels chaotic.
Form groups with a variety of student strengths. State what strengths each group member has with a special focus on helping all students recognize the special strengths of low-status students.	Students complain about partners
Ask students to provide general feedback on one another as opposed to actually scoring their teammates and make it anonymous. Ask students to grade themselves. At the very least, require a breakdown of all the work involved in the project and ask the students to say who did which parts.	Grading peers is uncomfortable.

Table 7.2: *Project Design Criteria That Avoid Common Group-Work Pitfalls Experienced by Instructors*

Cooperative Learning Design	Group-Work Challenge
Design work that *requires* a group to do it. There is no point in taking work that would be better done individually and making it group work.	Goals may be unclear.
Most people enjoy working with others. Design cooperative work that is intriguing and enjoyable.	Students are unenthusiastic.
Well-organized, well-planned cooperative activities often take less time than other methods. Design well from the start and keep tweaking.	It takes a lot of time.
Make it interesting. Hold each individual accountable. Have time limits. Circulate a lot. Assign a task master whose job it is to keep their group on task and practice how they will do that. Require frequent updates on how the work is progressing. Ask individual group members to demonstrate their learning via quizzes, independent write-ups, or other small assignments.	Students don't stay on task.
As the instructor, you should expect some conflict and welcome it as an opportunity to help students learn how to learn from conflict. (You may find the "Gracious Space" project from the Center on Ethical Leadership helpful.)	Uncomfortable conflict may arise.

You can't assume that students know how to work in teams effectively. Be specific about the types of behaviors that you expect students to use in their teams such as communicating regularly, maintaining a positive attitude, setting and meeting deadlines, time management, and treating others with respect. You may also need to provide students with tips on conflict management.

You can provide students with examples of common team problems, such as the three scenarios that follow, and ask them to decide as a group how they would handle such problems. In this way, you are empowering students to solve the problem themselves rather than immediately turning to you for an answer.

- Scenario 1: Gary is in your group. He is an enthusiastic team member but likes to bring up irrelevant topics during meetings. At first, you liked his jokes, but now these distractions are hurting your team's ability to complete tasks.
- Scenario 2: Lauren is in your group, but she is not contributing. She has done nothing for the group project, and other members of the group are complaining that it's not fair that Lauren will get the same grade as the rest of them.
- Scenario 3: Maria's family recently moved here from Colombia. She is trying but doesn't seem to understand English very well. You or another group member frequently need to rewrite her work. Your group has to give a group presentation next week, and you're worried that her language skills may affect the group's grade.

In Chapter 6, we emphasized the power of feedback and formative assessment for learning, and this applies to teamwork skills too. Just like you would provide feedback to students on their problem-solving or writing skills, it is also important to provide feedback on students' ability to work cooperatively. Midway through a group project, or more frequently for a longer project, check in with each group and ask for feedback on teamwork. In other words, formatively assess both the process (how students work) and product (the work they produce).

You may also find it helpful to help teams devise guidelines for group behavior. These guidelines will carry more weight with students if you allow them to come up with these themselves. Group guidelines can include things such as the following:

- A group policy outlining the format and frequency of group communication
- The expectation that all group members will come to class on time and prepared
- Expectations for active listening
- Ways to provide and receive constructive criticism

Now Make It "Transparent"

The work of Winkelmes and her colleagues (2016) on "Transparency in Learning and Teaching" or "TiLT" was a game changer for the four of us and has been adopted at many institutions across the country. When we teach the concept to instructors as part of our course design workshops, they are blown away by how a few simple shifts can create such surprising increases in student success.

But what *is* transparency? Transparency is increased any time an instructor

- makes the purpose of an activity or assignment clear.
- explains how the activity fits into the bigger picture of the course.
- explains how the activity will benefit the student.
- clarifies the steps required to complete the activity.
- provides clarification around how the work will be evaluated.
- provides students with annotated examples of past students' work or the work of professionals in the field.
- provides tools students can use to assess their own work or that of their peers.

Consider what happened in a study in which *instructors modified just two take-home assignments to meet the preceding criteria* while a control group continued to use the "business-as-usual" assignments that were not designed to be transparent. Students who received the more transparent assignments had higher academic confidence, a greater sense of belonging, and better mastery of skills that employers value compared to the control group. These gains were experienced by all students, but for first-generation, low-income, and underrepresented students, those benefits were greater. The faculty who assigned these more transparent assignments noted an increase in student motivation, better in-class discussions, and fewer grade disputes (Winkelmes et al., 2016). If you aren't already sold at this point that making your assignments more transparent is the right thing to do, the research also found that withdrawal rates were lower and retention rates were higher when students experienced transparent courses (Winkelmes et al., 2016). The original paper is beautifully written and not very long. Please read it. We also strongly encourage you to check out the TiLT website (https://tilthighered.com/) for additional resources, including assignment examples before and after they were "TiLTed." And note what a beautiful example of Universal Design for Learning (UDL) TiLTing is as it makes activities clearer to everyone.

It generally takes five to 10 minutes to make an activity or assignment more transparent. For a complex assignment, it may take a bit longer. In the research cited earlier, only two assignments were made more transparent. What would happen if an entire course were made more transparent? It doesn't take much time or effort, and the results could be extraordinary. If there is one thing entire institutions should be doing to foster no-cost improvement to learning, it might be this.

Common Concerns

The most common concerns we hear about TiLT are, "Isn't this too much spoon-feeding?" and "When I've given students examples in the past, they have used the examples to create something only marginally different from the examples."

We have a variety of thoughts on the "spoon-feeding" issue. The most important thing to recognize is that when we aren't as transparent as we could be in our directions and explanations, the students who have had the most advantages all their lives are the ones who are going to be able to read between the lines and be successful despite our lack of clarity. They may even have college-educated parents, friends, or relatives who can help them crack the code. It is likely to be the less advantaged student who, yet again, will struggle. If we truly believe in an even playing field, transparency will be necessary to give everyone an honest chance for mastery. In many ways, transparency makes the hidden curriculum more visible, and your transparency may even help students navigate more easily in other courses. However, we do believe that the level of detail you provide a first-year student will be greater than for seniors, even as you strive to incorporate the criteria for transparency.

Cynthia's Experience

I once attended a wonderful presentation by Mary-Ann Winkelmes. I don't recall her exact words, but basically, she said that we will sometimes want to present students with projects that are meant to mimic the messiness of real-world projects and problem-solving. Such projects may have pieces missing or require students to work out parts for themselves rather than being provided with support at every step, especially in the case of more advanced students. The trick to transparency in these cases is this: just be upfront about it. Say something like

> There are parts of this project that are designed to be messy; the projects and problems you will face in your professional life will rarely be neat. You will likely feel frustrated at some points during this project, and that's okay. Part of the PURPOSE of this project is to allow you to work through some of the problems on your own. If you get so frustrated that you can't move forward, come see me and I will help you.

Now what about providing students with examples—isn't this just telling them exactly what you want? We suggest that professionals utilize examples in their work regularly, and copying isn't a problem. When we were writing the book proposal for this book, one of the most helpful resources we had was an example of a successful book proposal—but, of course, the content and tone of our proposal was different from the example. If you've ever written a grant, one of the first things you likely asked your colleagues for is a copy of their previously funded grant proposals, but the research, data, and impact of the work you're proposing will be original. Imagine if you were fortunate enough to be asked to give a TED Talk; wouldn't you spend time studying examples? Don't sell students short by assuming they will copy examples.

The tricks to providing examples are as follows. One option is to provide the most wonderful examples you can get because most students will try to outdo whatever they see. Be sure to ask the permission of those students who created the examples and remove their names. Allow students to take a quick look at the examples, but not take them home, take photos, or otherwise have them in their possession. You want students to get an overall sense of what you think quality looks like, not get bogged down in "Mine must look like this." Hopefully you can provide several examples that, while all high quality, differ substantially one to the next so that students can see that quality can look many ways. Encourage students to view the examples as productive constraints.

Another option is to provide annotated examples that aren't the *most wonderful* but are on their way. Julia does this when teaching students to write lab reports. She takes an example of a lab report and annotates it with advice to the student for improving it. This approach provides a mechanism to highlight common mistakes students make *while also* giving them an example of what good-but-not-yet-great work looks like. A valuable side effect of this approach is that it reinforces to students that excellent work doesn't just emerge—you have to work at it.

Before and After TiLT—An Example

Now we're going to take the example performance task discussed earlier in this chapter (the History Channel script) and compare the project description before and after TiLT. Note that the TiLT website provides dozens of examples, so you may want to check those out as well.

Less Transparent

> The Sand Creek Project
>
> You are a team of writers for the History Channel, and your goal is to help your audience, a broad range of individuals ages 15 and up, understand how to make sense of conflicting historical accounts by writing part of an episode for a series on the American Civil War focusing on the Sand Creek Massacre. Some refer to the incident at Sand Creek as a massacre of the Cheyenne people while others insist it was not. To write this episode, you will have three weeks to read Senate transcripts and various conflicting firsthand accounts leading to your own 10-minute script that will present various points of view. The script should (a) explain the evidence for and against the "massacre" designation, (b) explain how the evidence might be weighed, and then (c) draw some conclusions as to whether the preponderance of evidence does or does not suggest a massacre. The final product is due Feb. 16.

These directions aren't terrible, but what if we applied the principles of transparency, clarifying the purpose, benefits to the student, steps in the process, and criteria for success and perhaps supplying exemplars and tools for self-assessment or peer feedback?

More Transparent

> The Conflicting Historical Accounts Project
>
> Project purpose: Many of us are crushed by a daily avalanche of news, buried under "facts" that are in conflict with each other. Or, if we aren't aware of conflicting facts or perspectives, maybe we live in too much of a bubble. This issue has been around since the dawn of human civilization, and it is an issue histori-

ans must frequently contend with. Historians must often weigh conflicting evidence, and the purpose of this project is to give *you* the opportunity to practice this important skill so you can use it for both the study of history and the living of life. In addition, professionals of all kinds must work productively on diverse teams, and this project will provide you the opportunity to hone your teamwork skills as well. Both weighing conflicting evidence and performing well as part of a team are goals for this unit.

Description of the Challenge

You are a team of writers for the History Channel, and your goal is to help your audience, a broad range of individuals ages 15 and up, understand how to make sense of conflicting historical accounts by writing part of an episode for a series on the American Civil War focusing on the Sand Creek Massacre. Some refer to the incident at Sand Creek as a massacre of the Cheyenne people while others insist it was not. In order to write this episode, you will have three weeks to read Senate transcripts and various conflicting firsthand accounts leading to your own 10-minute script which will present various points of view. The script should (a) explain the evidence for and against the "massacre" designation, (b) explain how the evidence might be weighed, and then (c) draw some conclusions as to whether the preponderance of evidence does or does not suggest a massacre. The final product is due Feb. 16.

Additional project information:

- Next week in class, we will review and discuss short transcript examples from several History Channel shows to help you get a feel for length and style.
- The class will work together to create a rubric that mirrors what a producer on the History Channel would be looking for in an excellent script so you will have a clear understanding of what quality looks like.

Steps in the project:

1. Individually read and annotate the provided primary source materials—due Jan. 27.
2. Discuss and analyze the primary source materials as a team in class on Jan. 27 and turn in your team analysis at the end of class for feedback.
3. Individually read and annotate several provided analyses written by historians—due Feb. 2.

4. Discuss and analyze the analyses as a team on Feb. 2 and turn in your team analysis at the end of class for feedback.
5. Weigh the evidence from both the primary and secondary sources using the methods learned on Feb. 4.
6. Use the time provided during class on Feb. 9 and 11 to create a draft of a 10-minute script that will lead your audience through a concise version of the experience you had of seeing both sides and weighing the evidence.
7. Individual team members polish their assigned portion of the script to turn in Feb. 16.

Reflect to Learn: What differences do you see between the less transparent and the more transparent examples? If you were an individual who struggled in similar courses in the past, how might the more transparent project description be helpful?

We want to take a moment and highlight the ideas from Chapter 6 that are showcased in this project. There is a significant amount of useful formative assessment built in. While the 10-minute script is a summative assessment and likely worth a significant number of points, along the way, students receive plenty of feedback and support, meaning that all students can earn an A. For anyone who balks at the idea of all students earning As, consider the amount of learning that is occurring. The students are becoming experts on a specific event, they are weighing conflicting evidence to draw a conclusion, they are writing about history in a concise and engaging way, and they are working on teams. This project demonstrates what connected assessment could look like in your course. One suggestion we might make for improving it is to provide students with different historical scenarios to choose from—this is motivating for students, gives them more opportunity to learn from each other, and prevents you from having to review multiple iterations of the same topic.

Activity: Evaluate for Transparency

Use the TilT feedback form (Table 7.3) to determine the extent to which the transparent example above does and does not meet the criteria. Is anything missing? Does anything need to be polished?

We hope we have convinced you to never give a project or assignment again without first evaluating it for transparency.

Table 7.3: *TiLT Feedback Form*

	Looking great	Polish this a bit	This is missing
The **purpose** of the activity is very clear.			
The activity is clearly related to the **goals** of the course or unit, and those are stated and explained.			
The **steps** required to complete the activity are clear and detailed.			
The **dates** various steps are due are listed.			
The instructions explain how the activity will **benefit** the student now or in the future.			
There is clarification around how the work will be **evaluated** (or a rubric is provided).			
The directions state that **examples** of past students' work will be provided.			
The directions state that **tools** will be provided so that students can assess their own work or that of their peers.			

Make It Happen: TiLTing Your Performance Task

Now it's time to "TiLT" the performance task you created earlier in the chapter.

Use the feedback form from Table 7.3 to check yourself. Then, give your project description to a colleague who is not familiar with this project. Ask them to evaluate the project as if they were a student. Would they know how to be successful? Do they understand the purpose of the project?

Then assess your project using the following questions:

1. Does this project align with what professionals do?

2. Can every student in the class succeed in this project? Have you considered the abilities of *all* students including physical, neurological, and cultural diversity? Return to the empathy maps you created in Chapter 3 for Juawn, Ameena, Isabella, and Jocelyn. Are there any specific elements of your project design that will present barriers for them? What strengths will each of these students bring to your project?

3. How long will this project take to complete? Have you built this into your course? Is the time commitment reasonable? Do you have built-in flexibility in case more time is needed?

4. How many of your SLOs are aligned with this project and do these SLOs feature portable outcomes?

5. Will the grade on this project convey mastery of the outcomes? What does a 60% mean versus an 85%? How will students know where they need to focus their efforts?

Wonderful Resources to Extend Learning

McTighe's (2004) ***The Understanding by Design Professional Development Workbook*** stands out for its helpful lists and activities, especially for developing performance tasks.

Want to know more about collaborative learning? Look no further than **Barkley, Cross, and Major's** (2014) ***Collaborative Learning Techniques: A Handbook for College Faculty***.

Start with this short article by **Winkelmes and her colleagues** (2016) to rev you up—**"A Teaching Intervention That Increases Underserved College Students' Success"**—and then head to the official TiLT website, https://tilthighered.com/.

We would all love for our students to grow from the conflicts they may face working with others, but how? The **"Gracious Space" Project from the Center on Ethical Leadership** can help.

References

Barkley, E. F., Cross, K. P., & Major, H. C. (2014). *Collaborative learning techniques: A handbook for college faculty*. John Wiley & Sons.

Bruffee, K. A. (1995). Sharing our toys: Cooperative learning versus collaborative learning. *Change: The Magazine of Higher Learning*, 27(1), 12–18. https://doi.org/10.1080/00091383.1995.9937722

Cargas, S., Williams, S., & Rosenberg, M. (2017). An approach to teaching critical thinking across disciplines using performance tasks with a common rubric. *Thinking Skills and Creativity*, 26(1), 24–37. https://doi.org/10.1016/j.tsc.2017.05.005

Chun, M. (2010, April). Taking teaching to (performance) task. *Change: The Magazine of Higher Learning*, pp. 22–30.

Hart Research Associates. (2018, July). *Fulfilling the American dream: Liberal education and the future of work. Selected findings from online surveys of business executives and hiring managers conducted on behalf of the Association of American Colleges and Universities*. https://www.aacu.org/sites/default/files/files/LEAP/2018Employer ResearchReport.pdf

Johnson, D. W., & Johnson, R. T. (n.d.). What is cooperative learning? Cooperative Learning Institute. http://www.co-operation.org/what-is-cooperative-learning

Larmer, J. (2015, July). *Project-based learning vs. problem-based learning vs. X-BL*. Edutopia. https://www.edutopia.org/blog/pbl-vs-pbl-vs-xbl-john-larmer

McTighe, J. (2004). *Understanding by design: Professional development workbook*. ASCD.

Meyers, M. C., van Woerkom, M., de Reuver, R. S. M., Bakk, Z., & Oberski, D. L. (2015). Enhancing psychological capital and personal growth initiative: Working on strengths or deficiencies. *Journal of Counseling Psychology, 62*(1), 50–62. https://doi.org/10.1037/cou0000050

Pink, D. H. (2009). *Drive: The surprising truth about what motivates us*. Riverhead Books.

Rashid, T., Anjum, A., Lennox, C., Quinlan, D., Niemiec, R. M., Mayerson, D., & Kazemi, F. (2013). Assessment of character strengths in children and adolescents. In C. Proctor & A. Linley (Eds.), *Research, applications, and interventions for children and adolescents* (pp. 81–115). Springer.

Scheidecker, D., & William, F. (2015). *Bringing out the best in students: How legendary teachers motivate kids*. Simon & Schuster.

Spencer, S. J., Steele, C. M., & Quinn, D. M. (1999). Stereotype threat and women's math performance. *Journal of Experimental Social Psychology, 35*(1), 4–28. https://doi.org/10.1006/jesp.1998.1373

Steele, C. M., & Aronson, J. (1995). Stereotype threat and the intellectual test performance of African Americans. *Journal of Personality and Social Psychology, 69*(5), 797–811. https://doi.org/10.1037/0022-3514.69.5.797

Wiggins, G. P., & McTighe, J. (2005). *Understanding by design*. ASCD.

Winkelmes, M. A. A., Bernacki, M., Butler, J., Zochowski, M., Golanics, J., & Weavil, K. H. (2016). A teaching intervention that increases underserved college students' success. *Peer Review, 18*(1/2), 31–36.

CHAPTER EIGHT

Strategies That Matter

Preflection

Instructors often say, "I really learned that topic when I had to teach it." How does that resonate with your own experience? What strategies can you use to enable a similar experience for students?

As you read this chapter, reflect on it, and engage with the activities both independently and with fellow readers, note that it has been designed to support you in the following:

- Choosing teaching strategies that are engaging, sticky, motivating, and culturally affirming
- Distinguishing higher quality strategies from lower quality ones

Our goal is to help you populate your lessons with teaching strategies designed to promote the most significant learning. When you're using backward design (Chapter 3), you first craft your student learning objectives (SLOs; Chapter 4), then design key assessments (Chapters 5 and 6), and then you figure out everything else, such as which resources will be the best match, what students will need to do day-to-day to prepare for success on your wonderful assessments, and how everyone will receive vast quantities of feedback without breaking your back. Teaching strategies are wide-ranging, and you certainly already have many in your teaching backpack. In this chapter, we offer criteria for choosing high-quality strategies and then present you with an amazing selection to add to your ever-expanding metaphorical backpack.

What Makes a Teaching Strategy High Quality?

We believe that high-quality teaching strategies are

- active and engaging,

- intrinsically motivating,
- sticky, and
- culturally affirming.

That's a tall order! Not all high-quality strategies will meet *all* of these items, but a great strategy should meet many of them. Let's delve into each briefly.

Active and Engaging

We wrote in Chapter 2 about the need for learners to be both active and motivated, but how does that apply to strategies? A statement that drives this home is, "The one who does the work does the learning." When instructors spend time preparing to teach a new topic, they make sure they understand it well and think about questions such as, "What is most important to know about this?" and, "How does this fit into the bigger picture?" If you are fortunate to have had enough time to prepare, by the time you are teaching you are fairly comfortable with the topic, and it shows. Afterward, you may feel good about your understanding. Is it possible that you fell into the trap of believing that because the topic is now so clear to you, it is also clear to the students? *You* did the work, so *you* did the learning. When we have to understand something in our own minds, that can trick us into believing that our students must understand it as well.

Cynthia's Experience

Years ago, I read a quotation that stunned me. Renowned educator Sheridan Blau (2003) was explaining an epiphany he experienced while teaching a college course:

> In the middle of teaching this particular class of freshman, all of whom had impressed me as stunningly bright and thoughtful young people (though not so much younger than I was at the time), I suddenly began to wonder why it was that I seemed so much more competent as a reader of the text than they did. I knew they were no less intelligent than I, and I could think of nothing in my education, in this particular essay, or in my interpretive skill that could account for why I was able to interpret for my students what they appeared to be incapable of interpreting for themselves. The difference between us, I realized (and promptly told them), lay largely if not entirely in our roles and in what we saw ourselves responsible for. . . . The experience of being taught was merely an experience of witnessing and possibly recording the teacher's learning, and not an experience of learning for oneself. (pp. 2–3)

It occurred to me that the majority of learning I had experienced was merely witnessing and recording the learning of others. Witness, record, memorize, regurgitate, forget. Witness, record, memorize, regurgitate, forget. How much of the 12 to 16 years most people spend in school is just that, over and over? Seriously. This is not a rhetorical question. Furthermore, to what extent might we be robbing students of the joy of discovery when we ask them to simply witness and record what we discovered and made sense of for ourselves?

Reflect to Learn: How much of your own education was largely "witness, record, memorize, regurgitate, forget"? To what extent do you regularly ensure that students experience the joy of discovery rather than simply witness and record what you have discovered and made sense of for yourself?

To grapple with new information and make it their own, *students* must do the heavy lifting; they must generate the answer rather than recalling it for optimal learning (Brown et al., 2014). This is referred to as "productive struggle," and studies in neuroscience back up the usefulness of hanging back and letting the learners grapple (Sriram, 2020). The instructor's role is to guide by keeping an eye on how learners are doing, providing feedback, at times pointing them in the right direction, supporting them just before the struggle becomes unproductive, and perhaps putting the right resource in front of them at the right moment. Just as teaching is not telling and memorizing is not learning, you are not there to do the work for them. The good news is that there are loads of strategies that allow you to move the ball into the learners' court, where the students have the joy of discovering new ideas, processing and making sense of their own learning, and applying what they have learned in ways that matter.

Reflect to Learn: Consider the things you know the most about including personal interests and hobbies. To what extent were *you* the one who actively undertook the work of learning those subjects, and to what extent were you mostly witnessing and recording someone else's learning?

In this field guide, we are trying hard to move more of the work of learning onto your shoulders (in a supportive manner, of course) for this reason. We know that reading a practical text like this feels like learning, but that type of learning can be easily forgotten. How many of the books on your shelf were inspiring at the time, but now you struggle to remember what was so great about them? How many conference presentations have you left vowing to incorporate some new idea, but then you dropped the ball? To what extent did you feel the difference in your own development when you opted to fully interact with this text and when you didn't?

Intrinsically Motivating

In Chapter 2, we explored the importance of intrinsic motivation to learning. When students ask questions about a topic, they become more invested in knowing what the answers are. When they have made guesses at what the right answers might be, they become more invested in knowing if they were right or not.

Cynthia's Experience

I can no longer recall where I heard this example, but I love it: A physics professor brings in one of those devices people sometimes have on their desks, five hanging metal balls. He lifts the one on the left and lets it fall. The three balls in the center stay still, but the fifth ball farthest to the right swings up, falls back, smacks the three still center balls, and sends the ball farthest to the left swinging. He lifts the two balls farthest to the left. They smack the other three, the one in the center remains still, and two balls on the right swing out in response. He asks the students, "What will happen if I pull back three balls? He asks them to make predictions. The students are ready to jump over their desks and grab that device, and he doesn't let them. He says, "Let's figure it out together." Many of the best strategies play on this human need to make guesses and find out, "Was I right?" Such strategies build on one of our greatest strengths as humans, our curiosity.

While maybe not quite as exciting as the example in this story, the anticipation guide at the beginning of Chapter 6 was similarly designed to tap into your curiosity.

Recall the importance of control and choice that you explored in Chapter 2? Humans crave that feeling of autonomy, so choosing strategies that allow students to have some choice in what they do or how they do it can be quite motivating (Pink, 2009). Note, however, that it is easy to overwhelm people with too many choices (Iyengar, 2010). Eight or nine tends to be the maximum before "choice overload" kicks in (Miller, 1956), but we have found that two or three is usually plenty.

Have you ever wondered what makes video games so addictive? Much of it has to do with the sensation of mastery. Humans enjoy that feeling of getting better and better at something. Video games make this growth obvious through increasingly difficult levels, allowing players to see themselves improving. What strategies might we use to provide the joy of clear growth over time for our students?

> **Reflect to Learn:** In education, we have long followed the pattern of "learn for a while, then quiz or test." We note whether students do well or not, then we move on to the next thing. How could you build in opportunities for students to gain a sense of that daily incremental progress that is so satisfying and motivating?

Perhaps the most intrinsically motivating quality of all is purpose, the feeling that what one is learning matters in some important way (hence the title of our field guide). Cynthia has joked that the best way to teach a foreign language is to get students to fall in love with someone who only speaks that language. Suddenly, the motivation for learning is sky high because love matters and the purpose of the learning is clear. We have already advocated for the importance of building meaning into *what* we teach through the incorporation of dilemmas, issues, and questions or DIQs (Chapter 5). There are also strategies that can bring meaning into *how* we teach.

Sticky

There are a number of recent studies that call into question much of what we thought we knew about how people learn (Callender & McDaniel, 2009; McCabe, 2011; Pashler et al., 2008). Here are some of those key ideas, but they are unlikely to stick, to become part of your long-term working knowledge, unless you take a deeper dive than this. (Check out the wonderful resources at the end of the chapter.) Still, we shall share some key ideas here so you can get a feel for how one might choose strategies that make learning stick.

Learning is deeper and more durable when it is effortful.

Many of the most effective learning strategies require effort and are sometimes even counterintuitive. Too often, struggling students imagine that everyone else in the class is sailing through an assignment with little effort. They read their own struggle as an indictment on their abilities. We must tell our students that significant learning can, and should, make their brains ache, that the struggle is often a sign of progress (Hall et al., 1994). To be able to run farther and faster, you must train at the edge of what is possible. The same is true with learning. When learning feels easy, that often means what you are doing in the moment is more akin to reviewing something you mostly knew or only adding in some small way to your understanding. Or learning may feel easy because we are merely witnessing someone else's understanding rather than truly processing it and making it our own—like listening to a great TED Talk. Deep, challenging processing is often at the heart of significant learning (Rohrer & Taylor, 2007). What does it mean to *process*? Chart it, concept map it, apply it, teach it—do something with it that stretches your brain. There is even a concept in the research called "desirable difficulty," the idea that individuals will learn more if they actively choose study strategies that require their brains to work harder rather than choosing study strategies that feel comfortable (Bjork & Bjork, 1992).

We are poor judges.

One of the most important takeaways from one of our favorite texts, *Make It Stick* (Brown et al., 2014), is this: We are poor judges of when we are learning well and when we are not. However, it is important to be sure that the reason our brains are aching is because the content is challenging, not because we are using poor strategies. Witnessing someone else's learning often feels marvelously clear; it can feel like learning when it isn't. Two favorite "witnessing" strategies for many college students are highlighting and then rereading the text or lecture notes. These tactics produce the sensation of, "Yes, this makes sense." Students often interpret the feeling of, "This makes sense," to mean, "I know this" (Gilovich, 2008). When you put the text or notes away and quiz yourself, that is when you will discover if you have truly learned. That is why retrieval practice through "self-quizzing" is one of the most effective learning strategies (Roediger & Karpicke, 2006).

For simple, factual knowledge such as definitions, key names, or dates, old-fashioned flash cards may be one of the best strategies around. Students can't fool themselves into thinking they know something when they don't, and they can make piles so they can practice the ones they are frequently missing. For more complex learning, students will need to put aside their text or notes and make sure they can explain critical theories or sequences to others. They need to practice or apply the learning to see if they are capable without the prompts.

Elaboration and Connecting

Another important takeaway from this research is that elaboration and connecting knowledge to a larger context increase learning dramatically (McDaniel & Donnelly, 1996; Willoughby & Wood, 1994). Elaboration suggests building complexity by taking an idea further in some way whereas connecting is about establishing relationships among ideas. Teach students a variety of ways they might elaborate on or connect to a new idea: Give an example, ask a question, wonder why, explain why it is so, critique, connect to lived experience or previous learning, or draw a graphic representation. You'll see that many of the strategies we introduce in this chapter rely on elaboration, and hopefully you've noticed that many of the activities we've asked you to do throughout the book also ask you to elaborate and connect.

Space, Don't Cram

Of course, some of what teachers have long preached still holds true. Namely, cramming doesn't result in significant learning. How many times have you begged students to spread their studying out? The more researchers test this, the more it becomes clear this is the case—spaced practice beats massed practice (Moulton et al., 2006). Help students learn to study more effectively by selecting strategies that build spaced practice into your course.

"POESIS"

To help students, remember these sticky concepts, we developed a mnemonic device:

1. Jot down ***P*re-questions** you hope a lecture, discussion, or resource will answer beforehand.
2. After the lecture, discussion, or reading, write key ideas in your **Own words** and then . . .
3. ***E*laborate** on those key ideas in some way, connecting them to previous learning, thinking of examples, considering why this idea is true, and so on.
4. ***S*elf-quiz** to check to see if you really remember what you learned or if you just felt like you learned.
5. ***I*nterleave** your learning by mixing multiple subjects, topics, or problem types rather than focusing on any one for a long period.
6. ***S*pace** your study over time rather than studying just before a test.

"Notes That Stick" are a terrific way of incorporating the POESIS steps. The concept is similar to Cornell Notes (Pauk & Owens, 2010). In this strategy, students use their notes to generate questions for self-quizzing. To start, students create three columns as depicted in Table 8.1. They record key ideas in their own words in the second column (Notes) during a lesson. Later, while studying, they elaborate on each idea in the third column (Elaboration)—students will need some practice in learning how to elaborate at first. Finally, they construct a question or two in the first column (Study Questions) that is answered by the notes.

Table 8.1: *Example of Notes That Stick*

Study Questions	Notes	Elaboration
What is "cognitive tunneling"?	Cognitive tunneling is a brain glitch that occurs in stressful conditions where the brain focuses on the most obvious stimuli instead of the most important stimuli.	For example, when you see a police car, you start paying so much attention to it that you almost hit someone.

Students may complain at first that taking notes this way takes too much time. Yes. Exactly. That desirable difficulty is what makes it stick. By taking something that is inherently pretty simple and therefore not sticky—copying down key ideas from a lecture or text—and using the brain to work to process it, the concept becomes sticky while also providing questions for the ever-important self-quizzing by again using the brain to craft associated questions.

You may notice how often and how insistently we invite *you* to reflect as you read this book. Why? Because reflection also incorporates multiple aspects of POESIS—connecting new understandings to your own life, elaborating on them, having to put them into your own words, and checking in with yourself to see if you are learning (Brown et al., 2014, p. 89).

Culturally Affirming

> *When someone with the authority of a teacher describes the world and you are not in it, there is a moment of psychic disequilibrium, as if you looked into a mirror and saw nothing.*
>
> —*Adrienne Rich (1994, p. 199)*

As we revise our teaching to make it consistently relevant to and effective for *all* students, modifying *what* we teach, the *content*, is fairly straightforward. Do the resources you use reflect a glorious diversity of individuals? Do students have the opportunity to see, and hopefully meet, individuals who are historians, chemists, artists, and doctors who come from a similar background? Making such changes takes time and effort, but the changes aren't difficult to conceptualize. The trickiest part is when those diverse voices don't exist for you to incorporate. That can present a teachable moment in which you can describe to students what you came up against in your search for diverse voices and how and when the voices you were seeking were excluded, silenced, or erased. You can collectively search for diverse people's responses to this omission.

But when it comes to the *how* of teaching in culturally affirming ways, the *pedagogy*, many individuals are stymied. What would it look like to incorporate methods and strategies that are consistently relevant to, and effective for, all students? In Chapter 2, we discussed how decolonizing, queer, feminist, antiracist, and culturally sustaining pedagogies all advocate for turning classrooms into communities of practice where teachers and learners collaborate to co-create knowledge. In this chapter, we provide you with strategies that are a good fit for these affirming learning communities. Such strategies tend to revolve around three key concepts: (a) the co-construction of knowledge through collaboration and discussion; (b) identifying, sharing, and incorporating students' strengths, lived experiences, and emotions; and (c) supporting students in navigating the hidden curriculum.

Culturally affirming pedagogies can only blossom in learning communities of trust and support. This doesn't mean a community that is always comfortable or conflict-free. It is often not possible, or even useful, to have conversations on topics such as race, gender, ethics, religion, or politics that are comfortable for everyone involved. Thankfully, we have strategies that can help create spaces where disagreement and tension are productive and can coexist with trust and support.

The Co-Construction of Knowledge

A cornerstone of affirming pedagogies is the co-construction of knowledge, a concept we broadly introduced in Chapter 2. Co-construction of knowledge is rooted in two ideas: that when we pool our knowledge and experience, we build understandings that are more solid than what we could have built alone and that everyone has something to bring to the table. As the authors of *The Guide to Feminist Pedagogy* note, "Students and teachers ideally learn with and from one another, co-constructing knowledge—both communal and contingent—together." (Valle-Ruiz et al., 2015, "Construction of Knowledge") As teachers, we are part of the community, not above it, sharing power to the extent we can and enjoying having our own assumptions questioned and our perspectives broadened. Because of the value of co-constructed knowledge, strategies that are designed to encourage students to pool their knowledge and experience, and strategies that also support students in using that pool to construct something new, are favored on our list of high-quality strategies.

Strengths, Lived Experiences, and Emotions

If our classroom learning communities are going to support students in undergoing a transformative learning experience, then we need to invite students to be their authentic selves. This means valuing their lived experiences, focusing on their strengths, and inviting emotions into learning. Emotions have always been there, but the academic culture of higher education, constructed from patriarchal roots, has traditionally viewed learning and the pursuit of knowledge as a rational process devoid of emotion. This makes little sense as emotions are powerful, and they can grab our attention, motivate, and contribute to deep learning (Cavanagh, 2016). We have long known that to ignore emotions in learning interferes with meeting our aims.

For students to be their authentic selves in your class and to take the risk of expressing emotions, we must first cultivate an affirming learning community that embraces the whole individual. Many strategies for developing an affirming and supportive classroom environment begin by inviting students to determine what a supportive classroom environment is, what it looks like, and their role within it. The D.E.E.P. model communicates expectations and facilitates the development of a learning community by "Developing appropriate language use, Encouraging open and honest dialog, Empowering students to share without ridicule, and Processing information shared by reconnecting it to course content" (Smith, 2016, p. 17). Another approach is to have a class discussion on sections of the student code of conduct that discuss civility, inclusion, and diversity to imagine what these behaviors would look like in class and what may be missing (Ott, 2016).

Reflect to Learn: Consider a time when strong emotions played a positive role in your classroom. What did the emotions contribute? Were you able to help the students (or yourself) analyze how those emotions were informing their perspectives or actions?

Navigating the Hidden Curriculum

Recognizing how students' knowledge bases might be different from our own can be a struggle. You need only imagine taking a trip to a country where strict norms for politeness are highly valued and where you are not well versed in those invisible guidelines to conceive of the struggle hidden curriculum can provoke! Such a situation is uncomfortable, a constant sensation that everyone else knows what they are doing and that all eyes are on you as you scramble to fit in. Likewise, it can be easy to assume that all students know the behaviors we are expecting and how to play the higher education game, but that is often not the case. Making our expectations as transparent as possible is a great first step toward helping students navigate what is often hidden. The process of "TiLTing" (Chapter 7) is a good example of this. Students who are knowledgeable about the higher education game can also be helpful in guiding peers to see what's behind the curtain. We have given preference to strategies that allow students to take mutual responsibility for one another.

In summary, ideal strategies should be

- active and focused around discovery, processing, or application.
- intrinsically motivating rather than relying on carrots and sticks.
- sticky, based on research-based principles for creating significant learning.
- culturally affirming.

Reflect to Learn: Consider some of your favorite teaching strategies. How do they align with these criteria? Can you imagine a strategy that fails to meet the criteria? Consider the diversity of students in your class, perhaps by returning to the "empathy maps" from Chapter 3. Which strategies are a good fit for all students? Which strategies might present barriers?

Strategies That Meet the Criteria

In the rest of the chapter, we describe the strategies we most commonly use because they meet many of the earlier-discussed criteria, promote significant learning, and have been field-tested in our own classrooms. These are the strategies we return to repeatedly. As you move through this chapter, notice when you come upon a strategy you've already tried in this book. When your interest is piqued by a particular strategy, visit our website for a multitude of supportive resources.

Students are sometimes frustrated by new strategies. They have spent so much of their lives in the "witness, record, memorize, regurgitate, and forget" cycle that these more active strategies feel like they require too much effort (Deslauriers et al., 2019). Just like someone who has started an exercise regimen after years of inactivity, the whole enterprise is quite difficult at first. How do you move students past that? First of all, be very explicit about why you have chosen a specific strategy and what you expect it will do for learners. Mention these benefits the first several times you use a strategy. Be consistent—don't abandon a strategy simply because you get resistance. Provide a great deal of explanation for how the strategy works and encourage students to ask questions. Let them know they may struggle initially with the strategy, but over time, they will become more comfortable. Use the strategy often enough that students master it but not so frequently that they grow tired of it. Be intentional about making their learning visible so they can see the benefits of the strategy in real time. Finally, debrief the strategy the first few times students use it by asking what went well, and how they could improve.

Over time you will likely find that a specific collection of strategies is a good fit for a certain course, and that collection can become your personal "signature pedagogy" for that course (Shulman, 2005). When students describe the course to others, they will note how your course utilizes a fascinating collection of meaningful strategies.

We organize strategies in four stages of learning. Most of what we do in any given course falls into one of these categories:

1. Strategies that prepare students for learning
2. Strategies that engage students with learning
3. Strategies for discussion
4. Strategies that make learning visible

A potential sequence might go like this. First, introduce the next unit or module by identifying relevant student strengths and lived experiences, building curiosity, and focusing on the unit's purpose, which helps students prepare for learning. Students discover and process new information by engaging with the learning. Strategies that make learning visible allow you to check for understanding and provide feedback, and if you discover students are progressing little and seem "stuck," you intervene with additional resources and opportunities to practice. Finally, students apply the learning in some way: creating, analyzing, evaluating, taking action, or the like while continuing to receive feedback. Let's consider strategies that might be a good match for each of these stages.

Strategies: Prepare for Learning

Inventories and Surveys

A simple survey can be one of the best ways to determine what relevant prior knowledge and life experiences students might have that they could build on or connect to. An electronic survey can be used year after year and will compile the data for you. Build your questions using stems such as, "Do you know anyone who . . . ," "Have you ever . . . ," "To what extent are you interested in . . . ," and, "How does this relate to your life, your family, or your community?" Write your survey questions so that you tap into student interest and emotions. If I'm teaching about setting in creative writing, I'm not going to ask, "Are you interested in writing about setting?" but, "Who do you know that tells stories that make you feel like you are there? How do they do it?"

Many science disciplines also have concept inventories, which are experimentally validated multiple-choice questionnaires designed to assess students' understandings and misconceptions (D'Avanzo, 2008; Hestenes et al., 1992; Libarkin & Anderson, 2005; Ngothai & Davis, 2012). Responses provide insights into students' current thinking, prior knowledge, or misconceptions. Use concept inventories to pre-assess student knowledge and understanding.

KWL

KWL is a simple but powerful graphic organizer. Students prepare a chart with three columns dedicated to what they already KNOW (K), what they WANT to know (W), and what they have LEARNED (L). As you progress through a lesson or topic, the (L) column will grow as they transfer items from the (W) column and add emergent learning. Have students combine their lists in a shared document or using sticky notes on the wall. Very quickly you have collected a formative assessment that can help you make well-informed decisions for future activities.

Private Journaling

Especially if your class includes discussions of controversial topics, then it is important to give students space to process and prepare. You can provide students in-class time to investigate their own biases and/or cultural experiences in a nonjudgmental way. These journal entries are not collected or evaluated. Professors are also not without our own biases, so you can model this type of reflection and do your own journal writing with students.

Graffiti Boards

Graffiti boards, also known as chalk talks, are a shared writing space, such as a chalkboard, a large sheet of paper, or a web-based graphic organizer where students record their comments and questions about a topic for five to 10 minutes. This strategy helps students observe and process each other's ideas, and it engages students who don't always speak up in conversation. Capture the board so you can refer back to it later. This technique works well in large classes or online by web-based tools. Try it out as a pre-discussion activity or as a wrap-up reflection.

Anticipation Guides

You experienced this one in Chapter 6. To create an anticipation guide, you'll need to write several statements that challenge or support students' preconceived ideas about key concepts. Students complete the anticipation guide before they know much about a topic to activate prior knowledge and build curiosity.

Strategies: Engage Students With Learning

The most common method of introducing new information to students is the lecture. Lecturing is not ideal for this purpose for a variety of reasons, but let's focus on three. First of all, as we have already pointed out, when students listen to a lecture, they tend to witness and record your learning rather than discovering it for themselves. Second, the human brain is not designed to focus for long periods—20 minutes is a good rule of thumb. Some learners will "zone out" from time to time, and others may lose focus for long stretches. Third, there is no way to know what students have learned. Some students may have missed crucial information they will need moving forward, and you'll be planning in the dark.

Lecture Supports

Obviously, we believe class time is best spent with students in active learning, but there are times when a lecture is needed. Lecture should not mean "passive." You can improve lectures by ensuring they are punctuated with frequent opportunities for students to engage with and process the information. Simply giving students time to compare notes and fill in gaps or perform a think–pair–share (Chapter 2) can be magical. You can also consider providing students with a graphic organizer or concept map template to track their learning. At critical points, pause to give students time to add ideas and compare maps so they can identify missing or incomplete ideas. These strategies help students identify what they have missed and fill gaps with peers.

Guided Group Processing

One of the simplest alternatives to lecture is providing students with resources they can interact with at their own speed on their own terms. If the resource is designed for self-instruction, students can first engage with it prior to class. In small groups, students respond to a series of intriguing lower order and higher order questions while you are there to provide feedback, support, and a diversity of perspectives—similar to a "flipped" classroom. For challenging texts or ideas, divide it into manageable chunks to read in class alternating between reading and processing. You will need to direct this so the whole room is able to read in silence.

Jigsaw

Jigsaw is a marvelous strategy when you have a plethora of resources, but you know there simply isn't enough time for every student to engage with every resource. Say, for example, you have three resources offering opposing or complementary perspectives on the same subject. Assign one resource to each of the three "expert groups." Students dig deep into their assigned resource before they meet in their expert groups where they identify the most important point in preparation for teaching their peers. Move the students into "breakout groups" that have one person from each of the three expert groups. These new groups build a comprehensive understanding by teaching each other the key takeaways based on their "expert" knowledge.

Co-Construction Circles

This strategy provides structure to support the co-construction of knowledge in small groups by ensuring that everyone has expertise to bring to the conversation. Unlike whole-class discussion, every student has many opportunities to speak, and no one is likely to tune out or become disengaged. The structure imposed by this strategy helps students keep discussion flowing and resist the temptation to veer into unrelated topics, which can happen in *unstructured* small groups. This strategy is effective in very large courses and can even be modified for online courses. The circles can last from 10 to 40 minutes. Visit our website for a detailed protocol.

After dividing into groups of four or five, each student is given a role: summarizer, questioner, focuser, connector, or linguist. Each role has a pre-conversation and during-conversation task. For example, the summarizer writes a short summary of the resource before the conversation begins and summarizes the conversation as it proceeds (in writing). We advise keeping consistency in the group membership over time so they can rotate assigned roles. Students not only discuss the resources but also hone their skills in co-constructing knowledge by playing roles and practicing improving the quality of their conversations. Save a few minutes at the end to debrief the quality of the conversation and the co-constructed knowledge by asking what they did well and what they would do differently.

Strategies: Discussion for Processing

Discussion can be an exceptional method for helping students process new information; one of the primary means humans use to discover what they value, believe, or come to understand about others is discussion (Rocca, 2010). We've devoted a significant portion of this chapter to structuring discussions because we believe conversation is at the heart of learning. Yet, discussions have the potential to harm students, especially those who are already disempowered. Freeform, whole-class discussion can be problematic. Some students may dominate while others don't contribute at all, the discussion may go in directions that are unproductive, or you might just hear crickets. Sound familiar?

Before you launch into a whole-class discussion, consider these five pieces of advice. First of all, prior to the first discussion, create an affirming, discussion-based classroom culture. Second, provide some kind of pre-discussion activity so that students can get some ideas flowing. Third, use a means to structure the discussion to promote equity of turn-taking and a higher quality discussion. Fourth, have strategies ready to handle heated moments. Finally, allow time for debriefing or reflection, at least sometimes. There are many excellent resources available for using discussions for learning. While we have highlighted some excellent strategies here, you'll need to do more work on this topic if discussions are a regular part of your course. We've given you a start at this with the wonderful resources at the end of this chapter.

> **Reflect to Learn:** Consider the last time you had a discussion in class. Who participated? Who didn't? What might this say about the structure of your discussions?

Preparing for Discussion: Creating a Supportive Culture

If discussions are a frequent part of your course, be transparent about how discussions align with the course SLOs. Elaborate on the skills that you want learners to develop and explain how discussions will lead to co-creation of knowledge. Remind students that the goal of discussion is dialogue, not debate. In dialogue, the group engages collectively to deepen their understanding of an issue, which is strongly contrasted to debate where individuals are required to take sides on an issue. Focus students on the skill of deep listening rather than forming a persuasive argument. Discussions are not conflict-free and, at times, may invite tension and disagreement (Ludlow, 2004; McIntyre et al., 1998). Explain that there may be times where students feel uncomfortable or frustrated during discussions, and that this indicates that the ideas are connecting to their emotions. However, being uncomfortable is very different from feeling threatened, so emphasize that at no point in class should anyone feel unsafe and that you will be there to support and protect students. Finally, equip students with the skills they need to engage in a dialogue and move through conflict productively while maintaining respect for one another.

Many students, and many faculty, would rather avoid discussing controversial topics. This can become even more fraught for students given the layers of power dynamics in the classroom. You need to invest classroom time in creating an affirming learning community for all students prior to venturing into discussions. You may want the class to consider questions such as, How can everyone in the learning community be supportive and push boundaries at the same time? and, What are productive ways to frame questions that avoid passing judgment?

Not everyone knows what it is like to participate in a productive discussion. Unfortunately, we see more examples of unproductive or disrespectful behavior than constructive examples on television and social media. Therefore, it is important to establish guidelines with students. We've provided a strategy for co-creating discussion guidelines through *learning community agreements*.

Before we transition into additional discussion strategies, we want to make a note about being careful with how discussion expectations may differentially impact students. Often, we want "civility" so that people are not "harmed" in the discussion, but sometimes we accomplish this by putting restrictions on behaviors, and those restrictions can end up being harmful. To engage in a conversation, students and their teachers must see each other as human beings who have value. For example, telling a Black female student to calm down or lower their voice reinforces harmful stereotypes about Black women in society. Similar to our discussion of professionalism in Chapter 4, signaling that there are "right" ways to show emotion or passion in a dialogue may communicate to students that they can't be their true selves and contribute to an intellectual conversation. There is a difference between a respectful dialogue and one that marginalizes some participants, although it can sometimes be difficult to know the difference by observing what is spoken. The strategies we present below can help to bring students into dialogue equitably and provide formative assessments for you to better understand how individuals are impacted.

Learning Community Agreements

An important strategy for creating and sustaining a supportive culture is through establishing agreements among the students in your learning community. These agreements, sometimes called discussion norms, are co-created guidelines for conversation. The act of co-creation is important because it builds collective responsibility among the group to uphold the agreements. It is wise to revisit every time you have a discussion. We also recommend you revisit the agreements with the class after each discussion to make improvements for future discussions. This might feel awkward at first, but as you make it a habit, it will become more comfortable for everyone. There are many styles for generating these agreements. Julia's favorite is a three-step process that uses an adaptation of think–pair–share:

THINK: Each individual prepares written responses to the following prompts.

- Participation: How will we encourage equitable participation? How will we ensure all voices are heard? How will we deal with conflicts when they arise?
- Expectations: What should we be able to expect of each other? How will we hold each other accountable?
- Mutual support: What will I do to affirm others in the conversation? What do I need from others to feel affirmed?

PAIR: Compare written responses and generate a list of 10 to 12 agreements to share with the group. Rank them from most to least important. They should start with the sentence stem "We agree to . . ."

SHARE: In a round-robin, each pair voices the first agreement on their list, which is recorded by a facilitator. This repeats until *all* agreements have been recorded. As you go, the facilitator should try to consolidate similar agreements.

VOTE: If a shorter set of agreements is desired/needed, each individual is given three stickers to select their top three to reveal the agreements that have the highest degree of support. Discuss as a group which agreements will be retained.

Pre-Discussion Activities

Just like a warmup before a run helps prevent injury and revs up your cardiovascular system, a pre-discussion activity helps get everyone's ideas flowing and primes the class for discussion.

Popcorn

Ask every student to choose one sentence from the reading they found particularly provocative or interesting and then one by one, read their sentence out loud. It is fine (and quite interesting!) if multiple students choose the same sentence. Encourage students to listen for patterns or themes in the sentences chosen. Looking for these patterns gives everyone some idea of where a conversation might begin. Let students know before they even start reading that they should be thinking about what sentence they will want to share.

Dialogue Journals

Give students five minutes to journal about the reading, lecture, and so on on the left side of a page. You may want to have a specific question for them to respond to or a more general prompt such as, "What thoughts and feelings arose for you as you interacted with this resource?" or, "What stood out for you in response to this news article?" Then have students swap journals and respond to their partner in the right-hand column.

Question Generation

This is a method described by Donald Finkel (2000) in his book, *Teaching with Your Mouth Shut*. In his classes, which emphasize discussion, the purpose is for students to deepen their understanding of something they have already seen—a story, an article, a lecture, a lab, a political event, and so on. The main idea is to allow students to formulate hypotheses and test them.

1. Ask a student to lead the process of brainstorming possible questions and discussion topics and listing those on the board. This should take at least five to 10 minutes.
2. The lead student asks the class to rank which questions and comments to discuss first.

A variation on this, especially when students are new to it, would be to ask students to spend a couple minutes jotting down questions and topics on their own prior to the brainstorming. Turn to a partner to share ideas *before* brainstorming. In another variation, students develop questions prior to class, write them on the board as they arrive to class, or use a shared document to share ideas virtually. It can also be interesting to have students discuss their questions in small groups prior to deciding which questions to discuss as a class. This allows students to contribute questions of interest that might not be chosen by the class, and the sensemaking that occurs through the interaction helps them determine which questions are particularly fruitful.

During Discussion

In discussions, structure is your friend. You may think that the deepest, most free-flowing discussions will happen if there is a whole-class discussion, but this is unlikely to be true. Many students will struggle with discussion if they have to create space for their voice to be heard or feel forced to participate. It is rarely wise to try to force participation because removing their autonomy is demotivating and can inspire performance avoidance. Deliberately structuring your discussion can help promote equity by providing a framework for all students to participate. While we're talking about structure, pay attention to the physical arrangement. Whenever possible, have students sit in a circle so they are all at the same level and can see everyone they are engaging with. Place yourself outside student circles to emphasize your role as an observer—or else you could end up with a "discussion" where students talk to you and not to each other. Julia once made the mistake of joining the circle during the first discussion in a first-year seminar class. After that, the students tried to speak directly to her in every discussion, and it took a lot of intentional restructuring to change that habit. Plus, sitting outside the circle gives you a better perspective to attend to the dynamics of the conversation by observing who is doing the speaking, if some students might feel silenced, or others might not be engaged.

Circle of Voices

The circle of voices is a technique used by First Nations people to discuss issues of importance equitably. Julia first learned about this strategy from the wonderful book *Discussion as a Way of Teaching* (Brookfield & Preskill, 2005), where the authors note that for some students, the circle can be liberating and, for others, it can be an ambiguous or humiliating experience. The circle of voices can help mitigate power dynamics in the classroom by providing equity in time and opportunity to speak. To start, place four to five students in a circle. After three minutes of silence to prepare, each student is given up to three minutes of uninterrupted time to speak. Students take turns by going around the circle or passing an object between speakers. You might think that this would lead to a stunted conversation, but often it is quite the opposite. For some students, the opportunity to speak, knowing they don't have to break into a conversation and won't be interrupted, is their chance to shine. If you find a class discussion has devolved to a conversation between just a few individuals, that would be a good time to stop and move into a circle of voices. When you make this move, be transparent. You might say, "I've noticed that participation in this conversation isn't equally shared among everyone, why don't we break into smaller groups so everyone can get an opportunity to contribute."

Task Assignment Discussions

Cynthia developed this strategy when she realized that some of her classes had great discussions because these students were particularly adept at playing roles rather than simply adding their ideas to the mix. Like co-construction circles, this strategy asks students to take on key tasks, but this strategy is designed for whole-class or large-group discussion rather than small-group conversations. Copy the task descriptions provided on our website, cut them into strips, and hand them out randomly to students. You can assign one student per role or give everyone in the class a role to play. At the end of the discussion, take a couple of minutes for students to guess what roles others were playing:

1. Keep us on track
2. Mediate
3. Make connections
4. Play devil's advocate
5. Compliment others
6. Summarize
7. Encourage others

Through the use of this strategy, students learn to take on all kinds of important new discussion tasks and break out of habitual roles. It will take a while for students to learn to do this well. At first, they may either forget to play their role or think so much about their role that they have trouble with the discussion. When used regularly, students develop a skill that will serve them well for a lifetime as they begin to take on the tasks well. After assigning students tasks for a while, you can generally switch to simply asking them to take out a handout that has all the tasks on it and ask them to incorporate the tasks naturally, as needed.

Two Cents' Worth

During a semester many years ago when Cynthia had a student who dominated discussions beyond anything she had ever seen before, she developed a strategy on the spot one day and has used it regularly ever since. Every student gets two pennies. During the conversation, when they make a point, they slide one penny forward to the edge of their desk or table. The goal is for every person to use both pennies, no more and no less, by the end of the discussion. Obviously, you could give students more pennies if it is a small group or you want to have a long conversation. This strategy is an incredibly valuable one for neurodiverse students who are less adept at reading social cues.

Partnered Circles

This strategy is useful for classes of 16 to 30 students where it is difficult to keep everyone engaged in a whole-class discussion. One third of the class, who will do the speaking, forms the central circle. Each individual in the circle has two people sitting behind them who pass notes to the student in the circle. One person provides feedback on "what"—ideas they would like the speaker to consider adding to the conversation. The other person provides feedback on "how"—processing feedback such as encouraging their speaker to talk more or less or invite someone into the conversation or noting when they perform a useful task (such as the ones in "Task Assignment" earlier). If time allows, students can rotate roles. Ideally, in partnered circles, students lead and direct the discussion, and the teacher attempts to stay outside the circle and take notes.

Signs

Another way to allow for all students to actively participate in discussions is to ask every student to make a "sign" when any other person has made a point. The class can come up with four hand signals representing, "I agree," "I disagree," "I have a question," or "I have something to add." This allows you to then say things such as, "Tannia, why do you disagree?" or "Felix, what would you like to add?" There is much to be said for discussions that just flow naturally with students taking the lead, but sometimes, if you are the one calling on people, you can better orchestrate equity in participation and draw out a wider range of perspectives. Furthermore, asking students to actively respond to every point ramps up the engagement.

Handling Heated Moments

As a transformative educator, recognize that you will be faced with unpredictable situations: a racist comment from a student is written on the board, a learner breaks down during a difficult discussion or begins yelling about her rights being violated, or the topic you see as completely unrelated sparks some unexpected, in-the-moment activism. When such an event happens, address it. If you feel your stress response kicking in or you see that someone is offended by what someone else said, then you can always say, "I heard this. I need time to process this." Ignoring the situation or pretending as though nothing has occurred can reinforce harm. Your silence might be interpreted as approval or an unwillingness to intercede in support of students' welfare.

One "go-to" strategy for addressing these moments is to take a collective pause and provide everyone an opportunity to process their thoughts and feelings in the moment—ask the class to engage in five minutes of silent writing. You don't have to go any farther than acknowledging and naming the issue in the moment. If you don't feel prepared to support further discussion without preparation, share that with students. This is an opportunity to model the value for vulnerability in learning. You might commit to creating a space in the next class for a discussion after you can prepare or promise to share some resources. In this way, you are not off-loading the responsibility or adding to harm, but you will have created the time to be thoughtful rather than reactive or defensive.

Another useful strategy is a communication protocol such as Open the Front Door (OTFD). OTFD is a communication framework for handling difficult conversations or for conflict resolution. You can use this technique if someone, intentionally or not, makes a statement that offends you or others. OTFD stands for

Observation: You state what happened in a factual, nonjudgmental way. "When we were discussing food deserts in low-income communities, two of you commented that Kiesha probably knows what this is like." (Kiesha is the only Black woman in the class, she comes from a wealthy suburb and went to a private high school.)

Think: Then you share your thoughts on what occurred. "I think that there are incorrect assumptions being made about Kiesha based on racial stereotypes."

Feel: Explain your emotions. "I feel uncomfortable moving forward in the discussion until we address this. I am frustrated that Kiesha is being spoken about in a way that ignores her lived experience."

Desire: State your desired outcome. "I want everyone to be treated with dignity and respect and for each of us to be seen as a complex human being. Following our community agreement, I hope someone can share their reaction and that we can have a productive discussion about that comment."

Tasha Souza's (2016) excellent, concise article, "Managing Hot Moments in the Classroom: Concrete Strategies for Cooling Down Tension," reviews the OTFD framework and provides other prompts that you can use to (gently) interrogate the meaning behind specific comments, such as,

- "I want to make sure I heard you correctly. Did you say . . ."
- "Can you please help me understand what you meant by that?"

We recommend that you practice these responses beforehand with a trusted colleague or friend, this way you build in some "muscle memory" for when a stressful situation presents itself.

After Discussion

Build in time for students to reflect on the discussion experience. This is especially important at the beginning of the course as the community is being built. Use this time to gather information about both the process and the learning. Return to the "Learning Community Agreements" to check in collectively on how well the group fulfilled their commitments. An easy way to do this is to display the agreements on the wall and give students two colors of dots. They can label each statement with a green dot if the agreement was well executed during the discussion and a red dot if they feel the conversation didn't quite live up to the agreement. This provides a quick visual assessment of the process and can be used to make improvements for future discussions. Post-discussion is always useful to help students process what they've learned, and it gives you the opportunity to view the discussion from their perspective. Ask students to write down how they feel it went, what new ideas arose, who helped them see something differently, what they struggled with, and how they felt the class did living up to their agreements. Gathering that information will let you assess the discussion and make choices about how to structure the next one.

Activity: Build Your Discussion

Picture a topic you would like students to discuss. Consider these questions: (a) How much warm-up will students need; is this a topic where students will walk in with loads to say, or will they need more of an opportunity to pull their thoughts together first? (b) How adept at discussion are students likely to be; do they need practice with the process of quality conversation, or are they ready to fly on their own? Now let your answers to those questions guide you as you choose a pre-discussion activity to get them warmed up for that topic and a structured discussion strategy to go with it.

Strategies: Make Learning Visible

Checking for understanding and providing feedback are sometimes more like afterthoughts when compared to other common parts of lessons such as introducing new information and assessing students. In some courses, the only feedback students receive is a mark for what they got right and wrong on a test or quiz. As we explored in Chapter 6, formative assessment and feedback provide some of the greatest return on investment for student learning. In other words, if you want to significantly increase student learning, spending more time on improving the quality and quantity of your checks for understanding and feedback are going to give you the biggest bang for your buck (Hattie, 2012). As you seek to make student learning visible so that you can determine their level of understanding and provide feedback, you may also find that students need more support or further instruction. We present to you here some strategies designed to help you check for understanding, provide feedback, and respond with further support or instruction if needed.

Gallery Walk

We are big fans of the gallery walk, which is why we encouraged you to do one to showcase your DIQs in Chapter 5. Gallery walks display student work like art pieces in a gallery. Students lay their work around the room, hang it on the walls with painter's tape, or share it virtually. What they share might be amazing finished projects or the answers to last night's homework. Using sticky notes or an online comment feature, students roam about looking at other students' work and provide feedback to one another. Consider teaching students to use phrases such as, "What if you . . ." to help them feel more comfortable giving constructive critique.

Three Pens

Quizzes can be wonderful for checking for understanding, but how do you take them from good to great? First of all, consider not grading them, but rather, let students know they are for their benefit. If you follow up a quiz with having students write for one minute about what they are getting and not getting and how they will go back to fill in the gaps, that drives the message home. Don't collect that writing.

"Three Pens" is a strategy to make quizzes more aligned with culturally affirming pedagogies. Most of the time, when we quiz students, we are just checking to see what students do and do not know. It is "assessment *of* learning." But students who don't have a firm grasp of the material generally don't perform very well, and by the end of the quiz, they aren't any more familiar with the material than when they began. Furthermore, students who struggle with the quiz may begin to feel frustrated, increasing the chances they will feel they don't belong in the class or aren't capable of mastering the material. What if we could modify the standard quiz to make it "assessment *as* learning" such that students could actually finish the quiz knowing more than when they started? And what if the process could also minimize frustration and build confidence?

Here is how it works:

1. Round 1: Students take a quiz using a black or blue pen, answering the questions as completely as possible in the time allotted.

2. Round 2: Students form pairs or trios (students could self-select, or you could group them) and talk about what they think the right answer to each question is and why. Using the green pen, students may add to or modify their answers as much as they like in the time allotted based on the discussion.

3. Round 3: Students remain in their small groups. In this round, they may use their notes (and/or their text, the internet, etc.) to further add to or modify their answers using the purple pen.

4. To wrap up, the instructor answers any remaining questions the students have.

While "Three Pens" can replace the standard "quiz at the beginning of the class period," it is also an excellent choice for a very short quiz at the end of a class to review the learning from that day. The end-of-class quiz is an exceptional practice for cementing learning before it fizzles away. When used in this way, the quizzes should be collected so that you get a sense of what students are and are not grasping, but they should not be graded (or if they are graded, they would be graded only for completion).

Peer Instruction for Conceptual Change

Many constructivist models present strategies for students to tutor one another and learn together. A particular strategy, called "peer instruction," has been developed by Eric Mazur based on his work in physics education (Mazur & Hilborn, 1997). In many science and math courses, there is a need for students to acquire a standardized understanding of specific concepts before they can move on. Peer instruction works well in any course where students need to come to a specific conceptual understanding to advance study in a topic. It can also be particularly appropriate for reinforcing the basic principles. Prior to coming to class, students interact with concepts at home and make an attempt to solve some problems. In class, the instructor asks everyone to individually solve a problem and then polls the class for their answers. Students can see how many chose each answer, but they don't know which answer is correct. If the responses are distributed among two or more choices, the instructor asks the students to justify their choice to one another in small groups before responding to the same poll a second time. If students are still not answering correctly, the instructor stops and conducts a short mini-lesson or asks a student to explain the concept (Crouch & Mazur, 2001).

Just-in-Time Teaching

Using a lecture to introduce students to new information is sometimes problematic, but a 10-minute or less "just as the students need it" lecture can work beautifully. At this point, students are in the middle of their learning and have a sense of what they find confusing. These pop-up lectures are generally "off the cuff." You are circulating and listening in when you realize there is a common problem or misconception, so you call the whole class together and talk it through. At that point, students are driven by curiosity to figure out how to do it, and you are helping them just as they need help. Motivation tends to be high at this point, and you aren't delivering an avalanche of information, just honing in on a confusing point. Lecture can work remarkably well in this type of scenario.

Observation

Observe students as they write, solve problems, work on projects, and so on. Take notes on a clipboard so you can truly keep track of progress and struggles. Whisper useful feedback or jot it on sticky notes. These may be simple strategies, but we find instructors rarely use them to the extent they could.

Checking in on Connecting With Others

While we often check for understanding of facts and concepts, you may also want to check on a different type of understanding: how well are students understanding the perspectives of others, developing empathy, seeing common interests, or feeling co-responsibility or the interconnectedness of the human experience?

Cynthia designed this strategy, shown in Table 8.2, based on the "Build Connections" strategy developed by The Character Lab (2020), which is also well worth looking at if students struggle to see the connections between the content you are teaching and their lives.

Table 8.2: *Building Connections: Providing Students with Prompts to Assist Them in Drawing Connections Between Course Content and Lived Experiences*

List here values and struggles that are essential to your life and your identity:	List here values and struggles that are central to the lives of those we are learning about:	Draw lines between values and struggles in column 1 and column 2 that you feel are connected in some way Now turn one into a sentence: ___________ (from column 1) and ___________ (from column 2) are connected because . . . Now take it a step further: I see I share a connection with the lives of the individual or individuals we are learning about because . . .

Practicing and Applying

Practicing and applying key concepts tend to be discipline-specific, so it is difficult to provide strategies that will work well across disciplines. Furthermore, the vast majority of the time, practicing and applying will take place through an activity or project, so head back to Chapter 7 when you are ready for this. We put this heading here to remind you that this is what the other pieces of your lessons—the warm-ups, the processing, the discussions, the reviews, the checks for understanding, and the feedback—lead up to. It is through observing students as they practice and apply that you truly know what they know and can do with their learning. Consider performance task activities and projects, cooperative team-based activities and projects, and mixtures of the two, then TiLT them, and you are good to go! Why, then, did we put the chapter on projects before the chapter on the other strategies? Because in backward design, you start by determining your major assessments and only *then* decide how you will need to design your daily lessons to lead up to success on those assessments.

> **Reflect to Learn:** We are about to say something that no one wants to hear. These strategies *do* sometimes take more time than the standard "lecture, quiz, test" sequence, but they result in deeper learning. Be honest with yourself, how much are students really retaining a few months after your course ends? Which would you prefer: that you teach 50 things and they remember 10 or that you teach 35 things and they remember 20? "But they have to know those 50 things for the next course in the sequence!" Yes, except they don't remember those 50 things, and the person who teaches that next course will confirm this for you. What could you combine, trim, or cut?

Make It Happen: Select Your Strategies

Review the DIQ-linked project you developed in Chapter 7.

Select two or more strategies from this chapter that you could use that would help students prepare and be successful in completing that project. Consider the following questions as you think of where you can include these learning strategies:

1. How will you introduce the module or unit to students? Which strategies could motivate students and connect to their prior experiences and knowledge?

2. How will students discover new information or ideas? Which strategies could build cooperation into this process?

3. How will they process what they discover so that it sticks?

4. How will you check students' understanding and provide feedback?
5. What will you do if many students aren't where you hope they will be? What if it is just a few students?
6. How will students practice and/or apply what they learn?

Reflect on what you have created. To what extent is the resulting lesson or series of lessons active and engaging, motivating, sticky, and culturally affirming?

Swap with a partner or team member. Provide feedback to each other.

As promised, in this chapter we've offered a plethora of strategies for you to fill your teaching backpack as you prepare yourself to put these practices into action. We know that we've bombarded you with a *lot* of information. Now might be a good moment to take a few deep, rejuvenating breaths to focus your mind. It is our intent that you will come back to this chapter and the resources on our website frequently when you are looking for high-quality strategies. The following summary outline will serve as a criteria rubric to evaluate teaching strategies before you adopt them.

High-quality strategies should

- Be active and focused around discovery, processing, or application. Students . . .
  - discover for themselves (discovery).
  - process and make sense of their learning, actively engaging with the material rather than simply passively receiving it (processing).
  - have opportunities to apply what they learn (application).
- Be intrinsically motivating rather than relying on carrots and sticks. Students . . .
  - feel their curiosity is sparked (curiosity).
  - have choice and autonomy (autonomy).
  - are able to track their progress (mastery).
  - recognize the learning as meaningful (purpose).
- Be sticky, based on research-based principles for creating significant learning. Students . . .
  - can distinguish between what they truly understand and what they merely feel they understand (checks for understanding).
  - elaborate on key ideas (elaboration).

- interleave and space their learning (interleaving/spacing).
- receive gobs of quality feedback (feedback).

- Be culturally affirming. Students . . .
  - collaborate to co-construct knowledge (collaboration).
  - engage in meaningful discussions to co-construct knowledge (discussion).
  - identify, share, and incorporate their strengths including their lived experiences (strengths).
  - are aided in navigating the hidden curriculum (navigation).

Reflect to Learn: What are some of the "go-to" strategies you have used in the past? Which of those meet at least some of the criteria summarized earlier? Which could be tweaked, and which might need to be discarded?

Wonderful Resources to Extend Learning

Incorporating emotion is motivating and can be culturally affirming. ***The Spark of Learning: Energizing the College Classroom with the Science of Emotion*** **by Sarah Rose Cavanagh** (2016) is ideal for developing these skills.

When you need the science of learning all wrapped up in one book, you can't go wrong with ***Make It Stick: The Science of Successful Learning*** **by Brown, Roediger, and McDaniel** (2014).

Teaching with Your Mouth Shut **by Donald Finkel** (2000) is an excellent example of how an individual professor can weave together a number of high-quality strategies into a personal signature pedagogy that defines a course.

Facing History and Ourselves (https://www.facinghistory.org/resource-library/teaching-strategies) and **The K. Patricia Cross Academy** (https://kpcross academy.org/) are two websites with loads of strategies you may want to consider.

For a deeper dive into the use of discussion, consider ***Discussion as a Way of Teaching: Tools and Techniques for Democratic Classrooms*** **by Brookfield and Preskill** (2005). This book is especially useful in developing discussions that are equity-producing *and* promote learning.

The apps **Parlay** (https://parlayideas.com/) and **Equity Maps** (https://equity maps.com/) are both useful for building equity into discussion.

Need some inspiration to step away from lectures? Check out **Emily Hanford's** podcast documentary, ***Don't Lecture Me*** (http://americanradioworks.publicradio.org/features/tomorrows-college/lectures/).

Pedagogy of the Decolonizing, a TedxUAlberta talk by **Quetzala Carson** will make you uncomfortable and might radicalize you a bit (https://www.youtube.com/watch?v=IN17Os8JAr8&t=2s).

References

Bjork, R. A., & Bjork, E. (1992). A new theory of disuse and an old theory of stimulus fluctuation. In A. Healy, S. Kosslyn, & R. Shiffrin (Eds.), *From learning processes to cognitive processes: Essays in honor of William K. Estes* (Vol. 2, pp. 35–67). Erlbaum. https://www.researchgate.net/publication/281322665

Blau, S. D. (2003). *The literature workshop: Teaching texts and their readers.* Heinemann Educational Books.

Brookfield, S. D., & Preskill, S. (2005). *Discussion as a way of teaching: Tools and techniques for democratic classrooms* (2nd ed.). Jossey-Bass.

Brown, P. C., Roediger, H. L., & McDaniel, M. A. (2014). *Make it stick: The science of successful learning.* Harvard University Press.

Callender, A. A., & McDaniel, M. A. (2009). The limited benefits of rereading educational texts. *Contemporary Educational Psychology, 34*(1), 30–41. https://doi.org/10.1016/j.cedpsych.2008.07.001

Cavanagh, S. R. (2016). *The spark of learning: Energizing the college classroom with the science of emotion.* West Virginia University Press. muse.jhu.edu/book/47958

Character Lab. (2020). *Character Lab.* https://characterlab.org/

Crouch, C. H., & Mazur, E. (2001). Peer instruction: Ten years of experience and results. *American Journal of Physics, 69*(9), 970–977. https://doi.org/10.1119/1.1374249

D'Avanzo, C. (2008). Biology concept inventories: Overview, status, and next steps. *BioScience, 58*(11), 1079–1085. https://doi.org/10.1641/B581111

Deslauriers, L., McCarty, L. S., Miller, K., Callaghan, K., & Kestin, G. (2019). Measuring actual learning versus feeling of learning in response to being actively engaged in the classroom. *Proceedings of the National Academy of Sciences, 116*(39), 19251–19257. https://doi.org/10.1073/pnas.1821936116

Finkel, D. (2000). *Teaching with your mouth shut.* Heinemann. https://www.heinemann.com/products/0469.aspx

Gilovich, T. (2008). *How we know what isn't so.* Simon & Schuster.

Hall, K. G., Domingues, D. A., & Cavazos, R. (1994). Contextual interference effects with skilled baseball players. *Perceptual and Motor Skills, 78*(3), 835–841. https://doi.org/10.1177/003151259407800331

Hattie, J. (2012). *Visible learning for teachers: Maximizing impact on learning.* Routledge.

Hestenes, D., Wells, M., & Swackhamer, G. (1992). Force concept inventory. *The Physics Teacher, 30*(3), 141–158. https://doi.org/10.1119/1.2343497

Iyengar, S. (2010, July). *The art of choosing* [Video]. TED Talk. https://www.ted.com/talks/sheena_iyengar_the_art_of_choosing?language=en

Libarkin, J. C., & Anderson, S. W. (2005). Assessment of learning in entry-level geoscience courses: Results from the Geoscience Concept Inventory. *Journal of Geoscience Education, 53*(4), 394–401. https://doi.org/10.5408/1089-9995-53.4.394

Ludlow, J. (2004). From safe space to contested space in the feminist classroom. *Transformations: The Journal of Inclusive Scholarship and Pedagogy, 15*(1), 40–56. https://www.jstor.org/stable/10.5325/trajincschped.15.1.0040

Mazur, E., & Hilborn, R. C. (1997). Peer unstruction: A user's manual. *Physics Today, 50*(4), 359–360.
McCabe, J. (2011). Metacognitive awareness of learning strategies in undergraduates. *Memory and Cognition, 39*(3), 462–476. https://doi.org/10.3758/s13421-010-0035-2
McDaniel, M. A., & Donnelly, C. M. (1996). Learning with analogy and elaborative interrogation. *Journal of Educational Psychology, 88*(3), 508–519. https://doi.org/10.1037/ 0022-0663.88.3.508
McIntyre, A., Colley, B., Jones, S., Smith-Mumford, P., & Weaver, B. (1998). Engaging in cross-racial dialogue: Does/can talk lead to action? *Transformations, 9*(2), 1–11. https://www.jstor.org/stable/43587110?seq=1#metadata_info_tab_contents
Miller, G. A. (1956). The magical number seven, plus or minus two: Some limits on our capacity for processing information. *Psychological Review, 63*(2), 81–97. https://doi.org/10.1037/h0043158
Moulton, C. A. E., Dubrowski, A., MacRae, H., Graham, B., Grober, E., & Reznick, R. (2006). Teaching surgical skills: What kind of practice makes perfect? A randomized, controlled trial. *Annals of Surgery, 244*(3), 400–407. https://doi.org/10.1097/01.sla.0000234808.85789.6a
Ngothai, Y., & Davis, M. C. (2012). Implementation and analysis of a Chemical Engineering Fundamentals Concept Inventory (CEFCI). *Education for Chemical Engineers, 7*(1), e32–e40. https://doi.org/10.1016/j.ece.2011.10.001
Ott, V. E. (2016). Set-create-reflect: An approach for culturally responsive teaching. In *Diversity and inclusion in the college classroom* (Faculty Focus Special Report; pp. 27–28). Magna Publications.
Pashler, H., McDaniel, M., Rohrer, D., & Bjork, R. (2008). Learning styles: Concepts and evidence. *Psychological Science in the Public Interest: A Journal of the American Psychological Society, 9*(3), 105–119. https://doi.org/10.1111/j.1539-6053.2009.01038.x
Pauk, W., & Owens, R. J. Q. (2010). *How to study in college* (10th ed.). Wadsworth.
Pink, D. H. (2009). *Drive: The surprising truth about what motivates us.* Riverhead Books.
Rich, A. (1994). *Blood, bread, and poetry: Selected prose 1979–1985.* Norton.
Rocca, K. A. (2010). Student participation in the college classroom: An extended multidisciplinary literature review. *Communication Education, 59*(2), 185–213. https://doi.org/ 10.1080/03634520903505936
Roediger, H. L., & Karpicke, J. D. (2006). Taking memory tests improves long-term retention. *Psychological Science, 17*(3), 249–255. https://doi.org/10.1111/j.1467-9280. 2006.01693.x
Rohrer, D., & Taylor, K. (2007). The shuffling of mathematics problems improves learning. *Instructional Science, 35*(6), 481–498. https://doi.org/10.1007/s11251-007-9015-8
Shulman, L. S. (2005). Signature pedagogies in the professions. *Daedalus, 134*(3), 52–59. https://doi.org/10.1162/0011526054622015
Smith, K. (2016). Teaching and learning 'respect' and 'acceptance' in the classroom. In *Diversity and inclusion in the college classroom* (Faculty Focus Special Report; pp. 17–18). Magna Publications.
Souza, T. (2016). Managing hot moments in the classroom: Concrete strategies for cooling down tension. In *Diversity and inclusion in the college classroom* (Faculty Focus Special Report; pp. 4–5). Magna Publications.
Sriram, R. (2020, April 13). *The neuroscience behind productive struggle.* Edutopia. https://www.edutopia.org/article/neuroscience-behind-productive-struggle
Valle-Ruiz, L., Navarro, K., Mendoza, K., McGrath, A., Galina, B., Chick, N., Brewer, S., & Bostow, R. (2015). *A guide to feminist pedagogy.* Vanderbilt Center for Teaching. https://my.vanderbilt.edu/femped/
Willoughby, T., & Wood, E. (1994). Elaborative interrogation examined at encoding and retrieval. *Learning and Instruction, 4*(2), 139–149. https://doi.org/10.1016/0959-4752 (94)90008-6

CHAPTER NINE

Supporting Students

Preflection

Rate your level of agreement with the following statements:

1 = strongly disagree, 2 = disagree, 3 = agree, 4 = strongly agree

1. When I was first teaching college courses, I felt like a bit of a fraud.
2. I tend to be more interested in learning something new when I see a clear purpose to what I am learning and how it might benefit me.
3. If I fail at a new task, I generally take that as an indication that I shouldn't have attempted that task at that time.

As you read this chapter, reflect on it, and engage with the activities both independently and with fellow readers, note that it has been designed to support you in the following:

- Examining the research base for supporting student learning through targeted supports
- Determining which targeted supports might be a good fit for the students you're supporting
- Reflecting on how your teaching methods, attitudes, and ideas may promote and hinder student learning

As you are coming to the close of this book (but not your learning), we want to tease out some ideas about student success with you. By this point, we assume you are at least interested in, if not dedicated to, equitable teaching and enduring learning as a holistic process based in relationship building. As you have traveled through these chapters, reflections, and activities with an inquiring stance, we hope that you have constructed understanding and a desire to continuously improve and expand your skill sets. Thus, we offer some guidance on supporting students as one of the more advanced considerations transformative educators undertake.

At the heart of supporting students is being able to recognize and acknowledge their humanity, both as individuals and collectively. This requires making conscious efforts to view learners in terms of both social and psychological dimensions and then building in supports and structures that address these dimensions as a part of the learning environment. Understanding learning in general, the varied motivations of those who pursue postsecondary degrees and credentials, and the implications of undertaking that learning in a public forum such as a classroom will enable you to begin supporting diverse learners. We have found that enacting teaching practices that build up students' sense of competence and that uphold "failure" as critical for transformative learning are fundamental to this process. In this chapter, much as we did in Chapter 6, we'll ask you to examine some assumptions you may have about why students do or don't do well in class and how you may be perceiving their performance. We also provide specific actions you can take to bolster students who could use attention or differentiation. We encourage you to move slowly through the content and call on the support of co-learners as you come to understand it is *people* you teach, not merely subject matter. We're first going to take on some potential assumptions you may have about student behavior.

Activity: Interpreting Student Behaviors

Read each of the following scenarios; then select how you would most likely interpret the behavior.

1. Kiera, a Black woman, always attends calculus class, which you know because she sits in the front row, actively takes notes, and pays attention. You were surprised when she scored a C– on the first exam. *What do you think is the likely cause of her grade?*

    a. Kiera did not spend enough time studying or practicing problems.

    b. Kiera experienced stereotype threat when the teaching assistant announced, "This exam will show if you really are a math person. Good luck—you're going to need it!" while he was passing out the exam.

2. Abdullah, a recent immigrant to the United States, rarely participates in class although he attends regularly. He sits in the back row, doesn't talk to his partner, and has yet to contribute to the weekly class discussions. *How would you interpret Abdullah's behavior?*

    a. Abdullah doesn't participate because he isn't prepared. Or perhaps he is struggling with the language.

b. Abdullah doesn't feel that he belongs in class. He is afraid that speaking will just confirm that he is not college-level material, which will disappoint his parents.

3. Kasey did well in high school, earning As and Bs without much effort. She was excited about her introductory biology course because it was her first step in becoming a medical doctor. After failing the first exam, she asks you to sign a drop form. *How would you respond?*

   a. Kasey didn't study enough and dropping this course is wise. Not everyone is cut out to be a doctor. You sign her form without much thought.

   b. Kasey hasn't experienced failure like this before and she may believe, mistakenly, that failing indicates that she is unable to learn. You convince Kasey to reevaluate her study habits (perhaps using the exam wrapper from Chapter 6) and tell her that she is capable of learning from her mistakes.

By now, you probably won't be surprised that we're going to lead you to consider why the reasons described in "b" are often overlooked, yet potentially key explanations for student performance. In the above examples, option "b" represents interpretations by educators who address the humanity of students and relate to them in ways that support their success. In this chapter, we offer strategies for supporting students in situations similar to these where targeted supports might be useful.

Reflect to Learn

1. Recall a time when your learning motivations were misjudged. What was that experience like?
2. Can you think of a time when a benevolent judgment or a direct suggestion would have helped you learn a confusing concept? How do you think it would?

As the evidence base for understanding how people learn grows, it is increasingly clear that factors beyond the amount of time learners spend studying have a profound impact on grades, success, and retention. Aspects such as students' motivation, sense of belonging, relationships with instructors and classmates, and connection to the course material are important to consider in your course design. Targeted supports are strategies that you can use in your practice to positively shape students' experiences by teaching more directly to these social-psychological factors. You may find that some students need more than others. We encourage you to incorporate targeted supports as a proactive means for addressing inequitable outcomes. Studies have shown that when provided opportunities and support, students from communities that have been underserved perform as well as traditionally-advantaged students (Harackiewicz et al., 2016; Hulleman et al., 2017; Jordt et al., 2017; Murphy et al., 2020; Walton & Cohen, 2011; Yeager et al., 2016; Yeager & Walton, 2011). Furthermore, there is an improvement in retention of first-generation college students (Hand & Payne, 2008); increased performance of women in science, technology, engineering, and mathematics (Martens et al., 2006; Miyake et al., 2010); and increased engagement and learning (Dweck et al., 2014; Yeager & Walton, 2011).

Targeted Supports

You might surmise that it would be quite difficult to help a student who feels like he doesn't belong with the other sociology majors to accept that he is an important contributor to class proceedings or to help a transfer student who gives up on difficult tasks to develop the persistence she needs to succeed. In fact, research suggests that a variety of small, simple, supportive actions can make sizable differences in situations such as these (Harackiewicz & Priniski, 2018). Part of the beauty of incorporating these interventions is that they are simple and take little time. These supports take perhaps an hour total, which might be done outside of class. If you're interested in learning more about the research around these targeted supports, then we highly recommend the review by Harackiewicz and Priniski (2018); it's one of our favorites.

We call these techniques "targeted supports." Other names used include "targeted interventions" and "psychosocial interventions." Targeted supports are actions or activities that focus on specific educational issues by addressing the social-psychological processes that underlie those issues at key points in the educational process. These supports can have powerful and long-lasting effects, especially for under-resourced students and those who in the past have not benefited from a "one-size-fits-all" approach, which, let's face it, was developed for affluent, cis, hetero, White men.

As we examine these targeted supports, we've grouped them into four categories according to their purpose:

1. Learners ascribe value to their learning.
2. Learners become confident in their capacity for growth.
3. Learners are secure members of a learning community.
4. Learners connect with their values.

If you are working through this book in a faculty learning community, we invite you to use the jigsaw technique described in Chapter 8 as a learning aid. If you can, you'll get the opportunity to experience firsthand community-building and co-creation of knowledge with your fellow learners.

Activity for Your Faculty Learning Community: Jigsaw

First, each reader is assigned a section to read from the preceding list. If you have enough people to double up, those with the same assignment should get together to compare notes. After experts have worked together, break into new groups to discuss the following questions:

- What similarities do you see among the categories?
- Which supports would be most appropriate for a course of first-year students? Or an upper level course in the major?

Learners Ascribe Value to Their Learning

Known as "task" or "utility value" interventions, these targeted supports allow students to explore and reflect on the value or importance of the course or tasks within the course (Acee et al., 2018; Harackiewicz et al., 2016; Hulleman et al., 2017).

You are probably not surprised to learn that students who see a purpose in a course—who find it intrinsically interesting or see how it will benefit them—tend to be more engaged and perform better. If, in the preflection, you answered "agree" or "strongly agree" in response to, "*I tend to be more interested in learning something new when I see a clear purpose to what I am learning and how it might benefit me*," then we don't need to convince you of this because it reflects your lived experience. *Frequently* telling students why you find the topic at hand interesting and how it can benefit them is a useful practice. However, when students learn how to ascribe this value for themselves, it has a measurably larger impact on their success (Canning & Harackiewicz, 2015). The following two examples demonstrate how you might lead learners to discover the value in learning.

Using Written Reflections to Make Connections

Use the following prompt as a writing activity (Hulleman et al., 2017). List a few topics that have been studied perhaps before the first exam or first big assignment. You could even make Prompt 1 the first question on an exam.

> Prompt 1: Write one to two paragraphs about how the material that you have been studying in class relates to your life. Don't summarize the material, just elaborate on its relevance to your life.

Then, a month or so later, assign this prompt:

> Prompt 2: (a) List course topics. Choose a topic from above that is personally useful and meaningful to you. In one or two paragraphs, describe how learning about this topic is useful to your life right now. (b) Choose a topic that is personally useful and meaningful to you. In one or two paragraphs, describe how learning about this topic will be beneficial to you in the future.

End-of-Term Connections

At the end of the term, students write for 10 minutes to explore how the material from the course relates to their current lives and/or how they feel what they learned will benefit them in the future.

Save the best of the writings each year and maintain a collection. The "best" could include writings that demonstrate deep connections, significant growth, career relevance, unique insights, and/or creative approaches. On the first day of class, lay out the collection around the room and ask students to circulate for about five minutes and then discuss what they discovered.

Learners Become Confident in Their Capacity for Growth

The supports in this section are used to shift a student's perspective about challenges or worries. For example, many students that performed well in high school are shocked when they struggle on their first college exam, like Kasey in the earlier scenario. If a student sees this grade and thinks, "I must be the dumbest one in this class; there is no way I can learn this," then one of these targeted supports, also called framing interventions, can help her shift her perspective to, "I didn't do so well on my first college exam, which sucks. I guess I need to figure out some new studying strategies." The first perspective can lead to a student dropping the course or giving up, while the shifted perspective can lead to the student attending review sessions, going to office hours, and utilizing better studying strategies. Encouraging students, and yourself, to develop a growth mindset is a powerful method for positively shifting perspectives.

Growth Mindset

Research by Carol Dweck and others (Dweck, 2008; Dweck et al., 2014) describes two different mindsets regarding learning: growth versus fixed mindsets. This work aligns with what we presented in Chapter 2 concerning goal orientation (whether we are motivated by mastery or performance goals).

A fixed mindset is the belief that an individual is either "smart" or "dumb" and that this is a permanent state. A person with a fixed mindset might say, "I'm just not a writer," and therefore approaches writing assignments with nonchalance or even fear, yet with an excuse for poor performance at the ready. Individuals with fixed mindsets believe that talent alone, without effort, creates success. If students have fixed mindsets, they believe failure demonstrates the limit of their abilities; thus, there's no point in trying again. When faced with failure, they tell themselves they won't ever be able to do it and make excuses to rationalize the failure. By interpreting one failed exam as an indication that she is unfit to become a doctor, Kasey demonstrated a fixed mindset.

A growth mindset is the belief that intelligence and other malleable traits continue to develop after birth through dedication and hard work. A person with a growth mindset acknowledges that challenge and perseverance lead to learning and that attitude and effort regulate abilities. Failure, especially failure with feedback, is viewed by someone with a growth mindset as constructive and as an opportunity to improve learning It's obvious that students with growth mindsets are advantaged. Here are some ways you can cultivate it in your classes:

- Break down large projects into smaller (achievable) steps or have students do this themselves (and submit this plan to you). They should also keep track of their completion of each component. In this way, students do not become overwhelmed to a point of inaction.
- Praise students' efforts and strategies that lead to learning rather than areas over which they have little control, such as inborn talent. Students with fixed mindsets may view effort as weakness; in praising effort, you're showing that you value and expect it. The aphorism "progress, not perfection" applies here.
- View mistakes as learning opportunities, normalize the idea that everyone makes mistakes when trying a new skill or applying a new concept and that the important thing is to learn from those mistakes. From the chapter on assessment, you may remember how important it is to expect students to revise early drafts and for instructors to avoid evaluating and assigning grades to work completed early in the learning process. Use teaching strategies (Chapter 8) that allow or even encourage students to make mistakes, and don't grade these learning attempts. Provide examples of your own mistakes and share how you learned from them. You might even reframe the word *failure* to have another meaning. We have heard of "fail" being defined as "first attempt in learning."
- Don't equate student performance with intelligence or worth. Tell students that their performance reflects their current skills and efforts and that grades are not a reflection of their intelligence or self-worth.
- Help students see how the application of feedback improves learning so as not to judge feedback as negative. For example, you might use examples from ath-

letics and music. Professional athletes and musicians are known to review past performances with their coaches or bands as a means for improvement. Explain that the reason that you are providing critical feedback is that you know that students can use it to improve, as pointed out in Chapter 6. Naturally, you should structure your course and assignments so that students do have the opportunity to improve from feedback.

Caralyn's Experience

In high school, I decided to take Russian for my required foreign language. It was a small class, which included a native Russian speaker and a few students whose families spoke Russian at home. I was in neither category. This was the first class where the material didn't come to me easily. I didn't know what to do, so I didn't do anything. I figured that I just "wasn't good" at languages, and the fact that everyone around me could learn this new alphabet and pronounce these foreign words only served to solidify that idea and make me even less likely to speak out loud in class. I finished my two required years and never wanted to experience that again. I even avoided applying to any colleges with a foreign language requirement because I was so fearful of failing.

I had an amazingly strong fixed mindset, and this is a great example of performance-avoidance behavior (Chapter 2). I viewed my need to practice pronunciations as a sign that I just wasn't good at learning Russian. My mindset prevented me from taking the steps needed to learn or from even recognizing how absurd it was to compare my Russian spelling skills to those of a native Russian speaker. If you ever hear yourself saying, "I'm not a [math, computer, writing, art, language, fill in the blank] person," stop yourself. Don't allow yourself to drift toward having a fixed mindset. If you hear students saying those things, help them correct their thoughts. Try "I'm not a language person *yet.*"

The first of the two targeted supports that follow help students develop a growth mindset by identifying their current mindset, learning about neuroplasticity and mindsets, and then putting this information into their own words through a written reflection. The second helps students overcome anxiety by changing their language about stressful events.

Mindset Letters

1. Ask students to take the Mindset Inventory—if you haven't yet, do so at https://blog.mindsetworks.com/what-s-my-mindset.

2. Teach a brief lesson about brain plasticity (the brain's ability to change throughout life) and the concept of growth and fixed mindset. Many useful resources for this are available online. In your lesson, emphasize the following:

    a. Failures and setbacks help us improve.

    b. Quality feedback from someone more knowledgeable is key to improving.

    c. People are better at something because they've worked harder at it, not because they were born that way.

3. Students write letters or videotape speeches for younger students about brain plasticity and how developing a growth mindset can increase success in school and life.

This type of activity can be used to emphasize a wide variety of positive strategies. For example, a professor trying to get students to space out their studying has his students write letters to high school students explaining why this works and when they've used it.

Self-Talk

Many students (and people in general) suffer from test, performance, or public speaking anxiety, becoming so anxious they don't perform well. This activity helps reframe that anxiety as excitement and introduces distance from stressful thoughts (Kross et al., 2014).

How? Encourage students to talk to themselves before stressful events using the following ideas:

- Use their own name and other non-first-person pronouns. "Why is Amy feeling this way? I think Amy is feeling this way because . . ."

- Use *get to* rather than *must*. For example, "Amy gets to give an oral presentation in front of class," instead of, "I must give an oral presentation in front of class."

This type of wording is more effective than telling students, or yourself, to be calm. Anxiety and excitement elicit similar chemical reactions in the brain, but the chemical signals released in your brain when you are calm are very distinct from those excitement/anxiety signals. If you, or students, are anxious about something, then it is easier to reframe as excitement rather than calm. If Amy is scared of giving a public presentation, then all the self-talk in the world is not going to convince her that she is calm. She can convince herself that she is excited: "Amy sure is excited that she gets to do this!"

Activity: Self-Talk

Now it's your turn. Consider an upcoming anxiety-provoking event. Talk to yourself about this using third-person pronouns and your own name. End by saying, "[Your *name*] sure is excited that [she/he/they] gets to do this!"

Your Mindset Matters Too

Not surprisingly, your own beliefs about how students learn matters. Students are less motivated and perform more poorly when their instructors hold a fixed "not everyone belongs in college" mindset compared to instructors who hold a growth mindset. Unsurprisingly, those from Black, Indigenous, and People of Color (BIPOC) communities bear more of this burden than their White or Asian counterparts (Canning et al., 2019; Rosenthal & Jacobsen, 1968). If, in the preflection, you responded "agree" or "strongly agree" to, "*If I fail at a new task, I generally take that as an indication that I shouldn't have attempted that task at that time*," now might be a good time to reconsider your attitudes and work on developing a growth mindset. Try viewing challenges as opportunities for self-improvement. If you, or students, fail at something, reframe it as a learning opportunity and not a comment on intelligence. Think of your brain like a muscle; it can grow and become stronger with practice and training. You wouldn't expect yourself to run a marathon without training, so you can't expect yourself, or students, to master a task without practice.

Learners Are Secure Members of a Learning Community

Believing that hard work and effort will lead to success is important, but how strongly students sense they belong is also important. Social belonging is the human emotional need to affiliate with and be accepted by members of a group and as humans, we are intrinsically motivated to be socially accepted (Walton & Cohen, 2011). Students, like all of us, need to hear that they are not alone and that they belong. If learners feel overwhelmed or isolated at the start of college or in a new course, then it is important for them to frame these feelings as normal feelings that most students experience and not an indication they shouldn't be in college. A lack of social belonging may be preventing Abdullah, from the initial chapter activity, from participating in class. Approaching Abdullah in a punitive or negative way will only reinforce Abdullah's sense of isolation. Instead, the professor should strive to help Abdullah become a valued member of the class and provide examples that frame those feelings of isolation as normal experiences.

Research shows that this feeling of "not belonging" can lead to poorer performance on exams, lower grades, and poorer health outcomes (Walton & Cohen,

2011). It is BIPOC and first-generation college students who are likely to experience these feelings of being outsiders in a typical non-historically Black college or university or four-year college or university. The support described in this section helps students see they are not alone in their struggles and that questioning belonging is common. Through social belonging supports, students can reframe the struggles, the feelings of isolation, and the sense of inadequacy that many students experience when transitioning to college.

Reflect to Learn: Recall your response to the preflection statement, "*When I was first teaching college courses, I felt like a bit of a fraud.*" How did your feelings as a novice impact your actions and behaviors?

Social Belonging Testimonials

This specific support involves collecting written testimonials from juniors or seniors, sharing those stories with incoming freshmen, and asking the freshmen to reflect on the testimonials (Walton & Cohen, 2011; Yeager et al., 2016).

Caralyn regularly utilizes this targeted support in her introductory biology class. The reflections she uses were written by junior and senior biology majors who describe how they remember feeling in their first biology class as freshmen and how that compares to how they feel now. Many described feeling overwhelmed and anxious about the large class size, although some said they valued the anonymity. Students from BIPOC communities remembered how White the campus was compared to high school. Others wrote they felt like everyone else was smarter and better prepared for college than them. In contrast, many discussed making friends, talking with professors, and determining what they needed to do to succeed.

After collecting the testimonials, the following prompt was provided to students in the introductory class:

> The purpose of this activity is for you to gain insight from feelings upper class Biology Majors expressed about Introductory Biology many semesters ago.
>
> First read "Reflections from Junior and Senior Biology Majors."
>
> Then write a 300–500-word response. In your response, be sure to explain what resonated with you from the "Reflections" and include your two favorite quotations. Consider why these students' experiences and feelings changed from their first to their final semesters on campus. Use examples from your own experience to illustrate this.

This intervention is best executed early in the semester, although it could be done at any time. If you were to use this intervention in your own class, then you would want to find appropriately relevant testimonials.

Caralyn's Experience

I have found reading through these reflections to be a moving experience. I have reached out to students because of what they wrote, and it helped us connect. Some students will share very powerful stories about themselves, and this motivates me to build in more supports and make my course as inclusive as possible.

Learners Connect With Their Values

These targeted supports, known as "personal values interventions," assist students in identifying core values and reinforcing what's important to them. They can be used in many contexts by activating the values that students hold in contradiction to negative stereotype threats. Many students have experienced negative stereotypes over their lifetimes, and it can be difficult not to be affected by those, especially in times of stress. By reflecting on their values and sources of self-worth, students are able to counter stereotype threats they face in academic settings (Jordt et al., 2017; Martens et al., 2006; Miyake et al., 2010; Steele, 2011).

Stereotype threat is when individuals worry that their behavior may confirm stereotypes about a group they belong to or feel themselves to be at risk of conforming to stereotypes about their social group (Steele, 2011). Claude M. Steele's (2011) book, *Whistling Vivaldi*, provides excellent examples of myriad ways that stereotype threat can negatively impact members of any group. Kiera from earlier in the chapter likely experienced stereotype threat in her calculus class when the male teaching assistant announced that the exam will sort students. She may have thought, "I am a Black woman. Black women are not expected to excel at math. This is a difficult math exam." These thoughts can lead to anxiety, distraction, and extra pressure to succeed that then harms performance (Spencer et al., 2016).

Creating learning environments that reduce or eliminate stereotype vulnerability can benefit all students. Avoid making the same mistake as the teaching assistant did when he announced how hard and evaluative the exam was by encouraging students to reflect on values that affirm their identity and provide resilience against stereotype threat (Spencer et al., 2016).

Values Affirmation

Students complete this activity, adapted from Jordt and colleagues (2017), at the beginning of a term and can repeat it again later in the course.

There are no right or wrong answers to this activity. Consider this list of personal values and select the two or three that are MOST important to you.

The most important values to me are:

- Athleticism
- Authenticity
- Compassion
- Confidence
- Creativity
- Determination
- Fairness
- Empathy
- Independence
- Honesty
- Humor
- Leadership
- Loyalty
- Patience
- Perseverance
- Popularity
- Religion
- Service
- Spirituality
- Success
- Wealth
- Wisdom

In a few paragraphs, answer the question: "Why are these values important to you?" You may include examples of personal experiences in your response

Indicate your level of agreement with each of the following statements. (Responses on a Likert scale: Strongly Disagree, Disagree, Somewhat Disagree, Somewhat Agree, Agree, Strongly Agree)

- The values I selected have influenced my life.
- In general, I try to live up to the values I selected.
- The values I selected are an important part of who I am.
- I care about the values I selected.

When to Use Targeted Supports

You may be asking yourself which of these supports to use when. Asking students to reflect on the value of their learning is good practice for all students, at almost any point in the semester. In addition to helping consolidate knowledge, it helps learners establish habits of introspection, observation, and mindfulness. Moreover, we believe developing a growth mindset and training oneself to view failure as a learning opportunity benefits everyone, ourselves included. Taking steps to minimize stereotype vulnerability by being affirming is always important.

There may be other times when you don't want to use an activity for an entire class because you are concerned about one or a few specific students. How can you tell if a student isn't participating because they don't feel like a part of the community, or is it because they couldn't afford to purchase the textbook and are too embarrassed to admit that to you? Might they have decided that this class is not important to them? We don't have a magic crystal ball that can help you elucidate these potential causes, but we do know that communicating genuine concern helps create a trusting atmosphere for problem-solving. We encourage you to go ahead and sit down with students and talk to them, virtually or in person. With such a platform, you are likely to be able to identify what they need. If you've already communicated to students that you care about them and their learning, that you've carefully selected course activities for motivation and engagement, and that you've worked hard to create a safe learning environment, then many students will be willing to have this conversation with you, enabling you to be responsive to individual needs with targeted supports.

Reflect to Learn: Are any of the targeted supports from this chapter ones you wish a professor had used with you at some point?

Taking care to support the emotional and psychological needs of students can go a long way toward helping all students feel they can take the risks needed to embark on transformative learning. Using targeted supports helps in creating learning environments that invite all students to see themselves as learners, colleagues, scholars, and leaders. While you might feel pessimistic when you consider the harm that stereotype threat has done to many, even when they had ability but lacked social belonging, which caused them to leave school, we choose to be hopeful. Considering the potential that might be unlocked or the many students you might help to succeed by minimizing or eliminating barriers is a further way to counter pessimism.

Make It Happen: Support Selection

Select two of the targeted supports described in this chapter that you wish you had used in a previous course where you are now recognizing there was a need. Are these general supports that you would incorporate in any course for all learners, or would you use them more specifically at a point in time or for particular learners? When during the term do you think the support would be useful?

Wonderful Resources to Extend Learning

Daniel Pink, has several short videos related to this chapter that you can share with students:

This Is How Not to Calm Your Nerves: https://www.danpink.com/pinkcast/pinkcast-2-18-this-is-how-not-to-calm-your-nerves/

This Is How You Motivate Yourself: https://www.danpink.com/pinkcast/pinkcast-3-01-this-is-how-to-motivate-yourself-when-you-dont-feel-like-exercising/

This Is How You Talk to Yourself: https://www.danpink.com/pinkcast/pinkcast-2-22-this-is-how-to-talk-to-yourself/

Mindset: The New Psychology of Success is **Carol Dweck's** (2008) rigorously researched classic that has spawned an industry of resources for helping learners achieve at higher levels through the application of a few simple strategies.

In ***Whistling Vivaldi: And Other Clues to How Stereotypes Affect Us***, **Claude Steele** (2011) explains how stereotypes influence identity formation and account for phenomena such as gender gaps in test scores.

In a short article in *Inside Higher Ed*, **Laura Behling** presents a great class activity for ***Helping Students See the Connections*** among their courses and co-curricular activities: https://www.insidehighered.com/advice/2018/01/30/helping-students-identify-connections-their-college-education-opinion

References

Acee, T. W., Weinstein, C. E., Hoang, T. V., & Flaggs, D. A. (2018). Value reappraisal as a conceptual model for task-value interventions. *Journal of Experimental Education, 86*(1), 69–85. https://doi.org/10.1080/00220973.2017.1381830

Canning, E. A., & Harackiewicz, J. M. (2015). Teach it, don't preach it: The differential effects of directly-communicated and self-generated utility–value information. *Motivation Science, 1*(1), 47–71. https://doi.org/10.1037/mot0000015

Canning, E. A., Muenks, K., Green, D. J., & Murphy, M. C. (2019). STEM faculty who believe ability is fixed have larger racial achievement gaps and inspire less student motivation in their classes. *Science Advances, 5*(2), eeau4734. https://doi.org/10.1126/sciadv.aau4734

Dweck, C S. (2008). *Mindset: The new psychology of success.* Random House Digital.

Dweck, Carol S., Walton, G. M., & Cohen, G. L. (2014). *Academic tenacity: Mindsets and skills that promote long-term learning.* Bill & Melinda Gates Foundation. http://k12education.gatesfoundation.org/resource/academic-tenacity-mindsets-and-skills-that-promote-long-term-learning/

Hand, C., & Payne, E. M. (2008). First-generation college students: A study of Appalachian student success. *Journal of Developmental Education, 32*(1), 4–15. https://search.proquest.com/openview/387e6235673f95ac562f32752546d1a3/1?pq-origsite=gscholar &cbl=47765

Harackiewicz, J. M., Canning, E. A., Tibbetts, Y., Priniski, S. J., & Hyde, J. S. (2016). Closing achievement gaps with a utility-value intervention: Disentangling race and social class. *Journal of Personality and Social Psychology, 111*(5), 745–765. https://doi.org/10.1037/pspp0000075

Harackiewicz, J. M., & Priniski, S. J. (2018). Improving student outcomes in higher education: The science of targeted intervention. *Annual Review of Psychology, 69*(1), 409–435. https://doi.org/10.1146/annurev-psych-122216-011725

Hulleman, C. S., Kosovich, J. J., Barron, K. E., & Daniel, D. B. (2017). Making connections: Replicating and extending the utility value intervention in the classroom. *Journal of Educational Psychology, 109*(3), 387–404. https://doi.org/10.1037/edu0000146

Jordt, H., Eddy, S. L., Brazil, R., Lau, I., Mann, C., Brownell, S. E., King, K., & Freeman, S. (2017). Values affirmation intervention reduces achievement gap between underrepresented minority and white students in introductory biology classes. *CBE—Life Sciences Education, 16*(3), ar41. https://doi.org/10.1187/cbe.16-12-0351

Kross, E., Bruehlman-Senecal, E., Park, J., Burson, A., Dougherty, A., Shablack, H., Bremner, R., Moser, J., & Ayduk, O. (2014). Self-talk as a regulatory mechanism: How you do it matters. *Journal of Personality and Social Psychology, 106*(2), 304–324. https://doi.org/10.1037/a0035173

Martens, A., Johns, M., Greenberg, J., & Schimel, J. (2006). Combating stereotype threat: The effect of self-affirmation on women's intellectual performance. *Journal of Experimental Social Psychology, 42*(2), 236–243. https://doi.org/10.1016/j.jesp.2005.04.010

Miyake, A., Kost-Smith, L. E., Finkelstein, N. D., Pollock, S. J., Cohen, G. L., & Ito, T. A. (2010). Reducing the gender achievement gap in college science: A classroom study of values affirmation. *Science, 330*(6008), 1234–1237. https://doi.org/10.1126/science. 1195996

Murphy, M. C., Gopalan, M., Carter, E. R., Emerson, K. T. U., Bottoms, B. L., & Walton, G. M. (2020). A customized belonging intervention improves retention of socially disadvantaged students at a broad-access university. *Science Advances, 6*(29), eaba4677. https://doi.org/10.1126/sciadv.aba4677

Rosenthal, R., & Jacobsen, L. (1968). *Pygmalion in the classroom: Teacher expectation and pupils intellectual development.* Holt, Rhinehart & Winston.

Spencer, S. J., Logel, C., & Davies, P. G. (2016). Stereotype threat. *Annual Review of Psychology, 67*(1), 415–437. https://doi.org/10.1146/annurev-psych-073115-103235

Steele, C. M. (2011). *Whistling Vivaldi: And other clues to how stereotypes affect us.* W. W. Norton & Company.

Walton, G. M., & Cohen, G. L. (2011). A brief social-belonging intervention improves academic and health outcomes of minority students. *Science, 331*(6023), 1447–1451. https://doi.org/10.1126/science.1198364

Yeager, D. S., & Walton, G. M. (2011). Social-psychological interventions in education: They're not magic. *Review of Educational Research, 81*(2), 267–301. https://doi.org/10.3102/0034654311405999

Yeager, D. S., Walton, G. M., Brady, S. T., Akcinar, E. N., Paunesku, D., Keane, L., Kamentz, D., Ritter, G., Duckworth, A. L., Urstein, R., Gomez, E. M., Markus, H. R., Cohen, G. L., & Dweck, C. S. (2016). Teaching a lay theory before college narrows achievement gaps at scale. *Proceedings of the National Academy of Sciences of the United States of America, 113*(24), E3341–E3348. https://doi.org/10.1073/pnas.1524360113

CHAPTER TEN

Your Turn: Self- and Collective Efficacy

> *Preflection*
>
> What are two or three of the more important ideas or concepts you learned from engaging with this book? Why have they had an impact on you?

As you read this chapter, reflect on it, and engage with the activities both independently and with fellow readers, note that it has been designed to support you in developing agency to promote change by doing the following:

- Continuing to build your knowledge of, competency with, and commitment to transformative teaching practices
- Feeling inspired, challenged, and supported to (re)calibrate your ideas about transformative teaching and learning
- Collaborating with others on the wonderful challenge that is designing and teaching a truly transformative course
- Cultivating your own community of change agents

We know that anyone who reads this book to this final chapter already cares about teaching well and is willing and eager to make changes that matter. Congratulate yourself on being that type of person!

Take a moment and reflect on the work you've accomplished—from student learning outcomes to dilemmas, issues, and questions to performance tasks. You had to think long and deep about your course, have been creative, provided and received feedback, and, we presume, have *really* stretched your brain. There may have been ideas presented in this book that you're not ready to tackle *yet*.

Keep Lea(r)ning

Throughout this field guide, we've indicated inspiring books that we love, as well as powerful research papers and intriguing resources. We're sure that there are great sources that we missed or that have since been published. Consider starting with one chapter or topic that intrigues you and commit to learning more about it. You may even want to organize a faculty learning community with colleagues (a *leaning* community?), where you can invite them to join you on your journey toward becoming a transformative educator—you could gather monthly and use a seminar format to explore one of the wonderful resources or visit each other's classrooms as you implement some of the strategies from Chapter 8. Consider sharing your learning and the changes you make to your courses based on what you've learned with students, your colleagues, and us. Model lifelong learning.

Self- and Collective Efficacy

Notice that the outcomes listed at the beginning of this chapter are affective in nature—that is, they encompass some dispositions we believe you have likely come to embrace as you've made your way to the end of this field guide. In short, those outcomes should say much about the type of teacher you're becoming and even suggest that you are ready for greater action. We hope you feel more confident and able to teach differently than when you started this book. We also assume that you acknowledge an obligation to support the success of every student. That "can-do" feeling is efficacy. Just as you support students in developing self-assurance, we expect your journey reading this book will have done the same for you. We know that if you are motivated, you will move forward in continuing to develop a transformational teaching practice.

First, a Bit About Efficacy

In the latter part of the 1970s, psychologist and social cognitive theorist, Albert Bandura (1997) coined the term *self-efficacy* to describe the capacity to exercise control over one's own motivation, behavior, and social environment to realize an aim. After noticing attributes of larger units such as communities, Bandura (2000) later developed a variation known as "collective-efficacy"—the perception of agency that groups of people apply to achieve a goal by undertaking a project with others. Noting that collective efficacy developed from more than simply being able to tap a variety of individual strengths, Bandura stated, "A group's attainments are the product not only of shared knowledge and skills of the different members, but also of the interactive, coordinative, and synergistic dynamics of their transactions" (2000, pp. 75–76). Being able to draw on others and knowing that they are in a process together develops the sense of agency that motivates members to act on situations and perform at high levels.

We highlight Bandura's work because all along we have encouraged you to find a partner, a small group, a virtual community, or someone(s) else to join this venture. We have stressed the importance of collaboration because it fosters innovation and consciousness. It doesn't occur in top-down, hierarchical organizations but where there is an environment of respect and trust—much like the classroom communities that we've been urging you to create. Interdependence is necessary in collaboration, which means that silos will fall, interdisciplinary perspectives will come together, and creativity can flourish. A collaborative ethos established in your classroom, that you then model for and with students, helps them build the 21st-century skills necessary for success in a globalized environment.

Collaboration is central to this work—collaboration with colleagues, with students, with administrators, and with the many communities that surround us. All of these are people who can support you, and you, they. When this type of mutuality exists, you will be willing and able to tackle bigger challenges and tap into more power, creativity, and satisfaction than you could individually. These benefits also mean that you have a responsibility to care for, empathize with, and empower those same colleagues, students, administrators, and fellows as you move out together building equitable societies.

By collaborating with others throughout this book, you will have built a faculty learning community that values your efforts and encourages your ongoing development as a professional educator. You have already committed time and energy to building relationships, so don't risk losing those bonds. Decide how you will stay connected with each other. To move from intention to commitment level, you must plan for these connections to take place, which brings you to the next step: the action plan.

Make It Happen: Your Action Plan

Now it's time to make an action plan for what you need to do next, decide on a deadline, *and* make plans with an accountability buddy for a check-in:

1. List three specific goals. While broad, aspirational goals are good to have, we suggest that these goals be more specific. For example, we'd all like to be better educators. What are the specific attributes that make someone a "better educator" you want to develop? Do you want to provide more effective feedback, do you want to learn and use the names of students, and/or do you want to see how small-group tests work in your discipline? Being specific makes it easier to monitor your own progress.

2. How will you know when you've reached your goals? What evidence could you collect that would inform you of any progress or need to revise?
3. What is your first actionable step? Make this a concrete action you can take in the next week. Taking this first step increases your chances of following through.
4. What are your deadlines? Again, be as specific as possible. You may tackle this goal in small chunks, so deadlines for each element are helpful.
5. Who is your accountability buddy who you can trust to hold you to account? Find someone who is willing to put your deadlines and goals on their calendar and contact you in advance of those deadlines to ask for an update.
6. How will you feel when you reach your goal? Build in some sort of celebration or self-acknowledgment of carrying out your plan.

Reflection

We purposefully included prompts for self-reflection throughout the book. During a hectic semester while juggling multiple classes, projects, and everything else in life, it can be difficult to build in time to stop and think deeply about your teaching and professional development. We believe this is important, and we hope you were able to give yourself time and brainspace to do this. That type of self-care is often not a priority and thus overlooked.

> **Reflect to Learn:** We are going to assume that you have benefited by giving yourself the gift of stopping, thinking, integrating, and applying your learning through reflection. How might students similarly benefit from moments of reflection in your course? How could you design a course to build in these moments?

Grow Your Community

> *The existence of Black feminist thought suggests that there is always choice and power to act, no matter how bleak the situation may appear to be. Viewing the world as one in the making raises the issue of individual responsibility for bringing about change. It also shows that while individual empowerment is key, only collective action can effectively generate the lasting institutional transformation required for social justice.*
>
> —*Patricia Hill Collins (2000, p. 290)*

You now know more about the many ways in which our current system of higher education is unjust. Rather than accepting the status quo, you have the ability to design courses and adopt teaching strategies that promote justice and equity. We believe we all have an obligation to teach, mentor, and inspire others to make these changes themselves. Systemic change won't happen unless we bring more people along, and we hope you're convinced that higher education is in need of major changes that you can play a part in realizing.

With a new set of knowledge, skills, and abilities that you can draw on, consider how you might grow a community of change agents who will support one another in a collective quest to become transformative educators. You appreciate the intellectual and emotional effort required to make a substantial change in your course design, so now it's time to help others take that step. Because you have begun this work, you are in a position to support and lead others. Even sharing what you found difficult and easy in this process can encourage someone else who may be on the brink of taking the step that you did. Remember that leaders don't dictate the work to be done, but they do empower others to join them in taking up the work.

In Closing

We've been writing these final chapters during the COVID-19 pandemic. Teaching through this extraordinary moment of generative change has strengthened our commitment to the teaching practices described in this book and highlighted how important the things we value in teaching are:

- We must reduce inequities in our courses. If we don't do this, then nothing else matters. The transition to online learning has put into stark relief the privilege experienced by many students compared to the racial, economic, social, and emotional hardships lived by others. We must not just be aware of these inequities but teach in ways that reduce and eliminate them.
- We believe that focusing on the bigger picture enables us to recognize what matters. What do you want students to know, do, or be 10 years from now because of what they learned in your class? Focus on that because the rest is just noise.
- We value students as full humans who live rich, complex lives. This belief elevates our courses because all students have something to add.
- We prioritize building relationships with students because a connected relationship can be the difference between students reaching out when they are having trouble versus students walking away, dropping out, or rejecting learning opportunities.

- We believe that ensuring that all students know they belong strengthens our classroom communities.
- We know we can't do this alone because a single course in a student's journey isn't sufficient to fulfill the promise of higher education and reduce equity gaps.
- We are committed to effecting change through grassroots movements. By supporting you in your journey to becoming an innovative course designer and transformative educator, you, in turn, can now support others as an agent of change. The potential for every person forthwith to enjoy the fruits of a meaningful education is thereby exponentially increased.
- We believe that equipping graduates with the skills and agency to tackle the important issues they will face in the world is worth doing well. This will require courses where students are able to grapple with important dilemmas, issues, and questions through multifaceted projects.
- We recognize the amazing expertise and humanity that faculty bring to their role as transformative educators as they inspire students to change their communities and the world.
- We appreciate the power of supportive and caring colleagues to keep us moving forward. As anyone who began the Spring 2020 semester teaching in a classroom and ended the semester spending way too many hours on Zoom, we all know that colleagues that support and appreciate all the hard work make all the difference.
- We invite you to partner with us in realizing transformative education for all.

Now it's your turn to make of your experience with *Learning That Matters: A Field Guide to Course Design for Transformative Education* what you will.

We leave you with two quotations from leaders and change agents who took on this work in education and in the wider world, thus have inspired and motivated us, and offer them knowing they can serve to energize you as well:

> *The teacher is of course an artist, but being an artist does not mean that he or she can make the profile, can shape the students. What the educator does in teaching is to make it possible for the students to become themselves.*
>
> *—Paulo Freire, We Make the Road by Walking: Conversations on Education and Social Change (Horton & Freire, 1990, p. 181)*

> *Our goal is to create a beloved community and this will require a qualitative change in our souls as well as a quantitative change in our lives.*
>
> *—Martin Luther King, Jr. (1966)*

Finally, know that we believe there is no more important work to be done right now. Also know that we are by your side and rooting for you as you step forward, joining us in becoming agents of change. We hope to continue our relationship with you and that you will interact with us via our website or on social media using the hashtag #learningthatmatters.

In community,
Caralyn, Cynthia, Karynne, and Julia

Wonderful Resources to Extend Learning

In her wonderful book, ***Emergent Strategy*, adrienne maree brown** (2017) offers ways to reshape our work and our communities, taking lessons from complex systems in nature. Her 10 core principles embody what we hope this book will leave you with: inspiration and motivation to lead human-centered change.

Small is good, small is all. (The large is a reflection of the small.)

Change is constant. (Be like water).

There is always enough time for the right work.

There is a conversation in the room that only these people at this moment can have. Find it.

Never a failure, always a lesson.

Trust the People. (If you trust the people, they become trustworthy).

Move at the speed of trust.

Focus on critical connections more than critical mass—build the resilience by building the relationships.

Less prep, more presence.

What you pay attention to grows. (brown, 2017 p. 41)

References

Bandura, A. (1997). *Self-efficacy: The exercise of control.* W. H. Freeman.

Bandura, A. (2000). Exercise of human agency through collective efficacy. *Current Directions in Psychological Science*, 9(3), 75–78. https://doi.org/10.1111/1467-8721.00064

brown, a. m. (2017). *Emergent strategy: Shaping change, changing worlds.* AK Press.

Collins, P. H. (2000). *Black feminist thought: Knowledge, consciousness, and the politics of empowerment.* Routledge.

Horton, M., & Freire, P. (1990). *We make the road by walking: Conversations on education and social change.* Temple University Press.
King Jr., M. L. (1966, May 4). *Nonviolence: The only road to freedom.*

ABOUT THE AUTHORS

Cynthia Alby has spent most of her career immersed in what could most accurately be described as "avid cross-discipline idea synthesizing." She studies pedagogy, sociology, psychology, neuroscience, and economics—anything that might yield useful clues to improving the art and science of teaching. Her primary research question is, "How might we reenchant learning for both students and faculty?" Dr. Alby received a PhD in language education from the University of Georgia, an MA in classical archeology from the University of Cincinnati, and an HAB in classical languages and philosophy from Xavier University. She joined Georgia College in 2001, where she is now a professor of teacher education and works extensively with the Center for Teaching and Learning. She is also the lead lecturer for Georgia's "Governor's Teaching Fellows," a program she has worked with since 2001. She and her husband raise a critically endangered breed of sheep on their farm, Shangri-Baa.

Searching for a purposeful profession after stints in both the public and private business sectors, **Karynne L. M. Kleine** came later to her career in education, which has now fascinated her for 35 years. Throughout that period, she has examined many of the taken-for-granted assumptions about teaching, learning, and how the world works to internalize her understanding of human nature and its intersection with growth and progress of the collective. Dr. Kleine's educational philosophy focuses on finding out "what is" and then imagining and realizing "what could be." She calls Georgia home, having traveled the United States and earning undergraduate degrees in interdisciplinary studies (Southwestern College) and business administration (San Diego State University) and advanced degrees in education from the University of Maine (MEd, Middle Grades Education; EdD, History and Philosophy of Science/Science Education.) As a former dean and current professor of education, Karynne collaborates alongside her colleagues at Georgia College as well as nationally with those in other fields to address issues of equity, particularly inequitable educational outcomes that serve to reinforce the status quo and limit life choices. She and the love of her life, Mike Gleason, together enjoy the pace of time and quietude found in the mountains of Appalachia.

Julia Metzker serves as the director of the Washington Center for Improving Undergraduate Education at The Evergreen State College. Julia received her first degree from The Evergreen State College, where she learned firsthand the value of a transformative liberal arts education. She obtained a doctoral degree in inorganic chemistry from the University of Arizona and completed a postdoctoral appointment at the University of York in the United Kingdom. In her 10 years as a chemistry professor at Georgia College, she discovered the power of community-based learning to engage students in learning that matters. After serving as the inaugural director of Community-based Engaged Learning at Georgia College, she moved to Stetson University as the founding executive director for the Brown Center for Faculty Innovation and Excellence. During her journey of discovering herself as an educator, she was fortunate to find a cohort of like-minded university educators who cofounded the Innovative Course-building Group (IC-bG)—a grassroots social network for learning that supports teaching faculty and staff across disciplines. She believes in reimagining and reclaiming the democratic potential of assessment, work she champions as a member of the Imagining America's "Assessing the

Practices of Public Scholarship" research group. She and her partner, Joe, raise chickens and bees with the help of an unruly Australian shepherd in the Pacific Northwest.

Caralyn Zehnder is a lecturer in biology at the University of Massachusetts Amherst. She discovered her passion for transformative teaching and developed her identity as a professional educator when she was a professor of biology and environmental science at Georgia College. It was at Georgia College where she realized the power and joy of collaborating with fellow educators to intentionally design courses. Dr. Zehnder facilitates course design workshops that help participants use evidence-based teaching practices that utilize the most recent research in education, cognitive psychology, and the social sciences to build learning environments that contribute to important student learning. She earned her BS in biology from Penn State and her PhD in ecology from the University of Georgia. For two years, she was the professional development coordinator at Springfield Technical Community College. On a good weekend, you'll find Caralyn out hiking and birding with her husband and daughter.

INDEX